'Fabulous. Brigid writes like a dream'

Joanna Lumley

'A wonderfully funny, mischievous account. It really did make me laugh out loud, startling the cat. Brigid Keenan is quite as hilarious a comic invention as Bridget Jones – only she's *real*!'

Julie Christie

'Life is what you make of it – you can't just sit there and let it happen to you, you've got to grab opportunities with both hands, or you risk boredom at least, depression and deathbed regrets at worst. Brigid Keenan rams the message home with hilarity. This is an important book, written by a very funny writer'

Shirley Conran

'Immediate and intimate, poignant and very funny; it is as if she is talking to the reader. Her eagle-eyed observation of human behaviour and far flung experiences made me laugh out loud'

Josceline Dimbleby, author of *A Profound Secret*

'What fun! Even in postings as remote and unlikely as Kazakhastan, or as bland and unpromising as Belgium, Keenan is incapable of boredom and therefore, she cannot be boring. She is the person you hope will be seated next to you at a dinner party: a companion of experience, vivacity and charm. To read her book is to meet her and to meet her, is to be enthralled'

Irma Kurtz, *Cosmopolitan* agony aunt and author of *Then Again*

'The story sparkles, flies, delights. What makes this book special is how, with a light touch, Keenan exposes the dark corners, the frustrations, the dilemmas of those who go forth to represent their country'

Yasmin Alibhai-Brown, journalist and broadcaster; author of *Some of My Best Friends Are . . .*

'There are a handful of books I should dearly love to have written myself, and this is one of them. By the end, I felt as if I had lived a whole new life in an unfamiliar and wondrous world that lies somewhere between that of Arthur Grimble's *Pattern of Islands* and Gerald Durrell's *My Family and Other Animals*. Like all the best memoirs, Brigid's book is endlessly engaging, full of delightful details, very funny and sometimes rather sad'

Christopher Matthew, author of *Now We are Sixty*
and *Now We Are Sixty (and a bit)*

'I am furious. I've just spent three whole hours chortling, giggling and wheezing my way through *Diplomatic Baggage* – and nary a pot washed or a keyboard key pressed all morning! Very few books these days make me laugh out loud – this one provoked loud hoots at the rate of three per page'

Mary S. Lovell, author of *The Mitford Girls*

'Brigid may have sobbed her way round the world in her diplomat husband's wake but her reward – and ours – is an inexhaustible stream of ludicrous events and witty observations. Her book has the authentic voice of a born storyteller and a very funny writer'

Lesley Garner, author of *How to Survive as a Working Mother*
and *Everything I've Ever Done That Worked*

'Always amusing, yet at the same time realistic, capturing the true feelings and flavours of the ex-pat life'

Hunter Davies

'Brigid Keenan is a new comic genius. But like so much of the best comedy, her humour is rooted in sadness and she writes with equal feeling about the loneliness and vulnerability of diplomatic life. Quite unlike anything else I have read: sad, touching, honest and observant as well as being very very funny'

William Dalrymple

Diplomatic Baggage

Diplomatic Baggage

The Adventures of a Trailing Spouse

BRIGID KEENAN

JOHN MURRAY

© Brigid Keenan 2005

First published in Great Britain in 2005 by John Murray (Publishers)
A division of Hodder Headline

1 3 5 7 9 10 8 6 4 2

A CIP catalogue record for this title is available from the British Library

ISBN 0 7195 6725 4

Typeset in Bembo by Palimpsest Book Production Limited,
Polmont, Stirlingshire

Printed and bound by Clays Ltd, St Ives plc

Hodder Headline policy is to use papers that are natural, renewable
and recyclable products and made from wood grown in sustainable forests.
The logging and manufacturing processes are expected to conform
to the environmental regulations of the country of origin.

John Murray (Publishers)
338 Euston Road
London NW1 3BH

This book is for all the women who live abroad
because of their husbands' or partners' work,

it is for Cecilia who inspired me,

it is for my mother, the first, best
and bravest ex-pat wife I knew,

and it is, of course, for AW − without whom,
it can honestly be said, it would not have been possible.

Contents

Introduction

People tend to think that ex-pat wives live in luxury compounds, drink a lot of gin and have affairs, so it's not surprising that we don't get much sympathy – which made the letter I received some years ago, very welcome. 'Dear Ms Keenan,' it said, 'I want to tell you how much I admire your courage and strength and resilience.' It went on in this vein for a while and I was glowing with satisfaction: here *at last* was someone who understood the sacrifices we ex-pat wives make. But then the author asked for a signed photo, which seemed a touch over the top, even to me, and then he mentioned my ordeal in Beirut, and I realized that the letter had been delivered to the wrong Keenan. The praise was (quite rightly) intended for Mr Brian Keenan, the hostage, and not for Ms Brigid Keenan the trailing spouse. Glumly I sent it on to Mr Keenan.

The fact is that no one understands the ex-pat wife's life, except another ex-pat wife. I hope that this book will strike a chord with my brave sisters in postings overseas; that they will recognize at least some of their own experiences in mine.

I apologize in advance to all who appear in these pages if their memories of the events I describe are different from mine. I have done my very best to tell it as it was, but as a distinguished American writer, William Maxwell, once warned, '. . . in talking about the past, we lie with every breath we draw.'

I have kept a diary on and off since we lived in Brussels in the Seventies, but maddeningly, when I came to go over it for this book I found that some pages had faded away to invisibility, and that on others, I couldn't read my writing. Most irritating of all was the fact that some stories – ones that must have made such an impact at the time that I thought I could never forget them –

were reduced to a few cryptic words which mean nothing to me now. What was 'the hilarious wasp and jelly baby' incident for heaven's sake? And who on earth was the 'small green VIP' that I made a note of twenty years ago and starred twice, meaning it was a particularly funny anecdote? You wouldn't think it possible for a person to forget such curiosities, but I have.

I would like to thank all the ex-pat wives whose friendship meant so much to me in Brussels, Trinidad, Barbados, India, Gambia, Syria and Kazakhstan. I have not been able to bring them all into the story, but they will know who they are.

I thank Andreas, Carmelita, Hari and Meena, Ceesay, Old Pa Momodou, Bakari, Sukai, Rabie, Marcelle, Bing, Khaled, Nabila, Nina, Ira and Yuri and all the people who have helped us around the world, so patiently and good-humouredly, making our lives not only easier, but richer. I am grateful to Michael Wynn Jones who asked me to write a column on ex-pat life for Sainsbury's *Magazine* some years ago – good training for this book.

I thank Christopher Matthew, Sue Fletcher and Barbara Toner for decades of morale-boosting and urging-on. I thank Claudia Shaffer, my agent and fond friend, and Gordon Wise, my editor – who is indeed wise, by nature as well as name.

Most of all I thank AW and Hester and Claudia for being the very best of all possible companions on the long journey described in this book.

Kazakhstan, November 2004

I

Homesick on the Steppe

Oh God, I don't know if I can bear it. This is my first morning in Kazakhstan and it is only eleven o'clock and I've already run out of things to do and I have another four years to go (that means one thousand four hundred and sixty days) until this posting comes to an end. How on earth am I going to get through it?

Actually, it's not quite true that this is my first morning here. I arrived in this alien world of snow and mountains and Mongol faces and incomprehensible languages and fur hats (even the street cleaners wear fur hats) at four o'clock on Saturday morning which was two and a bit days ago, but today is my first Monday, the day that every wife of a man working abroad most dreads; the day your husband goes to the office and you have to face your new life *ALONE*. I have a pit of misery in my stomach and I really do feel as if I am living in a bad dream and any moment I'll wake up and find myself in good old Pimlico. I could cry at the thought. What am I saying? I *am* crying.

AW, my husband, introduced me to the staff on Saturday when I came down for lunch, having slept all morning: that's Nina the cook who looks kind of tough but motherly – she could be a sergeant-major's wife, Ira the housekeeper who is young and pretty and as slim as a model girl, and Yuri, a huge, rather grumpy-looking man about eight foot tall who is the bodyguard/gardener/handyman. They are all Russians (nearly half the people in Kazakhstan are Russians left over from the days when the country was part of the Soviet Union) and they don't speak a word of English. The only Russian word I know is *niet*.

This is a bit worrying because in the early days of these foreign postings when the telephone never rings (or if it does, it's a wrong number), lonely ex-pat wives like me tend to lean rather heavily on our Ninas and Iras and Yuris since they are our only contact with the rest of the human race. We make them our confidantes and our soulmates – and then have to spend the rest of the time trying to put a respectable distance between us and them. For instance, in a fit of emotion in Syria, our previous post, I kissed Bing, the Filipino butler, goodbye the first time I set off home on leave, and then of course I couldn't *not* kiss him every time I went anywhere . . . the only person more embarrassed than me was him.

(This wasn't as humiliating as what happened when we left the Gambia years before. Then, as I was saying goodbye to Ceesay, our steward, I was suddenly filled with such affection that I leaned forward to give him an impromptu kiss. He saw what was coming and put up his hands to protect himself – which meant that as I got close, my two bosoms fitted neatly into his palms. We both screamed.)

In Ethiopia, our first stint abroad as a married couple, the maid, Andreas, offered me more than *moral* support. Every time AW and I had a row – which was about sixteen times a day – she used to appear silently behind him with a frying pan in her hand making shall-I-hit-him-on-the-head-with-this-now? gestures to me over his shoulder.

Well, obviously there'll be no such bonding here since we can't actually communicate at all, but then again there can't be any disagreements or frictions either, so perhaps that's a plus. And at least they won't be able to read my diary and see what I've written about them – as the staff did once in Damascus. That was truly mortifying because, needless to say, it was all about *them*. They were going to give in their notice, but we somehow forgave each other in the end and lived happily together for the rest of the posting.

When I woke up today it took me about ten minutes to work out who I was, let alone where I was. (*Kazakhstan!* – my stomach lurched.) I'd forgotten everyone's names, but the motherly cook-person brought me tea in a Tajik bowl on an English saucer at nine o'clock and then I plucked up my courage to come downstairs and face them all standing in the hall, beaming. I'm sure they are all ready to hate me though, as they have been looking after AW perfectly well for four months while I was in denial about the whole prospect of this posting and busy doing up our new flat in London. The last thing they want is some Memsahib from England who will be in the house all the time bossing them around.

In the Gambia, Ceesay – who, incidentally, was the living image of the comedian Eddie Murphy – pre-empted any possibility of this by somehow finding my weak spot, which is fear of entertaining, on the very first day. I can't have two people to tea without a panic attack, and Ceesay reduced me to a gibbering wreck of insecurity with his stories – dramatically told in pidgin English laced with French, Mandinka and Wolof – of our predecessor's wonderful dinner parties, the marvellous food, jovial company, etc. Until one day I nervously asked another ex-pat if she'd been to any of these glittering evenings and she said, 'Dinner parties? I don't think he ever had anyone to his house at all.')

After breakfast I looked up 'thank you' in my Russian dictionary – spaseeba – and tried it out on everyone, which seemed to go down well, then I bolted up here to the attic (where I have set up my computer) to avoid looking purposeless in front of them, or worst of all, bursting into tears. My unpacking is done, my clothes put away; I have no idea how to get to the centre of Almaty town and no experience of driving in real ice and snow, and as I can't actually speak to anyone, there is honestly nothing to do except telephone AW, my husband, in the office every hour or so (so far each conversation has ended with him getting annoyed and me crying), or look at emails. Thank goodness a nice young man from AW's office has organized the connection with Kazakhtelecom. This is the first posting we have had since the internet came into being (it was not permitted in Syria in our time) and it will make such a difference, especially when it comes to staying in touch with our daughters, Hester and Claudia.

Claudia is twenty-three and in her first year at Kings College, London. The reason she is rather old for an undergraduate is because this is her third go at university. The first time we settled her in at her Hall of Residence and then left for Syria – at which point she ran away to live with her boyfriend in Germany. It was weeks before we discovered what she'd done – whenever we rang her number we got someone called Helga's voice-mail and couldn't understand why Claudia hadn't changed it. It was all getting more and more mysterious and worrying, until our older daughter rang us and said, 'It's time someone told you what's going on . . .' The second time Claudia dropped out was in a slightly more respectable fashion, i.e. she told the university – and us – what she was doing, and went off to earn money as a teacher in an infant school.

Hester, twenty-six, is in Cairo where she is working on a refugee project. Later she plans to travel to Jerusalem to work for a Palestinian lawyer. This makes me feel uneasy because the Palestinian cause is something AW and I feel passionately about, and wittingly or not, we've probably encouraged her in this plan . . . I mean, she could find herself in danger because of us. She is training to be a barrister, and these jobs in the Middle East are to gain experience in human rights law before she starts her pupillage with a chambers in the autumn. Hester and Claudia are okay now, but both of them were such a nightmare when they were teenagers that, at the time, I was able to fill a monthly column in Sainsbury's *Magazine* with their misdeeds.

12 February

Ignore all the above about marvels of internet. I found I couldn't write any messages to the children this morning because I ended up sobbing into the laptop, then something happened to the computer (perhaps it got damp) or the line, or Kazakhtelecom – and it slowed down so that every message took hours to read and reply to. Gave up in despair and spent rest of day staring into space with wet eyes and feeling murderous hatred for AW, since of course I am only here because of him.

I first learned that he was to be posted as Ambassador for the European Commission to Central Asia (his countries are Kazakhstan, Kyrgyzstan, and Tajikistan) about nine months ago. Most people don't know that there is such a thing as a European Ambassador, but there is. He is the one that all the other ambassadors hate because he is the newest addition to the Diplomatic Service (i.e. an upstart) but, since he is representing all the countries of the EU, often has more power and prestige with the host government than they do. In my experience, British ambassadors in particular find it sticks in their throats to refer to AW as an ambassador and will fall over backwards to find another less exalted job description – 'Head of Mission' or 'Delegate' or 'EC Representative' – anything to avoid the 'A' word. In the course of our lives abroad together – especially at the beginning of his career when AW was actually working for the British Government – we often unintentionally managed to get up the noses of our ambassadors. The one in Nepal barely spoke to me at all – I think it was because I was living with AW in his camp in the jungle before we were married; the one in Ethiopia ticked me off for attempting to write a story on the famine for the *Sunday Times*; and in the Gambia we found ourselves at odds with the British High Commissioner because we felt he had gone about investigating the brutal murder of an English friend of ours so ineffectively. To be fair though, we did love the ones we knew in Brussels, Trinidad and Barbados.

But back to how we come to be in Kazakhstan. In June last year AW rang me from a business trip to Saudi Arabia. I should have been suspicious because he never rings when he is away – ever since the early days of our marriage when he was in Addis Ababa and I was working at the *Sunday Times* in London, where the switchboard operators were on a go-slow. Ethiopia had a telephone connection with Europe for only two hours a day, so poor old AW used to dial my office number and then listen to it ringing until the lines went dead. It gave him an enduring telephone phobia: he can't bear to make a long-distance call and what is worse, he can't bear me to make one either – though that is more for financial reasons. He says he doesn't mind so long as I have something important to say, but nonetheless, he still paces up and down sighing when I'm on an expensive call, and sometimes he puts his wrist under my nose and taps the face of his watch. This makes me so furious that I want to tap *his* face, preferably with a knuckleduster . . . Nearly all our most serious rows are about the telephone, mainly because his definition of what is 'something important' is about a million miles apart from mine.

When he rang from Saudi Arabia last June, he said, 'I've got good news and bad news . . .'

'Let me guess,' I said, 'the good news is that you have a posting abroad, and the bad news is that it is in . . .' I let my mind wander over the most remote and unlikely places in the world – the places I least wanted to go – and I came up with: 'Kazakhstan?'

'How do you know?' he said, amazed.

So I burst into tears and then spent most of the following months either sobbing or screaming at him.

The strangest part is that I had practically never heard of Kazakhstan, but once I knew that we were going there it cropped up all the time: I would pick up an ordinary English newspaper to find yet another weird story about the place. I read about two men who were sentenced to prison for killing and *eating* eight prostitutes in Kazakhstan, how a case of bubonic plague had broken out, how a new camel-milking machine was being tried out there. Then there was the first space tourist (an American billionaire) who took off and landed at the Russian cosmodrome in Kazakhstan – I watched it on the telly. Then the Pope went there. Then someone told me that Kazakh police had stopped a group of eccentric British hikers in the mountains and, not knowing about *Lord of the Rings*, held them for questioning when they said that they were looking for Mordor. Then, by chance, we met at a party the man who created Ali G and Borat, the hilarious Kazakh character, for television. He was thrilled when he heard we were going to Kazakhstan. Could we help sort out a problem? They had made an episode of Borat returning home to his family, but they had filmed it in Rumania pretending that it was Kazakhstan and the President of Kazakhstan was hopping mad and threatening lawsuits. I noticed AW slipping off into the crowd . . .

Then I heard of a plant historian with the wonderfully appropriate name of Barrie Juniper (what a pity his parents didn't go that extra mile and make it Berry) who had traced the origins of our ordinary English apple to Kazakhstan. He told me about the remnants of fruit forests in the Tien Shen mountains, and how the

Silk Route should really be called the Apple Route and how the
Mongol Hordes carried dried apple, full of vitamins, in their pockets
as they galloped down from Central Asia and ravaged the Middle
East, and how apple cultivation slowly moved west, and that grafting
was mentioned on clay tablets written in 2500 B.C. discovered in
Syria and, later, illustrated on a Roman mosaic.

Then I went to say goodbye to the butcher. 'I am off to
Kazakhstan,' I told him, whereupon there was a little yelp from the
rather good-looking Chinese woman behind me in the queue –
who turned out not to be Chinese at all, but Kazakh. Then after
lunch one day with a friend in a little restaurant in Pimlico, I
picked up my bag and said, 'Well, I suppose I'll see you next when
you come to Kazakhstan'; to our amazement the man at the next
table leaned over and said, 'I'm so sorry, but I couldn't help over-
hearing you mention Kazakhstan and I just want to say, I live there.'
He turned out to be based in the oil fields about 3,000 kilometres
away from Almaty, but we exchanged numbers anyway.

All this was most encouraging, in fact I was quite dazzled that
so much seemed to be happening in my new homeland. So when
I discovered that a writer acquaintance had researched part of the
Lonely Planet guide to Central Asia I rang him, all bubbly with
enthusiasm. At first I don't think he quite understood that I was
actually going to *live* in Central Asia for four years, because he told
me that possibly the happiest day of his life was the one when he
caught a plane out of the region and went back to London. But
then, valiantly trying to be more upbeat, he kept insisting that he
was there in the very early days of the Central Asian countries'
independence from Russia, and he was sure it would be better now.

After that I read Colin Thubron's book *The Lost Heart of Asia*
and, well . . . began to lose heart. This wasn't made any better by
cheery friends who kept saying 'You'll be okay Bridge, look how
you've made a success of all your past postings . . .', when all I
know is that I've been utterly miserable in every one of the six
countries across four continents that we've been sent to in the last
twenty years. But then again, I cling to the thought that – up until
now – I've cried almost as much when the time came to leave as
I did when I arrived. AW says I'd be grumbling in Paradise, and

William Dalrymple (who has been a pal since he came to spend one night with us in Damascus when he was writing *From the Holy Mountain* and stayed for *six weeks*) said I was an utter wimp and that Robert Byron, the great travel writer of the 1930s, would have given his right arm to have been allowed to roam Central Asia.

This is all very well, but people with normal lives can't possibly understand what it's like to be sent from England to Brussels to Trinidad to Barbados to India to West Africa and then to Syria without a break in between. We did have three years in Europe after Syria and before we were posted here, but that has only made it harder to tear myself away again. I know exactly what it feels like to be an autumn leaf – detached, insecure, tossed helplessly around in AW's slipstream.

Nothing links these postings of ours, there is no continuity; it's like being reincarnated eight times in one life (that's if you count Europe and now Kazakhstan). You arrive in each new place all naked (as it were) and friendless and vulnerable, you gradually build up a little world around yourself and then, bingo, you are suddenly sent off to the other side of the world to start all over again. No wonder I can hardly tell the difference between dreams and memories any more. Speaking of which, I have the most horribly vivid dreams here. They seem either to feature my mother – in which case I am letting her down in some frightful way, i.e. she is having Prince Charles to lunch and is in a total panic as I have not turned up, as promised, to help her, because my alarm hasn't gone off and I am still asleep in my flat sixty miles away. Or they are about my good friend Sandy (whose journalistic career is similar to what mine might have been, had I not been wrenched away by AW) in which case they are all about my failure, i.e. Sandy and I are both working on a big newspaper and she keeps writing front-page stories and being congratulated by the editor, while I try and try but never manage to write anything at all, and even fellow journalists are beginning to wonder out loud what I am paid for . . .

(Paranoia about my career – or rather about the lack it – is never very far away. In the Sixties I was a fashion editor on the *Sunday Times* and was once described as a Young Meteor, but now I'm more of a fallen star, or AW's satellite perhaps, or even, on bad days, a black hole. When we were posted to Barbados I can remember almost crying on the beach because I heard that Sandy had been offered the editorship of *Good Housekeeping* magazine. A friend who was with us was astonished: 'Be honest,' he said, 'wouldn't you rather be sitting in the sun on Sandy Lane beach with your children than in an office in London, for heaven's sake?' Of course, he was right, but since he was working full-time in a proper job he couldn't understand my feelings of inadequacy and failure.)

My most easily decipherable dream was two nights after I arrived here. I dreamed that I had created a really beautiful garden and invited Sandy and my mother to come and see it, but when we arrived we found that AW had got there ahead of us and dug up all the plants and put them in the earth upside down so all you could see was muddy roots. Hmmmmm.

Before AW left England to come here four months ago, he consulted – as he always does – the *I Ching*. If you don't know about this I should explain. It's a Chinese book that supposedly tells the future – you have to throw some coins and depending on how they land, you look up your destiny in the book. Well that's the theory, but the *I Ching* says such obscure things – 'The wild goose gradually draws near the cliff', or 'Within the earth, wood grows', or 'Progress like a hamster' – that I've always been pretty baffled about what's supposed to be going on myself. In the case of Kazakhstan however, it was suddenly rather disconcertingly blunt – the heading for AW's future in Kazakhstan read 'PIT OF BLOOD'. I am doing my best not to think about this.

13 February

Today I have decided to be more positive, but it is *really hard*. Put it like this: I am an age at which, if I saw my own obituary in the newspaper, I wouldn't feel *that* sad, and I don't want to spend my remaining years of energy and health wishing away time, here in Kazakhstan, when I could be doing . . . well, *what* exactly?

In my new positive-thinking mode I keep asking myself: what am I not doing here that I would be doing in London, except shopping at Marks & Spencer? So why am I miserable? First, of course, it is simple homesickness. I feel just like I did at boarding school: desperately lonely, missing family and friends and familiar things. This is childish I know, but I have discovered that I'm not alone: William Fiennes, the author of a new book, *The Snow Geese*, writes a lot about the misery of homesickness, or 'nostalgia' as it used to be called, and how it is 'more apt to affect persons whose absence from home is forced rather than voluntary'.

My own is a bit of both. AW and I discovered long ago that three months is the longest time we can be apart without endangering our marriage (I was pushing it, postponing my arrival in Kazakhstan for four months). In our experience, after three months we each become so used to being independent that no matter how much we have longed for each other in the meantime, being together again is really difficult – we find ourselves resenting our loss of freedom and the demands and interference of the other person. (Having to turn out the light before one o'clock in the morning, for instance.)

Secondly, my misery is to do with the fact that an ex-patriate wife is just an appendage. Indeed, we are officially known by the people who employ our husbands as 'trailing spouses'. We trail along behind, we have no identities of our own – we are only in Central Asia, India, Africa or wherever, because of our husbands. We may be engineers, pharmacists, journalists, business women, experts in antiques, geneticists, but when we meet each other we don't say 'What do you do?' – we ask what each other's *husband's* job is. We are only connected to the outside world through the umbilical cord of the Office – where newspapers and letters are delivered, and where the secretary keeps the engagement diary. Since usually we can't earn our own money, we have to ask our husbands every time we want to spend some. (AW is extremely generous and on the whole hands it over without asking too many questions, but there is still the matter of having to ask.)

Sometimes I feel like a large dog waiting all day for its owner to come home and take it out for a walk. When I hear AW's key in the lock I have an urge to rush downstairs barking and jumping up and down to lick his face.

I am not surprised that it is becoming more and more difficult for foreign ministries and international businesses to recruit men with wives who are prepared to sacrifice themselves on the altars of their husbands' ambitions (as I like to put it). It's okay for the husbands – they go to their offices and work at more or less the same sort of thing whether they are in Jakarta or Japan. But we woman are left on our own, wildly casting around for some sort of role for ourselves which isn't just playing bridge or golf, and having to fall back on our own inner resources – which in my case is rather painful as I feel they are a bit sparse.

From what I've seen during my travels, the women who slot in abroad most easily are the teachers and nurses – they can normally find proper jobs in any country. Here in Kazakhstan, I've come across another brilliant portable profession: our Admin Officer's wife is a hairdresser. She has set up a small professional salon in her house, through which she has made lots of friends among her clients, and earns her own money – and there's no reason she shouldn't go on doing this wherever her husband is posted. The nice wife of the Goethe Institute man here is a photographer, though that's a bit like writing – solitary, and entirely dependent on your own willpower and drive – but at least you get out of the house, which you don't if you are bashing away at a typewriter or computer.

In our own postings I have grasped at anything I could find to do – from making dressing-gowns to writing books to trying to save historic buildings to fund-raising (which is what we all do when everything else fails). Looking back, I loved every project, however random or peculiar, and was bitterly disappointed when AW was ordered on to the next place and I had to stop whatever I was doing.

Our house here – the ninth I have lived in over the last twenty-seven years abroad, not counting hotels and service flats – is on the outskirts of Almaty where the snow-covered mountains come down to meet the endless snow-covered steppe. We are on the edge of a low hill in a posh development with big new houses built much too close to each other and empty lots in between. Below us, at the bottom of the hill, is a village where people live in traditional wooden bungalows and we can hear their cockerels crowing and the odd donkey braying and the endless yapping of dogs. (It's been a constant mystery to me, travelling the world, why barking dogs don't seem to bother their owners as much as they do everyone else in the neighbourhood.)

I asked our Kazakh landlord what was here on the hill before they started building the new houses, and he said 'Oh, just old apple orchards and gardens'. It must have been lovely. Our roof has lots of triangular pointy bits sticking up out of it, which from a distance makes it look like a huge origami model of a house. The sitting room is enormous and looks over the city – but the décor is deeply depressing. The landlord has a passion for varnished ginger pine (ceilings, floors, banisters, doors); the good old EU has provided the usual Ikea-type furniture (in the humid heat of the Gambia we had grey knobbly tweed sofas). There is a lot of brown about – brown plastic parquet, brown bathroom tiles, patterned brown synthetic carpets – even the tap water is brown. The dining chairs are the worst things – they are a lurid orange wood with *black* upholstery. According to the EU rules nothing can be changed until it is more than eight years old and none of it is yet.

AW is very good at seizing the day, and before I arrived he got Yuri to hang all the pictures we brought with us so that there would be something of our own to look at. The trouble is, Yuri is eight feet high so they are all up by the ceiling. But I'm not really grumbling – at least there *is* a house and we don't have to spend three months living in a hotel while we look for one, as we have done in the past, and we've certainly come a long way since our first stint abroad together when AW and I lived in a sort of chicken shed in the jungle in Nepal. And we are lucky to be living in Almaty which is the 'old' capital of Kazakhstan (I put that in inverted commas because the town was only built in the last century) and not in the awful new capital, Astana, which is being created hundreds of miles to the north-west on the wind-blown steppe where the temperature can drop to minus 35 degrees in winter. All the diplomats have been instructed to move their embassies there as soon as possible and everyone is frantically trying to find convincing reasons why they absolutely *have* to stay in Almaty.

I have just discovered that Almaty is an earthquake zone, and that the town has been flattened twice – once in 1887 and once in 1911 – but AW says there is nothing to worry about because our house has been checked by experts to make sure it is earthquake proof. (When I mentioned this smugly to someone who knows where we live she said, 'Oh *your* house will just slide down the hill.') Apparently we are due for another big one any day now, and the American Embassy advises everyone to keep a suitcase packed with essential things like passports, to grab as you flee the shaking building, as well as keeping stocks of water and canned food accessible somewhere outside. AW seems to have ignored this; perhaps I'd better organize it.

14 February

A beautiful day, and the snow-covered mountains behind our house look very spectacular and picture-postcard-y. Our best view of them is from the bathroom window, and I noticed this morning, when I was brushing my teeth, that they look very similar to the illustration on the SR toothpaste tube. They are to the south, which is strangely disconcerting as I feel that mountains should be to the north, but north is the steppe, which stretches away for thousands of miles to the Arctic circle.

Kazakhstan is a huge country – two-thirds the size of India (but with only 14 million people) – and if you travel across it you go through three time zones. But today I made the truly depressing discovery that in the whole of this enormous place there are only a couple of historic old buildings still standing. The main one is a magnificent mausoleum that Tamerlane built over the tomb of a twelfth-century sufi, Khoja Yassawi, in a town called Turkistan, ten hours' drive away. So, no Old City to explore then, as there was in Damascus, and no weekend excursions to archaeological sites. In nearly six years in Syria we were only able to visit about half the places described in *Monuments of Syria*. In *Monuments of Central*

Asia, which I bought before coming here, Kazakhstan has less than a page, so we ought to be able to wrap that up in no time.

I feel very much aware of being in the middle of an enormous empty land mass thousands of miles from the sea. It's surreal.

Decided to waste no more time moping about and to get Yuri to drive Nina and me to the Zelioni Market (that means Green Market) to do some shopping. I love markets and this turns out to be a really good one: long trestle tables stretch down a huge covered hall selling all sorts of stuff. Babushkas wearing headscarves like those Russian dolls that fit inside each other stand behind these trestles selling mare's milk (fermented and unfermented – the fermented tastes better – or should I say, less awful – than the unfermented), camel's milk (not bad), cream, home-made cheeses, smoked chicken and fish, caviar in big plastic tubs, honey of all sorts, veg, fresh chicken etc. I said 'quack quack?' to Nina and she took me to the duck counter, where we bought one for supper.

A couple of metres of trestle table are devoted to all sorts of extraordinary mushrooms and fungi that you'd pay a fortune for in England, and there are certain things – some strange dried berries for example – that I had never seen before. The counters selling raw meat have pictures of cows, pigs, sheep and horses so you know what you are buying. I am sorry to say that the horsemeat stand is the biggest – one of the delicacies of Kaz is horsemeat sausage, the fattier the better. Towards the front of the market are jolly, gold-toothed Tajiks selling dried fruits (including the dried apple that Barrie Juniper talked about) and nuts from Uzbekistan, Turkey and Iran. If you buy anything from them you get lots of perks – I was given handfuls of dried apricots and sesame-sugar-coated peanuts. The Tajiks are much friendlier than the Kazakhs who don't smile much at all – one of the thinnest books in the world could be *Kazakh Charm* – though *Kazakh Road Sense* would run it pretty close (sometimes you're pushed to guess which side of the road people drive on here).

Then there is a whole section of the market where, to my amazement, they sell ready-prepared Korean food. This is because Koreans were one of the ethnic groups living in the Soviet Union that Stalin banished to the empty lands of Central Asia – along with the whole Russian-German community, the Chechens (every single Chechen was expelled from Chechnya), Kurds, Greeks and Armenians, and many others. Apparently more than a hundred different minorities are living here, and their presence is witness to the fact that fifty years ago the name Kazakhstan stood not for oil and gas as it does today, but for gulags, exile and suffering. (Dostoyevsky, Trotsky and Solzhenitsyn were each sent here at one time or another.) All these displaced minorities, together with Uighurs (from Xinjiang, Western China), Mongolians, Uzbeks, Tajiks and Kyrgyz who have migrated here from bordering countries, added to the native Kazakhs and the millions of Russians who stayed on after Kazakhstan became independent, meant that a new word had to be found to describe the people who live here – Kazakhstani.

The people here seem harsh with each other – in the market I tried to give a beggar with no legs some money and Yuri stopped me.

'But Yuri,' I pleaded, 'he has no legs.'

'Legs okay,' said Yuri mysteriously in his gloomy Vlad the Impaler voice, and that was that.

On the way home we drove past a huge stone blockhouse with oriental domes which turns out to be the *vanya* or bathhouse. One of the more attractive Soviet-style buildings in town, it was put up in the early Eighties by an extremely popular Kazakh Communist First Party Secretary called Kunaev. Apparently you can have a Finnish, Turkish or Russian bath there. I wonder what the difference is, and I would also like to know if you can get your legs waxed there. Must investigate but don't know who to ask.

Later. I have broken a tooth on the sesame-coated peanuts. This is odd, because I have just been re-reading the bit in *The Lost Heart of Asia* where Colin Thubron breaks his tooth on a kebab in Turkmenistan. Now I can't help feeling pleased with myself, as if I had passed some kind of test that makes me a real traveller. The enormous gap I can feel with my tongue makes me very aware that almost everyone here has at least one gold or silver tooth; some have a whole mouthful like Jaws in James Bond.

In spite of tooth, today has been much better, I don't know why; perhaps it was discovering that Yuri can drive me about so I can escape from the attic into town. Or perhaps it's just that I love markets. Anyway, I have not cried once and it is nearly six o'clock.

Still later. Well, that didn't last long. AW came back from the office and we went for a walk in the snow outside the house, but the surface is icy and it's easy to slip (AW measured his length dramatically in Panfilov Park just before I arrived) and suddenly I felt miserable again.

What am I doing in this frightful place in the middle of nowhere where you can't even go for a walk? AW made it worse by asking me why I was crying when I would have thought it was only too obvious. AW never listens to anything I say – though I notice that certain buzzwords get his attention – 'sex', 'thighs', that kind of thing; then he suddenly says 'What was that you were saying?' (I have got into the habit now of saying everything twice. I even say my night prayers twice over in case God isn't listening, either.)

But in spite of his infuriating ways, and our endless arguments, AW is my hero. I admire him more than anyone. He is disciplined, dutiful, hard-working, clever, thrifty, stoic, punctual and funny; I am the opposite.

No computer dating service would have matched us in a million years. He likes pasta; I like potatoes. He likes tea; I like coffee (and if I do drink tea, I like Tetley teabags, whereas he'll fiddle around with loose Darjeeling that clogs up the sink). He goes to bed and rises early; I like to go to bed late and sleep late. In all our years of marriage, I have never been allowed to read in bed. No matter how quietly I turn the pages, it's no use, he says he can't sleep if I'm reading. Sometimes he can't sleep if I'm *thinking*, for Pete's sake. How on earth did we get this far together? And will Kazakhstan be the last straw?

Was looking forward to ringing Claudia in London tonight but decided better not, as I would only upset her by howling down the phone.

15 February

Rang Claudia this morning and she told me that Princess Margaret died a few days ago. We haven't managed to sort out how to work our new World Receiver radio yet, but even so, I can't think how this news didn't filter through to us before – perhaps everyone assumed we knew. That's one of the problems with this ex-pat life: when you do finally get back to England you are just like Rip van Winkle, not knowing who has died, what scandals happened while you were away, who the new heroes are and so on. Usually, of course, we hear the main headlines on the BBC or CNN but we don't know about the small stories that make up a nation's folklore. When we come home on our annual leave and flip through *Hello!* or *OK!* magazine at the dentist, we realize with a shock that we've never heard of a single one of the celebrities they feature. We don't know anything about *Big Brother* or Beckham's flying boot; if we've heard of Halle Berry we might not know how to pronounce her name. Once, home for a few weeks, I found that Andrex had suddenly taken to calling itself 'the legendary toilet tissue'. I found myself worrying about what the legend was – had we missed something? Had 400 people escaped from a burning building on ropes of Andrex while we were abroad?

We ex-pats notice the changes at home far more acutely than people living there all the time. For us, everything seems speeded-up like those nature films in which buds unfurl into full-blown flowers before your eyes. I remember going off to India in the days when no one even whispered the word 'condom' in public, and then, one year later when we came home on holiday, watching a TV discussion in which people not only talked about condoms, but twanged them round the studio. AW and I decided long ago that it is essential to go to at least one film when we are on leave each year just to keep our shockability level in synch with the rest of the Western world. (It is almost as necessary to pop into your local newsagent from time to time to keep up with the rude things written in birthday cards.) Even so – usually starting in the baggage hall at Heathrow – I find myself flinching at the language I hear around me in England. (Presumably people in the developing world use bad language too, but we are protected by not being able to understand it.)

I think the staff must like us – Ira gave me a bottle of home-made wine today and Nina has taken to wearing lipstick. (I emailed Hester in Cairo: 'The cook is wearing lipstick' but as I forgot to specify what sex the cook is, I got a rather worried email back.)

Yesterday in the lunch hour AW and I went into town and bought a TV set and video, and this morning I set off with Yuri to buy a TV table to put them it on. (Yuri and I do these expeditions in total silence, which isn't as embarrassing as it sounds because we both know that conversation is impossible. He insists that I sit in the back of the Land Rover and though it seems daft, I don't resist because I remember the driver in India begging me not to sit beside him, explaining that his colleagues had teased him, saying that he couldn't be working for anyone important because the Memsahib didn't sit in the back of the car.)

I've never really thought about TV tables (in England, ours sits on a wooden chest) and I didn't know such a hideous genre of furniture existed until Yuri and I looked for one. In Kazakhstan there are seemingly no limits to the gilding, lacquering, wood carving, glass engraving and acrobatic swivellings that a TV table can achieve. We went to about ten shops to try to find something simple and ended up in the market selecting a Chinese-made one that only has carved pillars on either side of the glass doors of the video cupboard.

In the course of this search I had a good look at Almaty. It has some really pretty architecture: there are hundreds of charming wooden cottages with carved window frames and shutters all painted in different colours – these, I am told, were built by the Russian pioneers who, in the last century, came east to this empty land in search of a new life. They remind me of a children's book our daughters loved called *The Little House on the Prairie*, about an American family who went West to seek their fortune; the Central Asian version of the story would have to be called *The Little House on the Steppe*. I suppose most of these will ultimately disappear as the town is developed. I'll ask Yuri to take me round so I can photo-graph some of them.

Then there are the old Russian civic buildings of Almaty – long
and low, with columned facades painted in shades of yellow or blue.
Yuri pointed out the house where Brezhnev lived when he was First
Party Secretary here; it is ravishing, painted blue with white stucco
work. I wondered in sign language where Trotksy and his wife lived
when they were exiled here by Stalin, but Yuri didn't know.

In between all these pretty things are huge apartment blocks
which look semi-derelict: the President's new white marble palace
like a gigantic sugar cube (very similar to the President of Syria's
– perhaps they come in colossal kits), and huge Soviet-style edi-
fices such as the Palace of Youth and Culture, which has a tower
so phallic it would be better placed on an Institute of Human
Anatomy. Some of the Soviet buildings – such as the bathhouse,
and the neo-classical Opera House, and the enormous National
Museum, which looks like a mosque with a blue dome – are rather
wonderful.

I wish I could have been in charge of Almaty in the 1970s and
'80s and encouraged the old Russian style – especially the attractive Russian/Oriental combination they have here (basically clas-
sical but with little Oriental touches such as pointy Moorish
windows). Almaty could have become one of the prettiest places
in the world.

Came home, and AW and I had *solyanka* for lunch – this is,
apparently, the most popular Russian soup after borscht. It is made
of smoked chicken and pickled cucumbers, and when Nina showed
me the ingredients I thought it sounded absolutely disgusting, but
it was delicious. Nina is a very good cook – AW says that in all
the months he was here alone he barely had the same dish twice.
The service is a bit eccentric – mugs on saucers, guest towels for
napkins and so on, but who cares? Nina and Ira, and even Yuri in
his grim way, are so friendly and pleasant and obliging, I am beginning to love them.

(Speaking of 'service', our most hilarious experience was in the
Gambia a few years ago. AW was giving a big formal dinner for
the head of the bank there, when, in the middle of the meal, Ceesay,
the steward, disappeared. The first-course plates needed clearing
away, but Ceesay was nowhere to be seen.

'Ceesay?' murmured AW in a low voice – which got louder and louder as he became more desperate.

Suddenly Ceesay was back at his side.

'Where have you been?' asked AW in an undertone.

'Oh, sorry Boss,' said Ceesay loudly and clearly, 'I was just takin' a piss.'

The guests looked appalled.

'Well, I hope you washed your hands,' said AW deciding there was nothing left to do but make a joke out of it.

'Oh *no* Boss,' said Ceesay, indignant that AW should think he had wasted time. AW said he could see the guests flinch as Ceesay came round with the next course.)

Mind you, I am continually amazed that the people who work for us ex-pats round the world are able to come up with any service at all – belonging as they do to totally different cultures and often living in the poorest conditions. I remember going to a Ladies' Lunch in Delhi where we were given beef consommé as a starter and all of us were faintly surprised to find cherries in the bottom of our soup plates. What had happened, of course, is that the hostess had told the cook to put *sherry* in the soup . . . Cherries? Sherry? The ways of the foreign boss must seem totally extraordinary.

It used to be said that ex-pats talked about their servants the whole time – I can see why this might be true because most of the time their lives are much more exciting than ours. Marcelle, our cook in Syria, was an armed security guard in Manila before she came to us; her best friend escaped from cruel employers in Damascus by knotting sheets together and climbing four storeys down the outside of an apartment block. Our first butler in Syria, a really gentle man who was captain of the Sri Lankan cricket team in Damascus, came with glowing references about his honesty and trustworthiness etc, etc, but we discovered after he left that he'd been in prison in Syria (GBH), Italy (drug dealing) and Turkey (illegal immigrant). Even his departure was odd; he told us he had to take emergency leave and fly back to Sri Lanka as his father was ill, but the gardener, who saw him off, said he took a bus to Moscow. We never saw him again.

★   ★   ★

After lunch, Yuri indicated to me in sign language that we must go shopping again – I was not at all sure what for this time, but it turned out we were still looking for a TV table. I hoped we had committed ourselves to the Chinese one we saw this morning but apparently not. I don't seem to carry any money here, rather like the Queen. Up to now Nina has forked out of the housekeeping for everything we have bought, so somehow I thought Yuri had paid for the table and was collecting it later . . . He hadn't, so we spent more hours this afternoon looking at hideous and expensive tables, and then I somehow conveyed to Yuri that we should just buy the one we saw this morning.

I learned the Russian word for carpet – *covr* – a couple of days ago, so on the way home, feeling exhausted and depressed, I had an idea for cheering myself up.

'Yuri, Kazakh *covr*?' I asked, '*Old* Kazakh *covr*?'

Yuri got the message immediately and took me down a side alley to a dingy shop in a basement. We banged on the door and a jolly little man exactly like one of those fat china Buddhas you sometimes see in junk shops ushered us into a shop *full* of carpets and the particular Kazakh embroideries called Tuzkis which are made to decorate the inside walls of yurts (the circular felt tents that the nomads lived in here). I ended up taking two carpets on appro, and when I got home they looked wonderful, so I decided to hang on to them – as I keep saying to AW, we can always sell them when we go home. I can see Carpet Therapy opening up a whole new cheery world . . .

Later. Have worked out a new scheme for our hideous living room: lots and lots of bright red Kazakh carpets all over the floor, with white curtains and upholstery – and it seems there's a chance the office might contribute as the old upholstery covers are very worn, even if they are not yet eight years old.

TV is now on new TV table, so we decided to watch it this evening – but AW could not get it to work. Neither of us could understand a word of the instructions in any of the six languages they were in. We crouched in front of the telly all evening, twiddling knobs and pressing buttons, but nothing happened. Felt like chucking it out of the window. Oh, for the good old days in India when the TV just had an ON/OFF switch. Actually, it didn't really matter as AW and I can't bear to watch the news much anyway. We get too upset about George Bush and what is happening in the Middle East.

16 February

A Saturday! Thought I had AW to myself all day, but he had invited Gainee, a very pretty Kazakh girl from his office, to come with us to another huge market – the Baraholka – to translate, and after that to go riding. On the way to the big market she thanked me for the loan AW had given her to buy a car – I knew nothing about this and immediately became deeply suspicious. What on earth is going on? I now remembered AW calling me 'Baby' at lunch recently. He has never, ever called me baby before in the twenty-nine and three-quarter years we've been married and I did wonder about this at the time. The women here are extremely pretty and all of them have amazing figures with legs six feet long (especially the ones – all thirty of them – who work in AW's office). I think I should be careful about not leaving him alone here too much. Every man I've ever heard of who has been posted to any part of what used to be the Soviet Union has found a new wife there. I watched AW's and Gainee's body language carefully as we trailed through the vast market which mostly sells Chinese household goods and cheap clothes. *Think* it's okay . . .

I was hoping to find a dusty bale of some exquisite cloth left over from Silk Route days but the fabrics were mostly synthetic. Man-man fibres have done to textiles here what concrete has done to buildings.

Our next stop, riding at the Hippodrome, was definitely *not* okay. AW has become really proficient – this is what he did at the weekends when I was not here – so he got on to a huge horse and went off to do his own thing in the *manège*. When I went to the stable and was shown the horse I'd been allocated, called Eton, I felt quite relieved because it seemed much smaller than AW's, but this, as I discovered very quickly, was only because the stable floor was two feet lower than the surrounding ground. When they led Eton out he was colossal, and it took all the teacher Natasha's strength – as well as every sinew of mine – to heave me on top of him. It was agony: I knew I'd dislocated my left foot, knee and hip simultaneously but didn't dare say anything.

First Eton and I walked round on a leading rein and I tried to master my pain, fear and vertigo, but then, just when I hoped I'd be able to stop soon, Natasha said *Trot*. All I can say is I don't know why hundreds of people don't die in riding accidents every week – I could only stay on by holding the front of the saddle for grim death, but then of course, I couldn't control the reins. Natasha was cross: *Human One, Horse Two* she instructed, meaning the human has to master the horse. I could hear Eton chuckling to himself at these words. When the torture finally came to an end I tried to slide off elegantly but got my foot stuck under the saddle and ended up hopping round on one leg doing the splits vertically. Don't let anyone ever tell you that once you've learned to ride, you never forget.

Felt tearful as I watched AW galloping round *manège* in semi-crouch looking like a Grand National jockey, as I realized this is yet another thing we won't be doing together. How on earth are we going to spend our time here? Suddenly, with his horse going at full speed, AW fell off . . . my heart leapt. *Pit of blood!* Broken back: life in wheelchair. Broken neck: dead. Broken head: life as vegetable . . . But somehow he was perfectly all right.

That evening, bruised and sore, we decided we should try out the sauna that the landlord has insisted on building in our basement – we didn't need one, but it's a big Russian thing apparently. I've only had a sauna once, at a health farm, AW has never had one at all. We don't really know what you are supposed to do with it. People get a funny glint in their eyes when they talk about saunas as if there is some dark sexual secret involved . . . Are you supposed to invite friends round? Is it okay to have one alone? Should you wear a swimsuit? We have never learned sauna etiquette. We decided to wear towels for modesty going from bathroom to basement in case the guards at the gate could see us through the window, but we soon discovered that modesty doesn't come into sauna-ing at all. First of all you have to use your towel to lie on because the shelves are too hard, then you get so hot you don't really care any more, then you have to climb up and down a stepladder on all fours to get in and out of a big barrel of cold water. You end up seeing bits of each other you never even knew existed, even after years of marriage.

17 February

It's Sunday. AW became a Buddhist some years ago but he is always very accommodating about finding me a Catholic Church – somehow he'd tracked down the only one in Almaty, miles away from our house on the other side of town. It was built only five years ago. The Mass in English is on Saturday afternoons at five o'clock which sort of messes up both the afternoon and the evening. I might take to going to one of the two ravishing onion-domed Russian cathedrals – surely God doesn't make a distinction between Orthodox and Catholic.

18 February

It is a week since my first Monday – I could see absolutely no light at the end of the tunnel then, and not much now, though I don't seem to cry quite as often and I have had one phone call – from the Dutch Ambassador's wife inviting me to lunch to meet a Kazakh anthropologist.

Yuri has discovered that the TV didn't work last Friday because we hadn't switched on the digital box. So that solves that problem. But it doesn't work this morning either, even with the digital box switched on, because today is something called Prophylactic Day, when the whole system is overhauled and maintained. Don't ask me how I know any of this; I must have absorbed it through my pores because the language is completely beyond me. AW is working hard on it, but I realize in advance that there is no point in having lessons (though I did quite well at Arabic when we were in Syria – indeed, for some reason every time I open my mouth here per-fect Arabic comes out, which is such a waste). I mean, how can you cope with a language in which the word for 'stop' is '*ostanavlivite*' – by the time you'd got your tongue round 'OSTANAVLIVITE THIEF', for example, the culprit would be safely home with the loot. As someone said to AW, Russian is not a language, it's a conspiracy.

But in spite of all this, I have learned two Russian words this week. My technique is to link the impossible foreign word to something that sounds the same in English. In Syria, for instance, the essential greeting you have to know just to be polite is *kaifarlek*. I linked it to *Kaffe* Fasset (the artist and designer), and Pamela *Harlech* (who lives near us in Somerset) and I got Kaffe Harlech which was perfect and which I could never forget.

Here I have mastered *spaseeba* (thank you) by linking it to *placebo*, and now I have added *dobro outra*, which is Russian for 'good morning'. My link for this is *Deborah* Moggach, the writer, who is a bit *outré* (I hope she won't be offended by me saying this). Now that I've thought of it this way, it will be fixed in my brain for life. As for the rest, I just mutter 'Dostoyevsky' quietly if anyone says anything to me in the market.

There are some Russian words that we all know without realizing it – *bolshoi* for big (Bolshoi Ballet), *bistro* for quick (the story goes that when the Russians invaded Paris after the battle of Waterloo, Russian soldiers in French restaurants always wanted their food served quickly and would shout '*Bistro, bistro*' – until 'bistro' became the name of a place serving meals quickly). *Petroushka* (which I know as the name of the sad clown in a ballet) seems to mean parsley. Then there are English words which if pronounced in a Russian way actually become Russian – e.g. *biznizmien* means businessman, *narco biznizmien* means a drug dealer, and *trolleybus* means trolleybus.

The terrible problem with Russian is that some letters in their alphabet look exactly like ours but are not pronounced the same. For instance, the new big supermarket here (which has a skating rink inside) has PAMCTOP written across the front – but this translates as 'Ramstore' in English. (Just to confuse you even further, their plastic bags have a picture of a kangaroo on them.) When AW and I first drove through Almaty I was wildly excited because there seemed to be so many antique shops. On almost every street were shop signs saying АЛТЕК and I was thinking 'Oh, I'll have no trouble finding something to do here . . .' when AW, reading my thoughts, told me not to get excited because it means pharmacy.

One quirky thing about the language makes me smile – Russians say 'G' for 'H', so you have Luftganza, Golland, Robin Good, Gamlet, Gong Kong, alchogol, Guckleberry Finn, and best of all, Garry Potter.

Nina, Ira, Yuri and I keep a notebook in the kitchen because we don't need words like *biznizmien* or *tramvoy*. I need: 'Nina, do you know how to make a cake?' And she needs: 'Would you like beef stew for supper tonight?' So we have taken to drawing – just like that game, Pictionary.

Yesterday I drew a cake, a brilliant broad bean in a pod, and a potted palm tree (am desperate to get some houseplants), and Nina and Yuri understood perfectly. On the whole though, we only use drawing when all else fails. Most of the time we get by with acting and mime – if, for instance, I want to say chicken breast or chicken liver, I go 'cluck-cluck' and clutch my bosom or where I think my liver is. (I wish I'd paid more attention in biology – you need to know your anatomy with this system, or you might get served up with something appalling.) If Nina is giving us beef for lunch she says 'moo'; 'baa' if it's lamb – and we all fall around laughing. I know they are secretly longing for me to ask for pork so that I'll make a real fool of myself, snorting.

When we get seriously stuck we have to ring Gainee in the office for a proper translation.

So we get by, but I am a bit worried about what will happen to my speech after months of talking in pidgin English. I can see myself going back to London and saying to Claudia, 'Now we go Marks & Spencer buy vest, you know vest, shiver shiver, brrr brrr,' and then I'll take out a notebook and draw a vest. On the telephone to Hester I told her my fears and she said I was right to be worried – she's met people in her organization in Cairo who've worked so long with refugees that they have ended up SPEAKING VERY SLOWLY AND DELIBERATELY.

19 February

Asked Yuri to take me out to buy houseplants. We found some lovely palms eight foot high being sold in a theatre foyer (theatres all seem to have shops in them) – but they cost $400 each. Then Yuri drove me for what seemed like hundreds of miles through the suburbs of Almaty to various depressing nursery gardens with nothing to sell. To be fair, I suppose February is not the ideal month to be buying plants. (The suburbs – Orbita they are called – were a shock: just one enormous, grim block of flats after the other, set in a featureless landscape.)

I had my camera with me today so that I could start photographing the charming cottages. On the way home we spotted a particularly cute one down a side road – it was painted blue with pale green shutters and had a fringe of long icicles hanging from its corrugated iron roof. Yuri stopped, and I slithered off to photograph it.

Trying to get a picture of the cottage without showing the ugly hot water and gas pipes across the front, I discovered the first thing to know about snow – you can't tell how deep it is until you sink up to your waist and then look an utter fool thrashing around trying to get out again.

This has not been a good day for expeditions. After lunch I wrapped up again in my sheepskin coat, hat, scarf, gloves, boots etc (buying clothes for Kazakhstan in London took me into a whole new world of fleeces, layers and something called Gore-Tex which I'd never heard of before) and walked down the hill to photograph another pretty cottage we'd passed in the car. On the way back I was admiring the blue sky and the white snow all around and thinking it really wasn't that bad, when I was attacked by a scabby-looking white dog. I had to beat it off with my camera on the end of its strap. Must get Yuri to make me a stout stick; will probably have to get a new camera.

AW and I felt really sick this evening – idly wondered if it could be early stages of bubonic plague.

20 February

Obviously not, as both of us are perfectly okay this morning.

Lunch with Dutch Ambassador's wife today. That means contact with fellow human beings speaking my language . . . will I manage coherent sentences?

Later. In the event I didn't really have to, as the Kazakh anthropologist lectured us non-stop on the culture of the Kazakh nomads; the thing that touched me most was when she said that in the old days a Kazakh could tell from the particular jangle of each woman's jewellery who was approaching the yurt. The saddest part is that the nomad culture is virtually dead here, and all that is left are these stories.

When the Russians introduced collective farming at the end of the 1920s and early '30s it was an utter disaster for Kazakhstan – the nomads slaughtered their herds rather than accept this new and totally alien way of life, and then came a famine in which about two million people – half the population – died. Others were executed for not obeying orders, and many fled to Mongolia (where thousands of Kazakh nomads still live in yurts). In Kazakhstan the remaining people were gathered in *kolkhoz*, or collectives, and their ancient nomadic way of life with its customs and traditions was extinguished. All Kazakhs, though, are still very much aware of which tribe and which Horde – the Great, Middle or Lesser Horde – each family belongs to: the President, for instance, is Great, the Prime Minister is Lesser. (It crosses my mind that the Lesser could become the Greater – because theirs is the land in the west of the country, near the Caspian Sea, where all the oil and gas has been found.)

Since the country became independent in 1992, the *kolkhoz* have become more like ordinary villages, and in some, people have revived the habit of taking their herds up to the high pastures to graze in summer. There in the mountains, apparently, you still come across 'wild' yurts (as opposed to tame tourist yurts which have been put up in town as restaurants and coffee shops).

From what I glean from Nina and Yuri and Ira and from talking

to the Russians and Kazakhs in AW's office, it is clear that the rela-
tionship between the Kazakhs and the Russians still living here is
strained. The newly oil-rich Kazakhs are top dogs now, whizzing
round town in expensive cars with smoked glass windows, and the
Russians, who once ruled the place, have to find what jobs they
can − Ira and Yuri, for instance, are both university graduates, as
are many of the Russians in domestic jobs.

The Russians believe they developed this country and that
without them it would be nothing, and they tend to look down
on the Kazakhs. The Kazakh view sometimes veers towards the
Monty Python 'What-did-the-Russians-ever-do-for-us?' school of
thought, but most of them would acknowledge that Russia did
develop (or perhaps they'd say exploit) their country, though at a
terrible cost in lives − and in cultural identity, for Kazakhs have,
basically, leapt in a lifetime from yurts to shopping malls.

21 February

Yesterday I arranged with the Dutch Ambassador's wife that I
should tag along with her to the International Women's Club
meeting today (Dutch courage?). As if the ordeal of introducing
myself to a huge group of strangers wasn't enough, the lift to the
tenth floor in the hotel was made of glass, and I had to close my
eyes and hold her hand on the way up, crashing lifts and heights
being two of my many fears.

I had been dreading the meeting, but they were nice women −
or, in Club-speak, gals (or even 'guys' − the Club seems to be run
by American oil company wives). No obvious kindred spirits − the
British Council wife, Kit, who seemed the most likely, left early −
but it was an awful lot better than crying at home. All sorts of
activities are arranged through the Club: I could join the Bible study
group, the lunch-bunch, the cooking club, the hikers; I could learn
Spanish or yoga or do aerobics. I'm not really an organized activity
person though; I'll think about it.

22 February

Another terrifying prospect today – tea with the Diplomats' Club. I was dreading it even more than the other meeting because I hadn't really met any of the other ambassadors' wives yet. However, I got into conversation with a nice Canadian woman whose previous posting was Mongolia. She told me that one day when she was living there, she and two women friends decided to go and look at an ancient Shaman fertility shrine. It had once consisted of a huge stone penis and testicles, she said; incoming Buddhists had hacked down the penis so that it was only a stump, but the giant testicles remained. Anyway, the three friends were laughing and joking and larking about pretending to do the fertility ritual (which involved sitting on the penis stump), not giving a thought to what might happen . . . until a couple of months later all three of them discovered they were going to have babies.

Then I talked to a very friendly woman who, sadly, is about to leave (this is always the way). She had a terrifying story to tell about how she and her husband, fast asleep in their third-floor flat in Almaty, were gassed and then robbed by burglars. They were so drugged that they did not even hear the safe in the wall behind their bedroom cupboard being hacked out. It's never crossed my mind that I might be drugged in my sleep – this has given me a whole new worry.

26 February

Yet another women's bash today – this time, the French Group. It was held at the British Residence (the Ambassador's wife is French) which put me in a panic as I had made up my mind that – though I don't know them – I hate the Ambassador and his wife because they never invited AW round, even for a drink, in all the four months he was here without me at the beginning of his posting when he didn't know a soul and was feeling lonely. (AW says he doesn't care, but hell hath no fury like a woman whose husband has been scorned.) However, I went off to British Residence with Yuri driving (I really can't manage in all this snow) feeling

v. nervous about meeting my enemy, but she turned out to be pleasant and friendly and gave me the name of a curtain and upholstery shop.

In the afternoon I asked Yuri to take me to the shop she'd suggested where I chose some quite nice white fabrics from Turkey, and arranged for them to come round and measure everything. We have decided to pay for it all ourselves – the office may reimburse us in the fullness of time.

Tonight we had actually been invited out to dinner – only the fifth dinner invitation from diplomatic colleagues in *five months* – but it was cancelled this afternoon. Diplomatic society in Kaz seems to be rather dysfunctional. The French Ambassador is a recluse; the British, see above; the Japanese has suddenly been recalled because of some scandal; we avoid the Israeli; the American told AW that he spends most of his working time on the War on Terror (what did he do before? we wonder); and the Italian is so enormous that, as he jokes himself, he has to be given two chairs to sit on at dinner. I have been to only one diplomatic party so far – the Latvian National Day. I didn't know what to say to the Ambassador after congratulating him on the Day, so I just said something about how much we were looking forward to visiting his lovely country – he somehow took this to mean that we were going there imminently, like next Monday, and started to get all excited. I had to stammer out quickly that we hadn't actually quite decided *when* we were going to Latvia but we would surely be making our plans one of these days.

Looking around at the assembled Diplomatic Corps in the room, I realized that if they were all auditioned for a part in the famous Ferrero Rocher 'ambassador's party' advertisement not one would get a part. Oh okay, maybe the Frenchman, who is very handsome, would, even if he doesn't appear very often, and I must admit that the Spaniard is good-looking, but he wasn't at the party. And the Rumanian does look a bit like Alain Delon . . .

Mind you, there are oddities in the Dip Corps all across the world – the most unnerving we ever met was a German diplomat who had an artificial right arm. He usually kept it tucked by its thumb into his belt, but if you came up to greet him he would un-tuck his hand, and throw it at you to catch and shake. It was a nightmare: you had to have the concentration of a player at Wimbledon waiting for a serve, because if you missed, his arm was left dangling in a most embarrassing way.

Later. It has suddenly occurred to me, perhaps it isn't diplomatic society in Kaz that is dysfunctional, perhaps it's us – they are probably all functioning away quite happily but *leaving us out*. We are social pariahs.

Self-confidence has never been a strong suit in my family. When my mother was sent home from India (where her father was working as an engineer) to a convent in East Anglia way back in the 1920s, she accidentally overheard the most popular girl in the school complaining to her friends that too many others wanted to be in their group. 'We've got to draw the line somewhere,' my poor mother heard her say, 'so we'll draw it at Maisie Moss' (my mother). I don't think she ever quite got over it. By definition, an ex-pat is always an outsider – and this makes us even more vulnerable to paranoia and fear of rejection. Someone has only to ask me innocently, 'Will I see you at the Smiths' dinner tonight?' and I am plunged into a fever of worry about why the Smiths have not invited us.

Which reminds me, I must get on with planning some dinner parties myself, instead of sitting here, grumpily saying why should we invite the Canadians/Greeks/Americans/British/Spanish/French when they've never asked us. I would say that it is all my fault that no one has invited us because as soon as I've had a glass of wine I can't stop talking, but since we've hardly been out since we got here, no one could possibly know that yet.

2 March

Saturday, hurrah! But feel a bit odd today as last night I dreamt that I went to an incredibly trendy new restaurant in London and when I came to pay I saw that my waiter had written a description of me on the bill which said WHITE, SOLID AND PICKLED.

We have arranged a trade-off. AW can go riding on Saturday mornings if he will take me to church on Saturday evenings. Today this worked perfectly and we went to the museum in between. There is a huge section (which we skipped through) devoted to things that happened in what the locals call Soviet Time. Much more appealing were the showcases of costumes and domestic utensils from all the different minorities, with documents (which unfortunately we couldn't read as they were in Russian) giving the reasons they were exiled to Kazakhstan. But the best part of the museum is definitely the carpet shop in the lobby.

A weird thing happened at the riding school – we met a Frenchman whom we'd known in one of our first postings, Trinidad, thirty years ago. In fact his wife, Marie-Pierre, was my best friend there, but we lost touch a long while back. Sadly, she is not in Kaz, having decided to stick with her career in Paris. I can never forget Marie-Pierre – she was having lunch with me one day on our verandah in Port of Spain, and we were just gossiping about a woman we both disliked when the whole verandah began to shake. I had never been in an earthquake before, and it was so terrifyingly confusing that I thought that the woman we were talking about must have somehow got under the house and was shaking it. I tried to explain this to Marie-Pierre, but she said 'Don't be silly, *this is an earthquake.*' We got up to run, but by then it was already over.

A thin congregation at Mass – about twenty-five people, mostly American with a few Filipinos and Sri Lankans. The old priest is American and gave a rather odd sermon condemning Lesbians in Kyrgyzstan (I think, but the microphone distorted the sound so badly I might have got it wrong). But he is a bit of a hero – he drives 350 kilometres from Jarkent on the Chinese border to Almaty every Saturday to say Mass for the tiny English-speaking congregation, and then drives back again. He is in Jarkent trying to re establish a Catholic community there – the last one, a group of Franciscan friars, having been wiped out by Genghis Khan's grandson in the 1300s.

3 March

A lovely day, and we drove out into the snowy wastes of the steppe – sun shining, mountains gleaming in the distance, all very beautiful if you like empty landscapes.

When you see the snow-covered tree branches in the sun against a blue sky, you have the illusion that you are looking at apple or almond blossom. It turns out I am not alone in thinking this – there is even a fairy tale about it. A Portuguese king once married a beautiful princess from Norway, but when the princess went to live in Portugal she pined away all winter for the snow that she loved in her own country, and eventually took to her bed. Luckily, it was soon spring, and the king, who had realized what was wrong, carried her to the window of their castle so that she could look down over the vast orchards of fruit trees covered with 'snow', while their petals lay in drifts on the ground, and the princess recovered and lived happily ever after.

4 March

Ever since I head about the couple being gassed in their bedroom I have been nagging AW about getting a security system installed in the house. It was put in today because AW has to go to Astana tomorrow leaving me alone for the night for the first time.

6 March

Lay awake all last night worrying about what to do if the alarm actually went off – I would have got more sleep if I'd simply been listening for burglars. This is my security system dilemma: if the alarm starts ringing, do I assume it's a mistake and go downstairs to turn it off – and find myself face to face with the intruders? Or do I call the guard from my balcony? The problem with that is I can only say 'good morning' and 'thank you' in Russian, and neither of those quite fit the situation. Indeed, with the alarm jangling away in the background, the guard might simply decide to shoot at a dark shape on the balcony mouthing strange sounds. Will have to consult AW when he gets back this afternoon.

Before I came here I ordered the *Guardian Weekly* so as to keep up with what's going on at home, but in Kaz it seems to have turned into the *Guardian Monthly*. So last night, AW being away, I read *The Times of Central Asia* from cover to cover. I found a story that would put you off travelling in this region for life – on trains in Tajikistan, apparently, women and girl travellers are often subjected by drug patrols to 'searches of their most intimate and private body parts' . . . This can happen so often that, according to the paper, 'seasoned women travellers' bring a pair of rubber gloves for the customs officials to put on before they do the searches. Sometimes, though, the story continued, the officials just take the gloves and wear the same pair to search all the other women on the train . . . Yuck!

7 *March*

Have been wondering why my dearest old friend Meriel has not been in touch, so I rang her and discovered that she has been ringing the Almaty post code and not the telephone number.

Went to check out the *vanya* today before I actually commit myself to taking off my clothes and having a bath. After some confusion and lots of sign language about what I wanted, a v. nice woman who spoke some English took me round. She showed me the Turkish bath – a huge room under a domed roof with niches all around where you wash yourself with hot and cold water before stretching out to be massaged or to relax on a marble platform – all very much like a real Arab *hammam*. It was empty, but across the hallway the Finnish/Russian sauna section was absolutely packed with naked women of every conceivable size, age, shape and colour. I was stopped at the door and told I couldn't go in with my clothes on, but my guide managed to convince the wardress person guarding the entrance that I was doing serious research of some sort, so she dressed me up in a white coat and plastic slippers and then let me in. I couldn't work out if I was disguised as a doctor or a cleaning lady but either way, none of the naked women looked at me twice. The Finnish sauna room has steam and the Russian is 'dry' – but all customers end their session in a huge round marble swimming pool under another colossal dome. Looking down on the pool was like seeing one of those Orientalist paintings of harem ladies bathing come to life. The one thing I forgot to ask is what customers are supposed to do with the bunches of dried oak leaves that vendors sell along the pavement outside the *vanya*. I think they must be for slapping the skin to stimulate the circulation.

They *do* do leg waxing – in a rather dingy beauty salon on the ground floor. There are two beauticians, a Russian and a Kazakh who work on different days and won't take each other's bookings. I had the Russian who was very efficient, but all the towels are beige and I couldn't help wondering if they'd started off white.

8 March

It's Women's Day today. This is a cross between St Valentine's and Mother's Day; it is a public holiday, and is taken *very* seriously here. Prompted by Gainee, AW did his stuff – a party was held in the office this evening and every woman (including me!) was given a red rose. Men's Day was in February – it used to be called Red Army Day but has been de-militarized.

It's no use putting it off any longer – I must face my dragons, as they used to tell us in childbirth classes, and *plan a dinner party*.

One of the problems I have with entertaining is that my mind goes blank when it comes to the menu. Suddenly I can't think of anything normal like risotto or chicken stew; I can only imagine things like breasts of scarlet ibis in a sauce of cloudberries (of course I am making this up, but it gives you an idea of the dementia that sets in at the mere thought of entertaining).

The worst experience in my life as a hostess happened in Syria. AW planned a buffet dinner for fifty people in a hotel in Damascus, but the President's son was killed in a car accident, and all enter-taining in hotels was banned for the mourning period of forty days. AW decided that we should go ahead with the party and entertain the guests at home. In theory I had a cook, but in reality Marcelle had only just started working for us, and I was training her. It was a nightmare. There was a power cut that day so we had hardly any light and the blender couldn't work, and then of course, instead of choosing to do a nice simple curry with boiled rice and a few easy side dishes, I'd opted for some wildly elaborate Thai recipes which I'd never tried before. One of them involved lemon-grass – this was a new ingredient for me then, and I just chopped up all the stalks and threw them in. The curry tasted okay, but it was like eating prickly thistles, so we had to take out all the chicken, wash it, then sieve the sauce. The beef had to be lifted out of its sauce and washed as well because something we'd added made it horribly bitter.

We sweated nervously over that meal for hours, and then suddenly an old grey rat appeared from nowhere in the kitchen. I screamed and ran to fetch the gardener, but Marcelle grabbed a broom and beat it to death there and then amongst all the food, apologizing to it all the while, so that it wouldn't send its relatives to get revenge. Somehow the party was a success – no one knew about the rat blood all over everything of course – but I don't think I've ever been quite the same since.

Later. AW's secretary has invited twelve people to dinner on the fourteenth. We have chosen them carefully – a mix of diplomats, oil company bosses and businessmen. Thank heavens Nina seems to have assumed all responsibility for the menu. She says we are having smoked salmon, *coq au vin* and apple pie, and that's that.

12 March

Something so embarrassing happened today, it quite took my mind off homesickness and dinner parties. AW wanted me to get tickets for *Prince Igor* at the Opera House tonight (going to the opera here is as easy and cheap as going to the cinema in London). Yuri drove me down to the Opera House and when we got there I said 'You come with me?' meaning, to help me buy the tickets at the Box Office.

Yuri looked panic-stricken, went bright red, and said '*Niet, niet*' – and I realized with horror that he thought I was inviting him to the opera with me that evening. Then of course I had to flounder around trying to explain that *no*, I did not want him to come with me to the *opera*, just the box office. Oh God! He probably still thinks that I was inviting him, but got scared off by his reaction. What shall I do? Perhaps he thinks I have a secret crush on him.

13 March

I am never going to entertain anyone ever again. Just getting a clear 'yes' or 'no' out of the guests we've invited to our dinner party turns out to be the stuff of nervous breakdowns. One couple accepted, and then asked who else was coming. When they were told the names of the other guests they said they couldn't come after all.

Two couples accepted and then cancelled – one of them today, the very day before the dinner. A third couple said 'yes, probably, we'll confirm later', and they still haven't . . .

Personally I'd find it a great relief if it ends up being just AW and me sitting down alone tomorrow to eat the dinner for twelve, but it would be so humiliating if Nina and Ira and Yuri saw that no one wants to come to dinner with us.

Later. *Prince Igor* was terrific – cast of thousands in a glorious hotchpotch of exotic clothes that looked as if they'd come out of a huge family dressing-up box. The Opera and Ballet House was built in 1939 but has just been restored with masses of wonderfully over-the-top glitzy decoration inspired by Kazakhstan's national treasure, the Golden Man. (This is the body of a king or high priest dressed in an elaborate suit of gold; it was found in the 1970s when Russian archaeologists excavated a Sythian tomb not far from Almaty.) Some of the greatest Russian ballet stars and musicians have appeared in the Opera House here because, during the war, they were packed off to Almaty to keep them out of harm's way should the Germans invade Moscow. The legendary Russian film director, Eisenstein, was sent here in 1941, along with the whole Moscow film studio. In fact, he made *Ivan the Terrible* right here in Almaty (it is said that he only dared to give Ivan Stalin-like characteristics because he was so far from Moscow).

Yuri seems to be behaving perfectly normally in spite of yesterday's embarrassment. I am simply going to pretend it never happened.

15 March

At the eleventh hour, when I was beginning to hyperventilate about the dinner party, everything fell into place. Somehow, we managed to get thirteen people to come – only two of them from the original guest list – and it was all a howling success in spite of the unlucky number. Why do I get myself into such a panic? As Hester once coolly said about a family reunion I was struggling to organize for my parents' fortieth wedding anniversary: 'Why are you making such a fuss? They're only people.'

17 March

A strange coincidence: only last week I wrote about the rat in the kitchen in Syria and today we had our own Kazakh rat drama.

Last night AW and I were watching a video on the telly in the attic upstairs when we heard a little scrabbling noise. We looked up and, to our horror, saw a large rat walking across the plastic parquet. Since it was late and dark outside, AW shooed it into a room off the attic and shut the door. Being Buddhist, AW can't kill things, so this morning he told Yuri to catch the rat in a box and put it out in the garden, then he went off to work. Yuri spent hours and hours sweeping every flake of snow off the driveway until eventually I went out and suggested that perhaps we should do something about the rat.

'I get poison,' he said in his glum voice.

'No, no,' I said, 'we mustn't kill it.' He shrugged and went back to sweeping snow.

In the kitchen Ira, trembling with the thrill of it all, had got her dustpan and brush ready. 'It is red rat,' she said to me, in the voice of someone who was an expert on the subject.

It became obvious that no one was actually going to do anything until AW came home for lunch. As soon as he did, we all went upstairs in a little procession with AW leading the way carrying a cardboard box, and Ira, who wasn't going to miss a thing, at the back, excitedly clutching her dustpan and brush. The rat was hiding under a cushion but AW managed to get it into the box and then Yuri, looking triumphant – as though he had done it all – led the procession into the garden and released the rat.

When it was all over I said to Ira, 'So, that was what you call a red rat in Kazakhstan?'

Ira looked at me as though I was mad and said 'No, was grey rat,' leaving me utterly baffled.

Now that I come to think of it, our family seems to have had more than its share of close encounters with rodents. There was the time I went to the loo in Damascus: I just happened to glance down before I pulled the flush and saw the shocking sight of a rat's back under the water with its long black tail poking up the side. My friend Meriel was staying at the time and came running when she heard my shriek, but I don't think she's ever believed me because I had done about fifty maniacal flushings before she arrived and the creature was no longer there.

And then there was our horrible experience in Somerset. We had all just arrived home on leave and were starving. We'd picked up some bread and cheese at a garage on the way down, and then someone remembered Dad's Pickled Onions and rushed to the larder to get them out. AW pickles onions on our annual leave every year and puts them in one of those big wide-necked stoneware jars. We lost the corks long ago so we just put a piece of foil over the top. Anyway, Hester and Claudia and AW helped themselves to a dishful of onions and then disappeared to eat them watching TV, leaving me alone in the kitchen.

I don't much like pickled onions but I thought I'd try one anyway, so I was about to fish one out when I noticed something large and dark and smooth in the jar. 'I don't remember AW pickling aubergines,' I was thinking to myself, when the aubergine gently rolled over and I saw it was a big dead mouse. AARGH! My family had just eaten onions that had spent a whole year next to a dead mouse. Almost hysterical, we rang the doctor. He said that vinegar was one of the best antiseptics and everyone would probably be okay. Sure enough, there were no ill effects – except of course, mental ones for me, who had found it. I feel quite ill just writing this.

18 March

Oh God . . . the new white chair covers I ordered have just arrived and though they look great with the red Kazakh carpets, the upholsterer has added a hideous belt with a buckle around the lower corners of every chair and sofa. 'Modern style,' he said nervously, as he saw me wincing. How do things like this happen? We discussed these covers over and over but it never occurred to me to say 'Oh by the way, don't put belts and buckles round the corners' (the same way it never occurred to me to tell Hari, the cook in India, not to boil the lettuce before adding the vinaigrette the first time he made a green salad). It's weird, you think you've covered every possibility that even a doom-laden imagination like mine can come up with, but there is always something else you would never have thought of in a million years. Anyway, it turned out the straps and buckles were easy to take off, and now, miraculously, the sitting room looks marvellous − it has taken on the appearance of a place belonging to a cool, calm, self-confident kind of person and not an insecure depressive.

'Garmonie,' said Nina approvingly when she came to give her verdict.

19 March

I am going home in a few days!! AW and I are renovating a house in France and it seems that the builder needs me to make urgent decisions. It's strange, but even with a trip home to look forward to, I still can't get to grips with the idea of living here for the next four years. One minute I feel more or less okay, but then I am plunged into misery again. I need a friend, a kindred spirit; a friend would make everything all right. As P.G. Wodehouse once observed, to enjoy life, all you need is a couple of chaps to totter about with. I thought I had found one last week, but when I asked her to tea she said she'd have to leave early to go with her husband to their ballroom dancing class. I am not sure I can bond fully with someone who does ballroom dancing lessons.

My only friend at the moment is a literary one: Lady Macartney, the wife of the British Consul in Kashgar in 1898, who wrote a book of memoirs called *An English Lady in Chinese Turkestan*. She had never been abroad at all when she married at eighteen and set off for her new life in the wilds of Central Asia. Unlike me, she only complains once in the entire book, but her little outburst echoes just what I feel: 'How desperately homesick I was! And especially so when we got into Russia, and I found I could speak to no one. I could not read a word in a newspaper, or even the name of a station or a shop. And I had four long years of living in a strange land to look forward to . . .'

I have also been reading *Under A Peacock Fan*, about various British women who lived in India in the eighteenth and nineteenth centuries. I complain about the telephone being expensive and my email being slow, but how spoiled I am – they had to wait months and months just for a letter. A British traveller to India at the time sympathized with their plight and wrote that only a woman with a really energetic character did not become demoralized there. 'The first sign of deterioration is when a woman omits her corsets from her toilette and begins lolling about in a sloppy and tumbled tea gown.' I took a nap after lunch today and wonder now if this is the just the beginning of 'lolling about' for the rest of this posting – but, actually, I am far more likely to be found in a sloppy gown late in the morning in England, where there is no Nina to disapprove.

20 March

At the farewell party for the Papal Nuncio last night, AW brought over the pretty young wife of the Rumanian Ambassador and said, 'I think you two have something in common.'

It turned out that Cecilia is a doctor who has given up her practice in Bucharest to come with her husband to Kazakhstan (his first posting abroad) and she is *miserable*.

'You and I seem to be the only ones who are,' I said. 'All the other wives seem to be fine.'

'Of course they are not,' she said, 'they just put a good face on it.'

She doesn't know what to do: return to Bucharest, re-start her medical practice and risk losing her husband, or stick it out and be unhappy. 'This is my first experience abroad as the wife of a diplomat,' she said, 'but you have done it many times . . . what is your advice?'

Cecilia is only twenty-nine, her husband is clever and obviously has decades of postings ahead of him. It will be really difficult for her to continue her career – doctoring is not one of the portable professions because of the different qualifications, and more importantly, the languages, required. Here in Kazakhstan, for instance, she can't practise as a doctor as she does not speak Russian. She is rather like I was years ago when I didn't know whether to chose AW and an unknown future, or keep my marvellous job on a newspaper. I chose the unknown future, but did I do the right thing? Would it have been better if I'd opted for the job?

What on earth should I tell her?

Perhaps this is a good time to explain our French connection. It all began long ago, before I was married, when I was Fashion and Beauty Editor of *Nova* magazine. Out of the blue I was asked to do a TV commercial for Radiant washing powder. (Radiant seemed to disappear off the market soon after my appearance; I've always hoped the two events were not connected.)

The commercial was to be shown live, in three parts. In the first, I had to hold up a little white nylon dress and say 'Ugh, this dress is covered with egg, blood, gravy and sweat.' (It really was: they were sprayed on to the dress by two people called the Stain Team who had come from Port Sunlight specially.) Then I had to put the dress to soak in Radiant and say jauntily, 'Join me in the next break.' In Part Two, I had to lift the dress out of the sudsy water, act surprised and pleased, and say, 'Look! The stains have completely disappeared.' The final scene opened with me pressing the dress; then I had to glance up from the ironing board at the camera and say, 'Well, I really have convinced myself that Radiant gives the whiter white.' (It's deeply embarrassing writing this, even thirty-five years after it happened.)

All went well until the final rehearsal, just before we went on air. In the last scene I looked up, beamed at the camera and said,

'Well, I really have convinced myself that *Ariel* gives the whiter white.' I didn't realize what I had said and wondered why there was an awestruck silence. Then a desperate voice said, '*Jesus Christ* . . .' In the few seconds left before we had to begin filming the real thing, everyone wrote RADIANT on scraps of paper and held them up in front of me.

That last bit of the commercial was shown again and again – for a while, almost every time I switched on the telly I saw my own terror-stricken face repeating 'Radiant gives the whiter white' in a voice gone flat with fear. The worst part of it was that I had just met AW then, and he saw it too. It was mortifying. But the point of this story is that my fee was £1,000 ('Not much for your soul,' said Meriel) and with this I bought a tiny three-roomed house in a village in the Languedoc. AW has always suspected that I only married him to pay the builder who made it habitable. (It's true that I don't know how I would have paid the builder if I hadn't married AW, but that is not exactly the same thing.)

We have spent every summer holiday there since. Our children have grown up there – from babies in carry-cots to teenagers falling in love with Algerians in the local town. There was the summer Hester fell on a glass bottle which went through her hand, and the summer Claudia had her face bitten by a dog. Later, there were the summers of the village fêtes (fêtes worse than death I called them, as I had to drive the girls to whichever far-flung village was celebrating, wait for hours without a drink, and then prise them away from the boys they'd met and drive them home again). I don't recall AW clocking in for many French holidays in those years; I always seemed to be a single parent at the fêtes.

There was the summer I forgot I had rented out the house to other people. As we drove up to the village in our hired car, AW said, 'That's odd, why is there a light on in your top room?' and only then – with a hideous lurch of the stomach – I remembered that there were tenants in it. I had to go and knock on the door and explain that I was the owner and we'd come on holiday, and could they tell us how long they were going to be staying? Luckily it was only for one more night and they let us sleep on the floor. There was the summer we woke up and found that every single car without a local number plate had had its tyres slashed. There was the summer that Claudia and her friends, Laura and Jasmine, set fire to the vineyards by lighting bangers at the edge of the road – six fire engines came and it was only because Jasmine's father knew someone who knew the mayor who knew the firemen's boss that we escaped having to pay a fortune in costs.

And there was the summer that AW, in a tender mood, came and sat beside me on the bed one morning, whereupon both legs on that side of the bed gave way, and my sleeping body was catapulted into the bathroom. (Talk about not knowing where you are when you wake up.)

AW often says that if we sold the house we could use the money to go somewhere different and more exciting every year, but a) he loves being in France as much as I do, it's just that he hates having to do a year's worth of gardening and household repairs every summer holiday. And b) we tend to live 'somewhere different and more exciting' for the rest of the year anyway. And c) it's just *because* we lead such an insecure gypsy life that I love finding the same cast of characters on our holidays every year.

This is the place I have to go back to in a few days' time because the builder needs some vital decisions made.

London, 28 March

I don't know what happens to me when I go home from a posting – it's as if my body arrives back but my brain is delayed in transit, and I keep losing and forgetting things. It's always been like this – I have left a trail of coats, cardigans, typewriters and suitcases in planes, trains, buses and taxis all around the world, and I can't count the hairbrushes, sunglasses, paperbacks and gloves that have somehow slid down the side of the seat in the plane or been left in the back of a cab.

But my arrival back from Kazakhstan this time took the biscuit. It was *catastrophic*! My briefcase with all my most important possessions – including and especially my address book – was stolen off my trolley in Terminal Two ('Terminal' is such a sinister word, and for me it nearly always manages to live up to it). Of course I didn't notice until I'd got home. Then, after the first, stomach-churning realization that the case was not there, I prayed feverishly – and a sort of miracle happened. My address book, passport, tickets and so on were all found dumped somewhere in the luggage hall, and handed in. The jewellery, money and makeup – and the brief-case itself – had gone, though.

My trials didn't stop there. I got into the car (which I'd left parked in London) and found the battery was flat. Called the AA who told me I needed a new battery, bought one, drove to the airport to collect my things, and then continued on down to our house in Somerset. There I took a giant bite out of an apple I'd bought for lunch – and dislocated my jaw. Can now part lips only about a centimetre and, as a result, am speaking like ventriloquist. With difficulty (owing to mouth not opening) I telephoned the builder in France to announce my arrival in a few days – and dis-covered that he was going on holiday the very day I appear. (It never occurred to me to check his movements before buying my tickets on the Eurostar.) Most obligingly he offered to go a day later so we could make the necessary decisions about the work on the house – phew!

There was a message on the answering machine in Somerset from someone threatening to cut off our legs and pull our entrails out through our arseholes. Luckily I had heard about it in advance because it had already given Willie Dalrymple and his family a hor-rible fright when they came to stay in our house for the weekend not long ago while we were away. I thanked God I hadn't been the first to find it on some dark night arriving late and alone. Claudia came down (Hester is still in Egypt) and we had a lovely weekend and didn't quarrel once – not even about the fact that she hasn't yet, after a year and a half, got a part-time job, even as a babysitter.

Back in London a day or two later I lost the car key and had to call the AA again. (Soon afterwards I met the BBC correspon-dent Lyse Doucet at a party and – goodness knows why – I told her about losing the car key. She told me that she'd nearly lost her *life* the previous week in Afghanistan when there was an assassina-tion attempt on Hamid Karzai and she was standing next to him.

Then she paused thoughtfully and said, 'Actually, I think losing the car key is probably worse . . .' I felt I'd found a true soulmate.)

Apart from the trail of disaster I seem to drag in my wake when travelling, I find re-entering life in England really quite awkward. I feel surprisingly nervous – almost apologetic – telephoning friends to say that I'm home again. Sometimes I find it quite nerve-racking just trying to hold a normal conversation. Once, arriving in London soon after we'd bought our *pied-à-terre* in Pimlico, I stopped someone in the street to ask where I would find a 24 bus stop, except that what I actually said was 'Excuse me, could you tell me where to get a 24-inch bust?' (Mind you, this could have had less to do with re-entry, and more with having been a fashion editor for years – in my mind a number like '24' has to be followed by the word 'inch' and the world 'inch' has to be followed by 'bust' or 'waist', in much the same way that I can't say 'superfluous' without adding 'hair'.)

I seem to lose my confidence and become socially inept back in London. Years ago Felicity Lawrence, then editor of the *Telegraph Magazine*, asked me to lunch at Orso's in Covent Garden. I hadn't seen her for years and she'd married and had children in the meantime, so I was not altogether surprised, when I entered the restaurant, to find that I didn't recognize the woman walking towards me with a welcoming smile on her face. But I threw my arms around her and was kissing her enthusiastically when she suddenly said 'Are you for the table for two, Madame?' To my horror I realized I had hugged and kissed the Maître D. All I could do was pray that Felicity hadn't witnessed the scene – otherwise I was going to have to pretend all through lunch that the Maître D was my best friend. She didn't mention it, so I kept very quiet and gave the Maître D a knowing smile when we left, to make her think that I knew what I was doing all along.

Another problem with re-entry is the chaos factor. When your children have left your posting for school or university, the ex-pat wife's life abroad becomes a very quiet and silent one. You are alone with your husband – there is no mess apart from what you make yourself, no phones ringing all the time, no young people coming and going at odd hours, no one getting up at lunchtime for breakfast, no crumbs on the carpet. You get used to being in this oasis of serenity and peace, and then you return to your base in England and *WHAM*! It's like entering Bedlam.

A couple of years ago I got back to our flat in London to find both daughters had friends staying. They all went out that evening, so that was okay, but next morning there was utter confusion with bedding all over the place and five of us trying to get washed and dressed in a small flat. After the fourth try, I managed to get into the bathroom where, stressed out, I filled the glass by the basin with water and drank it down. Two seconds later there was banging on the door – 'Mum, Mum,' said Hester urgently, 'James needs his contact lenses, they're in the glass by the basin . . .' It was too late. I had drunk them. As Constance Gordon Cumming, a nineteenth-century woman traveller once wrote, returning home 'involves more wear and tear of mind and body than any amount of travelling in distant lands.'

It goes without saying that when you go home, none of your friends are remotely interested in hearing about your life abroad. I remember telling someone about how worried we, in Syria, were about the collapse of the peace talks with Israel, and she suddenly interrupted to say: 'Well, I can't really get worked up about all that; I've got a book to finish before Christmas.' Once, I stupidly blurted out to some close women friends at lunch that I didn't know what to do because my butler was leaving . . . I don't know how I ever lived that down.

'*Oh no!*' they shrieked. 'What a catastrophe! How on *earth* will you manage without your *butler*? What *are* you going to do? *HAR HAR HAR* . . .'

15 April

A good deal of my time on this trip has been spent visiting the doctor, dentist and chiropractor trying to get my mouth to open again, but I have managed to catch up with some friends, and I sorted out the house restoration in France.

All through this disaster-prone leave, poor Cecilia in Kazakhstan kept coming into my mind. What should I reply to her when I get back? Of course, right this minute, after a mere six weeks in Almaty, plus a stressful return home and, now, the prospect of once again tearing myself away from the people I love, I would tell her to forget all about her handsome husband and the diplomatic life abroad, go back to Rumania immediately, set up her medical practice once more, and never look back. But even I can appreciate that this would be rather irresponsible advice.

Do I regret my own decision to 'pack and follow', as the nineteenth century ex-pat wife, Isobel Burton, famously put it? If I knew then what I know now, would I have made the same choice? The fairest thing, it seems to me, it to go back over the last thirty years of postings abroad and then decide what I should tell her. I'll rewind to the beginning . . .

2

Love in a Chicken Shed

I heard of AW long before I actually met him, because my friend Sandy had married his best friend, Adrian – they'd been at school and university together. But AW was always abroad – it was 1970 and he was working in Libya then – so though I was told the odd snippet about him and his life in an oasis in the Sahara desert, I never met him face to face. Not even at Sandy and Adrian's wedding at which he was Best Man; he met my sister there – and rather took to her (he told me later) – but, somehow, not me.

A year or so later, when Sandy was expecting their first baby, AW came to stay with them in London for a few days. I heard all about it (I lived opposite Sandy and Adrian) – 'Adrian's friend has left his ghastly great desert boots in the cot I've just done up for the baby,' groaned Sandy, and I sympathized.

Then the baby was born and AW and I were asked to be its godparents. We met by chance, both visiting Sandy and the baby in the maternity ward at the same time (talk about fate) and shook hands over her bed. As we left the hospital, AW said, 'Wouldn't it be a good idea if we were to give the baby a joint present – we could buy something nicer than if we gave separate presents?' So we arranged to meet in the Silver Vaults in Chancery Lane, where our destiny was sealed by Mr Nathan, a silversmith. For, as we came to pay for the pair of wine coasters we had decided to buy, AW handed over his credit card and Mr Nathan said, 'Shall I put the whole amount on this card, or will your wife be paying separately?' *Your wife!* AW and I went bright red and tried to pretend we hadn't heard, but the strange thing is, we discovered later, that we both knew for certain at that moment that I would be his wife. Though quite how (I wondered) a sophisticated Women's Editor of the

Observer (which I was to become in a month's time) could ever marry this shy, desert-booted adventurer from Libya, was beyond me. And when he asked me out and we got to know each other, our chances seemed to grow even slimmer: he was younger than me, owned a pale blue Morris Minor (maybe chic now, but definitely not then), and knew London so little that when he took me to dinner at a Persian restaurant in Kensington he drove from Battersea via Aldwych. And I noticed that his eyes never glistened once during *The Railway Children*, our first film together, which I sobbed all the way through. (I've only seen AW cry once in all the years we've been together and that was when Hudson, the butler in *Upstairs, Downstairs*, offered to work for the upstairs family for nothing. AW says it's loyalty that gets him.)

Against all the odds, though, we fell madly in love – but our situation was desperate: he was taking up a new post in Nepal and was leaving in only three weeks' time. It was heart-rending, but there was nothing we could do, except promise to write to each other often.

I started my grand new job at the *Observer* after he'd gone. On my very first morning the lift broke down between floors and I had to climb out, so I arrived on my hands and knees which was pretty much the position I remained in for the next year and a quarter – mostly because, I still think, the Editor had hired the wrong Keenan. At that time, my older sister Moira was running the Women's Pages of *The Times*; she was married with children, marvellously clever, and the perfect Women's Editor for the *Observer*. I was not married and was working on trendy *Nova* magazine doing frivolous un-*Observer* things like re-vamping the Queen or interviewing the Best Dressed Woman in the World. To this day I believe that the *Observer* recruited the wrong sister – rather like that book *Green Dolphin Country* in which the nineteenth-century hero emigrates to New Zealand, and then sends back to England for his true love who is one of two sisters. Somehow, the wrong one steps off the sailing ship when it arrives months later, but he never dares tell her of the mistake, even though it breaks his and the left-behind-in-England sister's hearts.

There were some nice things about being at the *Observer*. One was that I inherited Shirley Conran's desk (she'd done the job before me) which had a fascinating list of 'dos and don'ts when writing' sellotaped to it – the only one I remember now is 'Never use the word "thus"'. (Excellent advice.) Other joys were making friends with Haro, the cartoonist, and Eric Newby, the travel writer. Eric kept his bicycle in the fashion cupboard; he was always jolly, and carried a whiff of adventure and places flung far from the office in Printing House Square, which was somehow comforting. Haro shared the Women's Pages room – his drawing board faced my desk – and he kept me from falling into a decline when none of the editors seemed to like anything I produced. (Haro was fired one day, but decided to continue coming in as usual and hope no one would notice. The *Observer* was that kind of place. After a time he found himself back on the pay roll as if nothing had happened.)

When *I* was fired not long afterwards, I was determined to make the Editor admit to the Keenan sisters mistake, so I asked him why he had taken me on in the first place. His answer was not exactly confidence-boosting: he said he hadn't been feeling very well the day he hired me. But, he added, 'We would not like to lose the sound of your little piccolo in our great orchestra,' and offered me a minor job on the *Colour Magazine*. I refused it, and cried on the shoulders of my ex-mates on *Nova* who sent me an enormous bouquet of flowers the following day with a note saying 'WE ALL KNOW YOU ARE THE BIG TROMBONE'. The *Observer* paid me a golden handshake (well, more like silver actually) and with the money I decided to visit AW in Kathmandu later in the year.

Very soon I heard from my ex-secretary, June, that the Women's Editor they hired after me had a nervous breakdown the day she arrived, and had started talking in numbers – 'June,' she would say, '18, 34, 90. Do you understand?' She only lasted a week at the paper, so I had a kind of revenge. I still occasionally dream that I have four blank newspaper pages to fill for Sunday's edition and it's Wednesday, and I have no ideas at all.

I wrote to Harry Evans, the Editor of the *Sunday Times* (where I had worked for years before leaving for *Nova*), asking if there were any jobs going on his women's pages, and soon after that, I went to Heathrow to meet AW who was coming home on his annual leave. I hadn't seen him for seven months. I stood in the crowd of happy, keyed-up people waiting at the arrivals barrier for hours and hours but there was no sign of AW. All the original crowd of expectant friends and relations and taxi-drivers came and went, except for one Hertz chauffeur holding a board with someone's name on it. Suddenly he approached me and asked if I would hold his board for him while he went to the toilet. 'I hope you don't mind,' he said, 'but I'm desperate. If my client turns up, just ask him to wait for a minute or two.' So I was holding the Hertz board when, to my horror, Harry Evans came through the barrier. Whether he saw me or not I never knew, but I did get a letter offering me the job of Beauty Editor on the *Sunday Times* a few days later, and I imagined him thinking, 'Poor Brigid, she can't get a job in journalism so she's had to become a driver for Hertz. Must be hard.' I agreed to start when I returned from Nepal.

AW never turned up that May morning – he had missed his plane (it left Kathmandu early, he said) and so arrived two days later. (I don't think I've ever had a successful meeting at London airport with anyone – something always goes wrong.) We went on holiday to France, blissfully happily, and made plans for my visit to Nepal in a month's time. He advised me on what I should bring – 'gumboots might be useful'. How ridiculous, I thought. What an idea. Gumboots in Kathmandu! I ignored his advice and packed a cocktail frock and an evening dress for dinners at embassies and such. Oh, and my hairpiece (hairpieces were big then), but at the very last minute I decided I had better not upset him, so I rushed to Russell and Bromley and bought a pair of red gumboots and chucked them into my case.

I had to change planes in Delhi where, for some unknown reason, there was a choice of two flights to take me to Nepal. Being terrified of flying, I knew one would crash . . . but which one? I tried to off-load the decision on to the huge Sikh at the ticket desk.

'No, no, Madam,' he said, 'it is you who must decide.'

'No, *please*,' I implored, you just tell me which one to take.'

'No, this is entirely up to you,' and so on, until I nearly missed both of them.

I arrived at Kathmandu airport safely after an amazing journey in which we could see the white peaks of the Himalayas (including Mount Everest) stretching as far as the eye could see, like petrified waves in an endless sea. In fact it was to be the only time I ever saw the mountains in Nepal, as a dust haze blocks their view in summer. AW was waiting on the tarmac. It was so romantic. I started towards him, beaming, imagining the scene in *Un Homme et une Femme* where the lovers run towards each other in slow motion, but he walked straight past me and shook the hand of the man who'd come off the plane behind me. This, it turned out, was his London boss who'd come out on an official visit to the project AW was working on – I'd had no idea he existed, let alone was on my plane. (AW told me later that the decision about which visitor to greet first had been an agonizing one . . .)

That night we all went out to dinner in a restaurant in Kathmandu called the Yak and Yeti. While we were eating, a rat came out and ran around the floor. No one did a thing.

'Goodness me!' I said brightly, trying to show AW and his boss how I wasn't fazed by anything the Third World could throw at me, 'in London if a rat came out and ran around the restaurant, everyone would be horrified, but here . . .' I laughed merrily, '. . . here it's just part of the scenery.'

'Just so long as it's not part of the soup,' growled an American hippie at the next table.

AW had a flat in a lovely old colonial-style house in the leafy suburbs of Kathmandu, but it turned out that we were to spend only two nights there because the British Government project that the Boss had come to inspect – and for which AW was working as the agricultural economist – was down in the Terai, the hot, flat, plains area between Nepal and India. The British were building a road through there – a loop on the Asian Highway – and AW and his colleagues were making a plan for the agricultural development of the land opened up by the road.

I was woken on my first morning by AW leaping violently out of bed and tearing out of the room. I couldn't imagine what was going on, but it turned out that the unmistakable smell from the kitchen had penetrated his sleep and he knew disaster had occurred.

Sushila, his young Nepalese cook, had chopped up, and was *currying*, the bacon and sausages I had brought out with me because AW had told me how he yearned for an English breakfast. It was a bitter blow as he wouldn't have another chance to eat bacon and sausages for months.

That day we explored Kathmandu – just as exotic as I had imagined it would be, with fantastic carved temples, and beautiful old wooden houses lining narrow streets – and we completed the mission we had been sent on by AW's boss, to His Majesty's Retail Hashish and Gunja Store. He had teenage children, he said, and thought he should try some marijuana so he would know what he was talking about in any future confrontation with them. (Marijuana was legal in Nepal then; it was eventually banned because of the huge influx of hippies and the problems they caused.) We bought a very small amount to try out with the Boss later, in the project camp. The Store, in an upstairs room of one of the old houses, looked just like a small old-fashioned grocery shop selling coffee or tea, but you could tell it wasn't by the numbers of desperately ill-looking Western travellers with septic nose-studs and matted long hair lolling around on the steps.

Next day we set off for the project camp along the Raj Path – the most frightening road I had ever been on, with sheer drops of thousands of feet on one side, vertical cliffs on the other and bends so sharp you had to do a three-point turn to get round them – not to mention the added hazard of lorries coming up from India in the opposite direction with drivers falling asleep, or high on *bhang*. Most of the time we were above the tree line – I noticed this particularly, not because I had done GCE geography, but because it was so obvious that there was nothing to catch us if we went over the edge. At one stage, when the road dipped a bit, we did pass rhododendron trees – they come as trees in the Himalayas, not bushes. Very romantically, AW decided to stop and pick me a spray of flowers. He leaned out from the edge of the cliff to grab a branch, lost his balance, and hung for a moment in space, before he somehow managed to scramble back. His signet ring was pulled off his finger in the struggle and plummeted into the abyss for someone to find, and puzzle over, some day in the future.

Hours later, my back stiff with leaning away from precipices, we arrived at Dumkauli, the site of the camp. I'd visualized this as a *macho* place full of white tents, with tanned Stewart Granger-like men strolling about in khaki, and Ava Gardner-type women with bush shirts tucked into the tiny waists of their jodhpurs. In fact it was a group of slightly larger-than-usual wooden chicken sheds, and the first man we saw was a weedy white one who had rolled up the legs of his cotton shorts higher than the pockets, so that these, which unfortunately were made of a pinkish-beige nylon, hung bulging on the outsides of his thighs, as though his private parts had become displaced.

AW showed me to his own particular chicken shed and my heart sank. It consisted of a meshed verandah about two and a half metres long, and behind that, one room with a bed, a couple of chairs, and a table to eat on – that was the living space. At the back of the hut was a cement lean-to, partitioned into a kitchen and a bathroom. It was all very crude and home-made-looking – which indeed it was: AW had chosen the tree it would be made of when he first arrived, and supervised his hut being built.

It got worse. The huts were built in a large clearing in the forest, and the area all around was apparently teeming with snakes, including one called the Banded Krait – also known as the Seven Step Snake, because if you got bitten you could only take seven steps before you dropped down dead. AW opened the First Aid kit to show me the anti-snake venom supplied by the British Government and reassure me that everything was under control, but when we read the label, we found that it was a) beyond its sell-by date, and b) specifically for African snakes, like mambas, not Indian ones.

There was a loo and a cold-water shower (from a water tank in the centre of the camp), but the shower water drained out through a hole in the outside wall – which also let in the snakes. (When I heard this, I put on my gumboots immediately and rarely took them off again.) AW, by virtue of the fact that he was brave and that he owned a long Gurkha *kukri*, had been appointed the camp snake killer, although the policy was not to harm the snakes unless they were a clear and present danger. Once he'd been called to kill a snake that had *fallen off the top of the bathroom door* on to the naked shoulders of his neighbour, Malcolm, as he stepped inside to take a shower.

Some time after I arrived, a krait was found just outside our hut. It was deemed too dangerous to ignore, and, since kraits are very quick and difficult to kill, it was arranged that the Gurkha drivers would shoo it towards the drainage hole in the bathroom, while AW would wait inside and chop off its head with his *kukri* when it came through. What actually happened – I was standing on a chair at the time, observing from a distance – was that the snake shot through the hole so fast that AW only managed to cut off the end of its tail. So then we had a dangerous angry krait whipping round inside our house, instead of a relatively calm krait dawdling about outside. Ever since Kipling's terrifying story, 'Rikki Tikki Tavi', was read to me when I was a small child in India – belonging to an English family just like the one menaced by the cobra in the book – I have been scared of snakes, and so I stayed on my chair, screaming unhelpfully, until AW had managed, not without risk, to kill it.

The camp's only communication with the outside world was by Morse code to Kathmandu or, locally, by runner. The fridge worked by kerosene and the flame was always blowing out. I can't remember what we kept in the fridge, because even though AW had employed a cook in the camp (his name was Penny, for some reason), every-thing we ate, apart from *dhal* and rice, seemed to come out of a tin. (Till then the whole alternative world of tins had passed me by; now I was amazed to learn that *everything* came in cans – butter, bacon, whole Christmas dinners, anything you wanted.) I liked Penny a lot, in spite of his cooking – AW admitted that he had only hired him because he could play the flute. He was a Sherpa, and had been on lots of mountaineering expeditions; his shorts and T-shirt and socks all had EVEREST 1968 or ANNAPURNA 1970 written on them. I thought that was thrilling.

It was a couple of days after I got there, that I came face to face with the worst hazard of all: the giant jumping spiders. I was having an argument with AW in the kitchen when one of them appeared on the cement wall behind his head. I couldn't believe it – it was the size of a small saucer. My voice died in my throat, and our row ended abruptly; we had to comfort each other in the face of this new and horrible threat. For some reason AW had never seen one before, perhaps they were seasonal – whatever, they seemed to have it in for me: one jumped out of my spongebag a few days later, and once, when we went to visit a family in the local village, I could swear I felt one crawling up my leg inside my trousers; it took every ounce of self-control not to get up and run screaming out of their hut, but squash it against my knee instead.

Our project leader, or Camp Commandant (as I thought of him) insisted the camp generator was turned off promptly at 9 p.m., so our evenings became a desperate race to get inside the mosquito net before we were plunged into darkness, unable to see whether one of the spiders had got into bed with us. I used to check inside the mosquito net with a torch about ten times a night before I could relax enough to sleep. When I was sure we were alone in it, the mosquito net was blissfully secure and comforting. In fact, I rather wished I could go round in one all day long. Lying cosily under the net, even the eerie racket the jackals made on the edge of our clearing did not seem too threatening. Whatever the name is for this noise – howling, yelping, giggling – you would not believe how like a cocktail party that has got seriously out of hand it sounds. Night after night it would be just as if raucous neighbours were throwing yet another wild get-together.

There were tigers near Dumkauli too – a boy from a nearby village was killed, and AW, driving back from the road engineers' camp one evening, was brought to a halt by an enormous tiger padding across the road in front of him. He sincerely wished, as he sat there, that he hadn't been in an open jeep, but the tiger clearly didn't see him as a late-night snack, and continued on its dignified journey.

The London Boss was anxious to try the marijuana before he left, so one evening we invited him to supper in our hut and then, feeling incredibly silly and self-conscious, passed a joint round between us. Goodness knows what was in it – all I can remember is that at one stage the Boss made some sort of feeble joke and I began to laugh politely, but then found I couldn't stop. I went on laughing for about three hours – not a mild chuckle or a giggle, but a vulgar, swaying-to-and-fro, stomach-holding, falling-off-the chair kind of loud belly laugh. The Boss looked surprised; even he must have known that his joke wasn't *that* funny. I had to leave the table and go and lie on the bed, but they could still hear me shrieking and cackling away to myself. It was agony, my head was jangling – it seemed to be full of shards of broken glass. I thought I was going mad, but still I couldn't stop laughing. Next day, AW, the Boss and I all found ourselves plunged into the deepest of depressions. I often wonder what he told his children in the end.

The day after we arrived in the camp AW had to go to work weighing rice grains and measuring crops, and I got my first taste of what it would be like to be an ex-patriate wife. It was desperately hot, my feet were sweating in the gumboots, and there was nothing to do except wander listlessly around in the dried-up scrub looking for discarded snakeskins to give my nephew when I got home. I did discover that when snakes shuffle off their skins, even the transparent outside layer of their eyeballs comes off. Later, when the Boss from London wasn't there, I could occasionally persuade AW to take time off and play battleships with me, using project pay sheets that were conveniently ruled into squares, but on the whole the days passed without anything happening at all.

Then a colleague invited us to dinner outside the camp – I was quite excited, and got dressed up in one of the until-now useless outfits I had brought from London. I almost wore my hairpiece except that somehow out there in the jungle it looked more like a dead animal than a glamorous accessory.

It wasn't quite what I had expected – for a start, it was in a small tent on a lonely Nepalese hillside, and secondly, the dinner was all Heinz baby food. Our host's wife had gone back to England with their baby, leaving him with dozens of tiny tins of stew and pureed apple, so he gave us the chicken and beef stews (mixed together) as a main course, with the apple for pudding. (When AW and I discussed it later, we were thankful that at least the baby had got to the small lump stage – a whole pureed dinner might have been too much to bear.) AW got mildly irritated because our host, John Makin, and I spent most of the evening describing our perfect meals: 'Veal kidneys in mustard sauce in a brasserie in Paris,' I suggested.

'Mmm, delicious,' said John, 'but what about *truite meunière* with a glass of chilled Sancerre in a restaurant by a river in France?'

'Oh, do shut up you two,' said AW.

The only other social engagement we had in the Terai was when the British Ambassador came on a visit. The camp received a Morse code message to say he was arriving on some kind of inspection and would be expecting dinner. As the only woman in the camp at that moment, I was unanimously elected to be in charge of the meal. Even then I had my fear of entertaining, besides in those days I couldn't cook anything grand enough for a dinner party without a recipe book, and of course I had not taken one to Nepal with me. I mean, a cookbook is not the first thing you pop into your luggage when you are off to stay with the man you love. I know better now, of course.

But I vaguely remembered a dish my mother used to make called Chicken Blanquette, which was nice pieces of chicken cooked in a deliciously flavoured white sauce, and I thought we might be able to do a version of that, so I sent Penny off to the nearby village to buy the chickens, and the Gurkha drivers in the camp queued up to be allowed to kill them. We borrowed an extra table and chairs from our neighbours and laid everything out on the verandah as it was so hot. I arranged some flowers in an empty Nescafé jar (without the label) and, while Penny heated up some tinned vegetables and potatoes, I made the white sauce with tinned butter and powdered milk, and put on the long dress I had brought with me for all those embassy dinners I thought we'd be going to.

The Ambassador arrived, unsmiling, and after everyone had been introduced we sat down rather nervously to the Chicken Blanket (as Penny had taken to calling it). It tasted exactly like bits of string boiled in wallpaper paste, but luckily no one really noticed the food, for a small typhoon blew up. Everyone hung on to their plates except the Ambassador, who had that hairstyle in which long strands from the side are combed over a bald pate. He hung on to his hair, so his plate was blown off the table.

It was a disaster, but we all decided that at least he'd gone away with an accurate picture of the conditions we lived in.

Soon after that AW announced that he had to go and talk to villagers in the hills about their crops. How lovely to get out of the hot dreary plains – and the camp – even if only for a couple of nights, I thought . . .

We arrived at the hill village after a long drive through glorious scenery, and were shown to a wattle-and-daub hut with two string beds in it. Then AW had to go off to call the neighbouring villagers to a great meeting. They were, quite literally, called: the Headman stood on top of a hill and yelled out through his cupped hands something like, 'Everyone please come here at eleven o'clock tomorrow morning for an important meeting', and his voice echoed around the surrounding valleys. Fat chance, I remember thinking to myself, that anyone is going to turn up, but next morning hundreds were assembled.

I retired to our mud hut down the hill, wondering idly what to do about going to the loo because, of course, it didn't have one. Later, when my need became more urgent, I thought I had better stroll out and find a bush to hide behind. But when I emerged from the hut I found dozens of people crouched outside – news that a white woman was in the village had obviously got around, and I was a big attraction. Trying not to show any embarrassment I smiled at them, and set off to look for a bush – but the crowd followed me. I must have looked like the Pied Piper as I walked up hillsides and down valleys with a huge chattering gaggle of people behind me. Every now and again I stopped and faced them. I tried being nice: 'Please go away and leave me alone'; I tried being nasty: 'Bugger off, can't you?' I was becoming hysterical; it was impossible to go to the lavatory. In the end I decided that the only thing to do was go back to the hut and wait there until they all got bored and went home, and then I'd be able to creep out in private. I went back and waited, and so did they – I could see them through the chinks in the mud walls. Finally, in desperation, I went into the darkest corner of the hut and squatted down on an airmail edition of *The Times* we happened to have brought with us. When AW came home that evening and I told him my humiliating story, he was very sympathetic, but couldn't help being sorry about the cruel waste of an unread copy of *The Times*.

A couple of weeks later we left the camp on another of AW's business trips – this time to an agricultural research station in a different part of the hills. There was no road to the research station; we were going to have to walk there from the nearest town, Pokhara. The idea of walking a great distance – not for fun, or for exercise, but because it was the only way to get somewhere – seemed exciting. We asked the others in the camp how long it would take. 'Oh, it's nothing,' they said nonchalantly, 'probably do it in a couple of hours or so.'

I hadn't brought any proper walking shoes with me, so I had to wear plastic flip flops. As AW and I neared the end of our gruelling ordeal of staggering up and down hills for about six hours, I happened to look down at my feet, and saw that they had acquired extra fat black toes in between all the pink ones. Leeches. But I was too tired even to feel disgusted when the porter carrying our overnight bag burnt them off with a cigarette butt.

In spite of the exhaustion and the sunburn and the thirst and the leeches, we loved the path we were on – the Jomsom Trail. It was a medieval highway, like the road in the *Canterbury Tales*, only with all the characters making their journeys for different reasons, and with the most spectacular panoramic views over the hills and terraced valleys. There were Gurkha soldiers coming home on leave with a light step, carrying their cardboard suitcases jauntily on one shoulder; going in the other direction were the ones leaving to join their regiment. There were relatives visiting families they'd not seen for a long time, people travelling for weddings and funerals, traders and porters with their goods loaded on donkeys, or into conical straw baskets carried on their backs. Once we passed a whole mule train, with jangling bells and gaudy pompoms, carrying salt down from Mustang, a mountain province on the edge of Tibet. At regular intervals, just when we were desperate to stop, a teashop would come into view where we could flop down with relief, and, as far as we were able, chat to our fellow travellers.

When we finally limped into Lumle research station, which was high enough in the hills to be shrouded in cloud, with dense, dripping vegetation, we were shown our rooms by the manager and found that while AW had been put into the main house, I was in a sort of guest garden shed. At the time I was reading Somerset Maugham's short stories about desperately unhappy British Memsahibs in colonial days, and I lay awake in my lonely room for hours thinking how true they sounded, and miserably wondering how AW and I could possibly have a future together.

Back in the camp in Dumkauli the days got hotter and hotter, and I became more and more obsessed by two problems. One was the future, which I had started agonizing about in Lumle. I knew that if this had been a simple holiday with no strings attached, I would probably have enjoyed the adventure of living in the wilds of Nepal, but it wasn't a simple holiday, it was a sort of trial period for the rest of my life if I married AW, and I didn't think I could face the rest of my life in a place like Dumkauli. I truly loved AW, but his career in the developing world would always take him to some kind of Dumkauli, so what to do? On the other hand he hadn't actually asked me to marry him, so I decided to put that worry on the back burner, and concentrate on the other, which was my career.

There is a compulsion attached to being a journalist, which is that you can't help seeing everything in terms of 'stories' which you have to write and get published – and if no obvious stories are at hand, you ought to be out looking for them. If you aren't doing either of those things you are a hopeless failure. I kept thinking to myself, Oh God, if a *real* writer were in this situation they would have done five interesting pieces by now and I am just sitting here like a slob.

A month before, when we'd briefly explored Kathmandu, AW had shown me the temple inhabited by a real life Living Goddess, and I'd thought 'That's a good story, I could do something with that,' but we left Kathmandu the following day, and there wasn't time. Then one day someone passing through our camp mentioned that an aged Gurkha called Lachiman Gurung, who'd won the VC in Burma during the war, lived in the hills not so very far away.

A *story*! AW sent a runner to Gurung's home asking if he would meet me in a village at a halfway point, and lent me the Land Rover and a driver who could translate.

Gurung was a local hero and when I finally arrived at our meeting place, he was sleeping off the rum-fuelled reception he'd been given on arrival at the village. I sat on the verandah of his house until he woke up and told me his story: Lachiman Gurung, alone, had beaten off an attack by seventy or more Japanese. He and three other comrades had been positioned in a foxhole guarding the path to the main body of their platoon, when the Japanese came down the track. His comrades were killed and he himself had his right arm blasted off, but he managed to keep loading his rifle and firing, until the Japanese, not realizing that all this opposition was coming from only one seriously wounded man, withdrew. When he finished his story, Lachiman Gurung fished around in his bag of things, took out a plastic envelope, and proudly showed me the Victoria Cross that he kept inside. I was so moved by his story and his dignity, and the loss of his arm and his poverty, and the beauty of the medal, and the strange circumstances we were in, that I almost lay on the floor and sobbed.

My article about him was published in the *International Herald Tribune*. That in itself was a piece of luck – there wouldn't have been much of a market for my piece on the heroic Gurkha if it hadn't been for the fact that a reunion of VCs was held in London not long after I returned. Lachiman Gurung didn't attend, but it was enough of a 'peg' for the paper to use my story.

Soon the monsoon was approaching. The camp would be completely cut off from the rest of the world during the rains, so a skeleton staff was to stay and hold the fort while the rest of us had to leave while we still could. It was already too late to go back to Kathmandu the way we had come – the Naraini river (we had originally crossed by loading the car on to a platform ferry which was winched across the river) was already too turbulent, and though AW toyed briefly with the idea of putting the Land Rover on to two canoes lashed together, he opted (to my relief) for an alternative route.

We loaded up and set off, all keyed up and excited to be on the road again. Penny offered all the empty spaces in the Land Rover to some pretty Sherpa women whom he said were his sisters, which annoyed AW, but then as we drove along Penny played his flute and the 'sisters' sang a lovely song about Mount Everest – or Sagarmatha, as it is known in Nepal – and he was appeased. Everything was fine until we came to a river where the bridge had, just that morning, been swept away. So now we were trapped between two raging rivers, and I began to panic. How was I ever going to get back and start my job on the *Sunday Times*? I suddenly felt desperately homesick; I needed my sisters and my parents. I wanted to go home *now*.

Quite a traffic jam had built up on the road leading to the broken bridge, which was good, as it meant we were not the only ones wanting to use it. There was a local bus with an elderly English woman on it heading for New Zealand. New Zealand! I felt ashamed of my fears. AW went off to discuss the situation with the Chinese engineers in their Mao suits who were in charge of the bridge. Somehow he convinced them to repair it and, after a very long wait, we finally crossed, feeling triumphant. But that only lasted until we came to a landslide on one of the precipitous mountain roads. Rocks were actually falling, but AW made a dash across in the car, and we finally reached Kathmandu late that evening.

There were two weeks to go before I was due to leave, so AW hired me a bicycle (he already had one) and every morning I used to free-wheel down the long shady slope from his apartment into the town, passing a pretty Hindu shrine in a tank of water on the way, and occupy myself exploring. I tackled the Living Goddess story: I wasn't allowed to talk to the little girl currently occupying that role, because a Goddess doesn't give interviews, but I found the previous one who'd been retired (as was the custom) when she reached the age of puberty. It was rather sad: after years of being pampered and, literally, treated as a Goddess, she was now back with her ordinary family. They were all finding it difficult, and it seemed she would be on their hands for a long time because in Nepal it was considered unlucky to marry an ex-Living Goddess.

In the two weekends we had together AW and I biked to some

of the old wooden towns in the Kathmandu valley, with their Buddhist *stupas* ringed with prayer wheels and painted with huge stern eyes watching over the four corners of the earth. And in the evenings we used to walk along the *bund*, the embankment along the river in Kathmandu, and look down on the *ghats*, where the dead bodies were burned on funeral pyres.

Just before I left AW told me, quite excitedly, about a job he'd heard about that would be coming up when his present one ended. It was in a place called Pakribas, which was three days' trek on foot from Kathmandu (which was already a day's journey from London). I could just imagine inviting my friends to stay: 'Oh do come. It's only three days' walk from the airport with your suit-case . . .' I boarded my plane forlorn and with aching heart. I couldn't face Pakribas; what about my family – not to mention furniture, pictures, books, food? If and when AW finally got round to asking me to marry him, the answer would have to be no.

3

Always Tie the Knot Before Six O'clock

I went to work at my new job as Beauty Editor on the *Sunday Times* among friendly former colleagues, which was fun, compared to the *Observer*. Shortly after I arrived, I was invited to meet Estée Lauder on one of her visits to London. 'Oh my word!' she exclaimed when she saw me. 'Look at Yesterday's Girl!' She took off my make-up and redid it with her own hand, giving me blue eyelids and bright pink cheeks and lips. I slunk back to the office hoping I could get to the cloakroom before anyone saw me. On another visit she did the same thing to my friend Meriel, who worked on the *Sunday Times Colour Magazine*. Meriel walked out of Claridges with her new Technicolor face, praying no one she knew would see her, but as luck would have it she bumped into an old gay friend who shrieked with delight and began whooping like a Red Indian brave.

AW came home three months later, and moved into my flat. The first thing he told me was that he had not applied for the job in Pakribas. 'Living together' was still considered rather shocking in 1972, and we had to keep it a secret from our parents. AW couldn't answer the telephone in my flat in case it was my mother or father, and any time senior relatives were planning a visit, we had to rush round hiding all his things and putting the bedside table in between the single beds again, before he disappeared to stay somewhere else. Then one day I came back from the office and found that – though I had no one visiting – AW had packed up all his stuff. His suitcase was in the hall. As I stood there wondering what was going on, he asked me to marry him. 'If you say no,' he said, 'I am leaving, and you won't see me again.' I was dumbfounded. I couldn't *bear* not to see him again, so I said yes, thinking to myself that I might get out of it later. Then he said, 'I can't promise you'll be rich but I do promise you will never be bored.'

He was right. There have been times in our travelling circus of a life together when I have been frustrated, homesick or desperate, but never actually plain bored.

AW went to ask my parents' permission to marry me. The main emotion at home was immense relief: I was thirty-two, for years my parents had longed and prayed for me to settle down. It wasn't so much a question of them agreeing to give my hand in marriage, AW told me later, as needing convincing that anyone would want it. 'Are you really sure you know what you are taking on?' said Dad. Later, on our wedding day my aunt accosted AW and said, 'You may have bitten off more than you can chew.'

I went to stay with my future husband's parents in Somerset for the first time. To prove what a hard-working daughter-in-law I was going to be, I rushed to the sink to do the washing up every five minutes. At one moment my eye was suddenly caught by a brown chemist's bottle on the narrow shelf above the taps. On the label it said, 'Valium 5 mg. Four tabs in emergency.' Oh my God! my brain whirred, someone in this mild, nice family could turn into a monster at any moment and need this massive dose of Valium. Which one is it? I tried to avoid being alone in a room with any of them until I could ask AW what was going on. It turned out that the tranquillizers were for the dog, a huge Rhodesian Ridgeback that was prone to fits.

Two months later, my beloved sister Moira died of cancer. She was my best friend and the person closest to me in the whole world; I couldn't even begin to imagine life for me, or her husband and children, whom she adored, without her strength and love and wisdom and humour. AW was a rock that I clung to through that dreadful time, and I forgot about all about escaping from my engagement.

AW convinced his employers in the British Government's Overseas Development Administration that he should not be posted abroad for a couple of years. We reckoned that that would give me enough time to get used to the idea of leaving the paper and living abroad, and so we fixed the wedding day. Since I was an older bride of thirty-three, I thought I might look a bit odd in the full white bridal outfit, so I opted for a long navy blue dress with silver stars on it – very simple, no veil and no bridesmaids.

So many strange things happened during our wedding ceremony that I sometimes wonder if we are really married. I'll start at the beginning: we wanted our wedding to be in the evening, by candle-light, but there turned out to be an ancient law in England which says you have to tie the knot before six o'clock so that you can't claim later that you couldn't see who you were marrying because of the dark. We arranged with the priest at the London church we had chosen that our wedding would start at 5 p.m. so that we could meet the deadline. Then the priest remembered that daily Mass was held at 5.30 p.m. each day in his church. 'Oh, never mind about that,' he said finally, 'we'll make an announcement that the Mass is postponed to 6.30 that day.'

My parents came up to stay in London. The day dawned. I was terrified. Let me just say that, in my experience, on your wedding morning you are just as unsure about whether you are making the right decision as you are at any other time – the only difference being that it's too late to do anything about it. Mum (known in our family as Doomwatch because she always expected the worst) set off for the church in a mild flutter – which grew into full-scale panic when her car overtook a taxi being pushed up Piccadilly by AW and his Best Man in their morning coats. Later I asked AW why in heaven's name had they not simply got out and found another cab, and he said they felt sorry for the driver.

Dad and I, on the other hand, left my flat in a hired Rolls-Royce with about four hours to spare. I managed to persuade Dad to get the driver to go slowly round the block about twenty times so that I didn't arrive at the church before the groom. Even so, we arrived early, and the service started so punctually that we were followed down the aisle by a crowd of latecomers who'd been held up in the rush-hour traffic. As Dad and I progressed towards the altar, I heard one of the guests whispering 'How extraordinary, she's in black,' and I wanted to stop and say, 'It's not black, it's navy blue,' but nothing would have halted Dad.

Our service hummed along beautifully until the bit when the bride and groom have to go into the vestry to sign the register. While this was happening, I noticed another priest with two altar boys going into the main church. I mentioned this to our priest who was slow to take in the implications of what I had said. Then – 'Oh my God!' he said, 'they must have started the 5.30 Mass.'

We returned to the church in disarray, to find that the strange priest with his acolytes had taken over the altar, the choir had stopped singing in the middle of a hymn, and all our seats, including the special kneelers for bride and groom, had been filled up with dozens of little old ladies in black.

We shuffled about not quite knowing what to do, while our priest went into battle with the priest at the altar and persuaded him to leave so that he could give us the final blessing. Then to thunderous organ music (luckily) we elbowed our way down the aisle past more little old ladies coming in to find seats. The Rolls that was to purr us to the Hyde Park Hotel for our reception set off down the road, but was almost immediately caught in a traffic jam, and slowly all the guests who'd been with us in the church overtook us on foot.

After some time my mother-in-law's cleaning lady from Somerset went by, looking anxious. 'Shall we give her a lift?' suggested my new husband. '*Are you mad?*' I said furiously, but when our car got stuck again, a little further up the road, and she walked past looking even more worried than before, I capitulated and she joined us. After that I gave up caring who was invited in – I know AW's Dutch uncle was among them because I'd never met him before, and we solemnly shook hands in the back of the car.

When the Rolls finally pulled up at the red carpet, and the elegant, tail-coated Banqueting Manager opened the car door, he was practically trampled underfoot by the crowd who got out before the grumpy, crumpled bride. But, though I say it myself, our reception was terrific. In fact the only problem was how to bring it to an end. Since AW and I were staying the night in the hotel, we were not 'going away', with the result that no one else was going away either, and my poor father was looking more and more taut round the eyes as he visualized the size of the bill we were running up. We decided we'd better leave, even if it was only to drive round the block. Then we had the brilliant idea of going with our Best Man, Adrian, to visit Sandy (his wife and my friend), who was in hospital having had her second baby the day before.

I can't remember much about it, but Sandy's version of the story is that she was happily dozing off in her bed when, in what seemed like the middle of the night, a nurse came and whispered that a noisy party of a bride with two grooms and a bottle of champagne were waiting for her by the lifts. Poor Sandy, she hobbled gamely out of the ward to celebrate with us.

Next day, AW and I, feeling horribly depressed and hung over, lamely took a taxi from the hotel back to my flat, where we had to wait for two weeks before setting off on our honeymoon in Egypt. A delayed honeymoon is not a good idea: you don't feel properly married. One evening a boyfriend I hadn't seen for a while telephoned and asked me to go to the theatre with him. 'That sounds lovely,' I said, 'but I'd better go and check.' I suppose he thought I was checking my diary, but in fact I was going to ask AW if it would be all right.

'Don't be daft,' he said, 'you can't go to the theatre with other men – you're married to me.'

I went back to the phone feeling rather silly, and said, 'My husband says I can't really go to the theatre with you.'

'*Your husband?*' yelled the boyfriend, 'I didn't know you'd got married . . . I would never have called . . .'

AW had chosen a cruise up the Nile for our honeymoon – he wanted to get right away from my world of fashion and newspapers and into neutral territory. But as we stepped on board our steamer in Luxor, hand in hand, so much in love, so looking forward to relaxing alone and away from it all, we were greeted by a piercing voice: 'Darling! How wonderful! Don't tell me . . . you're not doing the same cruise? How divine!' It was a friend of mine who ran a very grand travel company. Our hearts plummeted. Not only was she on board, but so were her 'group' of fashionable folk, including the wife of Giovanni Agnelli (who owned FIAT, the car company). I mention her because she had just been nominated Best-Dressed Woman in the World by *Woman's Wear Daily*, so I was secretly dying to see what she would wear.

We needn't have worried; it was the perfect honeymoon with blazing sun, romantic ruins to look at every day, and the added spice of famous travelling companions to stare at (rather like living in *Hello!*). But four days into the boat trip, Mrs Agnelli was still in the same blue jeans and red T-shirt she had worn on the first day. I was fascinated. It just shows, I thought, that when everyone *knows* you are the Best-Dressed Woman in the World it doesn't matter a hoot what you wear. I explained this theory proudly to my friend of the very grand travel company, and she said, 'It's not that at all. Mrs Agnelli's luggage was lost in Cairo and she only has the things she stands up in.'

Our own tour group consisted of just AW and me and a charming middle-aged man and woman we met on our first night in the hotel in Cairo. They were at great pains to assure us that they were not a 'couple' – oh *no*. She was the wife of a businessman who couldn't get away, and he was the husband of a woman who was in England waiting for the birth of her first grandchild. But in the corridor of the train taking us to Luxor to meet our cruise ship, we came across them locked in each other's arms. As a wise woman once said to me when I was wondering what one of our daughters was up to: 'Things are always further down the line than you think they are.'

In Luxor we had had to transfer from the railway station to the boat in a horse and trap. As we climbed in, this felt very wobbly and insecure, so I asked AW who had done Arabic at university, as well as Farsi, to request the driver not to go too fast. Nonetheless we set off at such a spanking pace that I said, 'Oh please, ask him again to go slowly.' AW spoke to the driver who then whipped up his horse until we were hurtling through Luxor like contestants in the chariot race in *Ben-Hur*. I began whimpering in the back, and AW was on his feet yelling at the driver to slow down – but it turned out that what he was actually saying was '*Go faster! Go faster!*' as he had got his Arabic words muddled up. The driver must have wondered what kind of maniacal speed freaks he'd got landed with. We didn't manage to sort out the breakdown in communications with him until we skidded to a halt at the dockside.

When our steamer stopped at the great funerary temple of Abydos, AW and I split off from the others (our group, being so small, had been amalgamated with the posh lot by that time) and went to find an old Englishwoman we'd been told about, who lived in a hut there. Apparently she thought she was the reincarnation of the mother of Pharaoh Seti; indeed, she was known locally as Umm Seti – mother of Seti.

This was the first thing we asked her about, and she was distinctly put out – 'It's a silly idea,' she said in an unmistakable Cockney voice, 'A Pharoah's mother? I'd never presume such a thing. I was a cleaner, a handmaiden, in this temple in those days, that's all.' Her real name was Dorothy, and her story was extraordinary. It went something like this: when she was fifteen or so she had a bad fall in her family's flat somewhere in the East End, and was knocked unconscious. When she came to, she felt strange and detached, as if she didn't belong any more, until one day she was passing the British Museum, and as it had begun to rain, she decided to go inside. In the great hallway of the museum, Dorothy said, she found herself drawn to the Egyptian section and once *there*, she felt that at last she had arrived home. She knew she must get to Egypt, and somehow she met and married an Egyptian student and went to live in Cairo. But it still wasn't quite right; only several years later, when she saw a postcard of Abydos, did she absolutely know where her destination should be. She left her family in Cairo, and had lived in Abydos ever since.

Umm Seti could read hieroglyphics without being taught, and the archaeologists reconstructing the temple at Abydos when she arrived there (who began by thinking she was a bit of a nutter) found that she also knew exactly how the layout of the temple should be – she became a valuable assistant on the site.

We were sitting outside her little house as she told her story, when a boy came up selling a small carving of a scarab.

'Let's have a look at that,' said Umm Seti. She examined it, and read out the name of the owner in the engraved cartouche on the back. 'You should buy this,' she told us, 'it's not a fake.' AW gave it to me, but sadly I lost it in Ethiopia two years later – creating another mystery for future archaeologists.

AW and I happily bickered our way around Egypt as we have bickered our way round the world ever since. Our most frequent argument was about the newspaper. When we got back to Cairo our hotel gave us a free one every day but somehow AW always lost it before I could read it – I couldn't believe he could be so careless. But back in London I discovered there had been a terrible Egypt Air crash in the headlines and AW was simply trying to hide it from me, since we were flying back with them.

Coming home from our honeymoon was an awful letdown. For some reason I imagined we would be met at the airport by friends and relatives with cries of joy, but of course no one was there – why should there be? We took the bus into London on a grey February morning and went to our freezing little flat to begin boring old real life as a working married couple.

It didn't last long. Three weeks later AW was posted to Ethiopia on another British development project. He couldn't disguise how thrilled he was, but I had an agonizing choice. I would either have to give up my wonderful job – I had been promoted to Fashion Editor just before our wedding – or live apart, and miss not only AW, but the whole Ethiopian adventure. In the end, I was incredibly lucky: my Editor said I could take ten months' sabbatical leave. (I came and went from the *Sunday Times* so often over the next four years that when I finally did leave for good, some people refused to contribute to my leaving present.)

AW flew off to Ethiopia; I was to follow three months later. In the meantime, a writer called Ted Simon, who was preparing to set off round the world on a motorbike, needed a place to stay, so I put him up. He and I rarely saw each other as I was off at the *Sunday Times* writing about fashion and beauty, and he was out practising on his bike.

One day I brought home some toffee balls sent to me by a Middle Eastern reader who wrote that removing leg hair with a kind of toffee ('sugaring', it is called) was much easier than using melted wax. The instructions were to warm each toffee ball in your hands, work it a little to get it really sticky and stretchy, smear it on to the unwanted hairs, and then rip it off. I thought I would write about it if it worked as well as she described, so one quiet evening I tried it out on my legs, and found that it did. Then I rolled all the toffee strips back into balls again and put them in the jar, ready for next time.

A couple of days later, I came home and found a note from Ted saying 'Sorry, couldn't resist the toffee', and a half-empty jar. I was appalled – Ted had eaten my leg hairs. It didn't bear thinking about. I just prayed that he wouldn't produce a fur ball, like a cat, while he was away in some benighted corner of the world.

Soon it was time to think about my own journey to Ethiopia. We had always assumed that I would go to Ethiopia by air, as AW had done, but my fear of flying was now so acute that I didn't think I could get myself on to a plane. I decided I would have to travel there overland, so I bought an ancient and very cheap Land Rover, which became known as Tansy, and somehow talked my cousin Simon, who was in the army, and Lesley Garner, a fellow journalist, into coming with me.

We never thought it would be *easy* to drive to Ethiopia, but we hadn't realized quite how difficult it would be just to get started. Every time we planned a route we'd discover that for some reason a border we needed to cross had clanged shut: Egypt's with Sudan, Syria's with Lebanon and so on. We'd heard there was a cargo boat going from Aqaba in Jordan, down the Red Sea to the Ethiopian port of Massawa – but we couldn't get the Land Rover into Jordan from any Mediterranean port. (I remember the Jordanian Ambassador saying to us, 'My friends, I am afraid you are caught in the shifting sands of Middle East politics.') Then we thought: maybe there's a similar boat leaving from Israel – after all, the Israeli port of Eilat is just across the bay from Aqaba . . . But how to find out?

We were in the *Sunday Times* office discussing this (you could sit on desks then, because they didn't have computers on them) when I had a *Eureka*! moment. I remembered that ten years before, during my first incarnation on the paper as Young Fashion Editor, one of my duties had been to attend the first Israeli Fashion Fair. There, through Cyril Kern, owner of Reldan suits in London, I had met an Israeli army officer called Ariel Sharon. (Cyril Kern is the 'wealthy South African businessman' who came into the news in 2003 when his loan of a million dollars to General Sharon came under brief scrutiny just before the Israeli election.)

This was in the early Sixties; I didn't know anything about Sharon or his reputation then, and – though it sticks in my throat to say so now – I have to admit that I had quite liked him, and felt sorry when I heard later that his young son had accidentally shot himself with his father's gun.

Anyway, we rang him and he remembered meeting me, and agreed to check out cargo boats leaving Eilat for Ethiopia. Pretty soon we heard he had found one, sailing in the not-too-distant future, so we booked ourselves, and Tansy the Land Rover, on the Italian ship *Enotria* leaving Genoa for Haifa in a couple of weeks' time. Simon and Lesley drove Tansy to Italy; I joined my parents in France for a sad few days' farewell, and then we rendezvous-ed in Genoa and watched Tansy being loaded on to the ship in a giant steel string bag.

It was a pleasant voyage. We stopped in various places on the way: Naples, Athens, the Corinth canal and Rhodes, where Lesley, Simon and I, carried away by the sun and the sea, drank two bottles of Retsina over lunch in a café on the harbour, then went swimming. Hardly surprisingly, I was knocked over by the first big wave; frantically scrabbling around on the seabed, trying to find my feet, I lost my wedding ring. I was so ashamed: I felt almost as if I'd been unfaithful to AW, and was consumed by remorse. Worse, it seemed like such a bad omen – I'd only been married for four months and already lost my ring – something horrible was sure to happen.

I scrutinized the safety instructions on board the *Enotria* and discovered an extraordinary thing. In Italian, the instructions read: 'When you hear the emergency signal of one long whistle followed by seven short whistles, ABANDON SHIP.' But in English they said: 'When you hear the emergency signal of one long whistle followed by seven short whistles, passengers are requested to assemble in the First Class lounge.' In other words, while the Brits were busy assembling, the Italians would be getting away in the lifeboats.

When we arrived in Haifa Lesley sent a telegram to her parents saying 'HAIFARRIVED'; this gave me a complex about how much cleverer she is than me, which has survived to this day.

I discovered only recently that Simon and Lesley and I have very different memories of our trip through Israel in 1973. This seems odd, but I suppose it's not really that surprising – memory is so subjective, the incidents that leave a vivid impression on one person might go quite unnoticed by others. Someone should do a scientific experiment on the three of us. In the meantime, Simon and Lesley will just have to forgive me for writing what *I* remember.

None of us had particularly wanted to go to Israel: we only ended up there because there was no other way to get to Ethiopia with the Land Rover. But now that we were actually in the country, with a vehicle, we had a unique chance to drive to St Catherine's monastery in the Sinai Desert (which the Israelis held then), seen by few people at that time. Before that, though, we had been told to present ourselves at Ariel Sharon's office in Tel Aviv.

Sharon was not at all as I remembered him from ten years before: he was fatter, more authoritarian and aggressive. He had Arabs working on his farm in Beersheba, he told us, and knew very well how to deal with them (implying a good kick kept them in order), and he boasted about how one day soon the Israelis would cross the Suez Canal into Egypt and that would show everybody. When we talked about how, during British rule in Palestine, Jewish extremists had blown up the King David Hotel (where we were to stay) and killed many people, he said: 'One man's terrorist is another man's freedom fighter,' which is certainly not what he is saying today.

On the other hand when I complained that my back was hurting (probably my seabed experience) he organized a medical corset, in an unlikely shade of flesh pink, for me to wear. I never gave it back – Ariel Sharon's corset is still lurking somewhere in the attic in Somerset.

It was clear from our meeting that we would not be allowed to do our own thing in Israel. A programme had been arranged for us, and it certainly did not include driving to St Catherine's monastery. Oh no, we had to go and stay in a kibbutz so that we could see how the Israelis had made the desert blossom, and above all, Sharon insisted that we visit Masada, the mountain stronghold where the Jews committed collective suicide rather than accept defeat at the hands of the invading Romans. Our first stop, though, was the King David Hotel in Jerusalem (the only thing left from our own programme) for a couple of days.

I wore the corset when we went sightseeing; it did help, but then I cricked my neck, had my wallet stolen, and got painfully sunburnt in the hotel pool. I knew it was all a punishment for losing my wedding ring, so I prayed like mad in the Church of the Holy Sepulchre, and at least my neck got better.

We did the Masada trip. The others went up in a cable-car; I was too cowardly, and walked. Lesley remembers the power of the site, and how Sharon had seemed positively obsessed by it; I remember that my sunburn was such agony that I couldn't wear a bra, and consequently became the tourist hit of the day. Then we went to the Dead Sea, and photographed each other reading newspapers while floating on top of the water – and we did our compulsory stay in the kibbutz nearby where we had to stand up in the canteen and introduce ourselves (and where we discovered that Sharon was deeply unpopular for the violent methods he'd used putting down the rebellion in Gaza not long before). And then at last we were allowed to drive to Eilat to catch our boat. But as we bowled into the resort, Simon driving, we couldn't help noticing that the harbour was empty of large, Red-Sea-going ships. Sure enough, it turned out that our boat was four weeks behind schedule – and we could only afford to stay in Eilat for a couple of days.

Lesley remembers a handsome Israeli major who arranged various outings for us in that time. I can only remember being seized by panic as it became obvious that we would have to fly to Addis Ababa after all. To me it was like a morality tale – no matter how hard I had tried to avoid being involved in a plane crash, no matter what lengths I had gone to, there was no dodging my Fate. It seemed like the fable of the man who sees Death in the market-place in Baghdad. He is terrified, and decides to get away as fast and as far as possible, so he gallops off to Samarra. There, when he feels safe, he leaves his lodgings and goes out into the street – and the first person he meets is Death, who says, 'Oh there you are. I was surprised to see you in Baghdad, for I knew we had an appoint-ment together, today, in Samarra.'

We left Tansy on the dockside with a note on the windscreen saying it had to be loaded on to the cargo boat for Ethiopia when it turned up. (I suppose one of us must have told the Israeli major as well – which is presumably why it arrived safely in Addis Ababa a few months later.)

I wrote a farewell letter to AW (it would reach him after my death, I thought) explaining about losing the ring and how sorry I was, which made me feel better, and then we we took the bus back to Tel Aviv to catch the plane to Addis.

4

Drama and Trauma in Ethiopia

AW's and my new home was in Awassa, a quiet town in the Rift Valley, about five hours' drive south of Addis Ababa. AW had rented a bungalow in a garden that overlooked a lake with storks and hippos and anaconda snakes. And he had hired Andreas, a rather scrawny and fierce woman, to cook and clean for us. Andreas had been married to a violent husband – which explained her protective feelings towards me – and had left him, bringing her young son, Solomon, to live with her in the compound behind our bungalow. Andreas wore the demure national Ethiopian dress in white muslin edged with embroidered braid; it always looked to me as if it had been designed by a missionary, and perhaps it had been for Ethiopia was one of the first countries in the world to become Christian.

Our house had a room with a sitting area on one side and a dining space on the other, and there were two bedrooms. AW had made the inside quite cosy – we even had bookshelves made of planks balanced on piles of bricks – but the roof was made of corrugated iron, on which dozens of pigeons scrabbled around at crack of dawn each day and woke us up. (We used to chat companionably at four o'clock in the morning about ways of exterminating them. AW had the best idea: to electrify the roof.) But apart from that, even I couldn't find much to complain about, except possibly the telephone, which you had to wind up frantically, all the time you were speaking, to make it work.

Of course there was the same problem as there'd been in Dumkauli, of how to fill in the days when AW was out at work, with no job, no friends, telly, radio or newspapers, but I decided to teach Andreas English, and Solomon to swim in the murky green pool that belonged to the local 'big' hotel (you couldn't swim in the lake because of the danger of catching bilharzia). Besides, it was a much prettier place than Dumkauli, and there were local markets to visit. These didn't have much in them to buy, but were fascinating because of the other customers: our local tribe were called the Sidamo, and they wore skins decorated with cowrie shells. Most cheering of all, of course, was the fact that I only had a few months there, so I could enjoy it without worrying about the long term.

AW's project was something to do with draining one of the Rift Valley lakes and establishing a market garden in the fertile soil that would be revealed when the water went down. I don't think he had much faith in it, but a whole team from England was involved, and there were two wives – Jackie and Sue, which was nice for me. I did find Jackie a bit passive, though – I remember her asking one day whether she should be worried when her husband developed a temperature of something like 108°. Sue on the other hand made me feel like a bit of a wimp because she chose to have her first baby in the local hospital while we were there.

There were two office drivers: Tradda, who was tall and thin, dressed immaculately and had perfect manners, but who would occasionally go on spectacular drinking binges that would land him in jail for a few days – and Mulligator. Oh poor Mulligator, he probably assumed we were all touched by the sun: time and time again when we said goodbye to him we'd say, 'See you later, Mulligator,' and then clap our hands over our mouths dramatically as we realized we had done it yet again . . .

There was a slightly older Englishwoman in Awassa, working on another project – Helen Inkpen. I liked her a lot. Some time after we left, I heard that she had married someone called the Reverend Hogg and gone to live in a place called Piggs Peak in Swaziland. Is it just me, or does everyone keep meeting people with peculiar names? In Barbados, the Canadian Ambassador was called Noble Power, which sounded more like a novel by James Clavell than a person, and the boss of the Freedom from Hunger Campaign in the Gambia was inappropriately called Mr Fatty. In Syria I was introduced to a Korean lady who, if my ears did not deceive me, was called Dung Heap, and in Trinidad we once met Bum Suk Lee, the Korean Foreign Minister, at a reception. In Ethiopia there was a doctor called Trots and a priest called Father Hilarious. And here in Kaz one of the ambassadors is called Mr Turdicool. My mother always swore that she knew a couple called Rose, who whimsically called their daughter Wilde – the only trouble was that she grew up and married a man called Boar.

Across the dirt track from our bungalow was a small hotel run by a plump Italian signora called Angela. She telephoned one day in a great flap: a hippo was lying in her driveway and she wanted AW to remove it. AW had been warned about hippos and how dangerous they were if you got between them and the water they live in, so he took his time – about an hour actually – explaining to Angela that he was just working out which angle to approach it from, when luckily it lumbered off back to the lake by itself.

Next door to us on the other side, in a similar bungalow to ours, lived a Scottish couple on a coffee rehabilitation project. The wife invited me to tea when I arrived. It was a strange scene. There in the African bush, miles from anywhere, she'd laid a table in her garden with a white lace cloth, fine bone china and a silver teapot. We sat down and then my hostess formally opened the conversation. 'Don't you think Prince Philip has brought the Queen out wonderfully well?' she said. She was sweet to me and I liked her, but relations between us became slightly strained later on, after she caught me doing an impersonation of her for my cousins who had arrived for Christmas. I didn't hear her coming into the room and continued with my act wondering vaguely why my cousins had stopped falling about at my side-splitting jokes, and were just sitting there, looking appalled. Of course she could never be completely sure about what I had been doing, but I felt so guilty that I took care to be extra-nice from then on.

The Emperor of Ethiopia, Haile Selassie, had paid a visit to Jamaica in his youth when he was known as Ras Tafari, and had become something of a cult figure there – which is how the Rastafarians, or Rastas, got their name. He'd given a group of them land in the village next to Awassa, and you'd occasionally see them with their dreadlocks and knitted hats looking totally out of place among the tribespeople at the market. The locals didn't have much time for them, considering them a bunch of layabouts.

One day, to prove what a capable wife I was, I went to the market with Andreas and bought wheat; then I husked and winnowed it myself, took it to the town mill to be ground into flour, and made a loaf of bread as heavy as a stone. I was so proud, but AW, after chewing it for hours, tactlessly let slip how he longed for a nice slice of Mother's Pride spread with Marmite. Andreas used to cook us Ethiopia's national dish of *injera* – a flat, rubbery, sour-tasting, gritty bread made out of grass seed, on top of which was served *wat*, a beef stew so burningly chilli-hot that they add hard-boiled eggs to cool your mouth down every now and then. You had to tear off pieces of bread and use them to carry the stew to your mouth. At first I thought both were practically inedible, but soon I became addicted, and even now, as I type this, my mouth is watering.

One day we heard that someone had been murdered in our local butcher's shack. (Dorothy Parker might have asked, 'How could they tell?' since the place was full of blood and flies at the best of times.) We never knew the story, but presumably the butcher wasn't the culprit because he continued in business. He used to kill a cow a day and hang it up, and customers asked him to chop off the bit they wanted. Andreas and I always got the fillet for about 20p as no one else liked it – Ethiopians preferring a nice bit of gristle and fat. Apart from the murder, Awassa was quiet and peaceful, and our lives should have been an idyll of tranquillity – but in fact my Ethiopian experience turned out to be nothing but drama followed by trauma, or the other way around.

Not long after Lesley and Simon had left, AW had business in Addis so we went up together and stayed at the Ras Hotel ('ras' meaning 'king'). We were getting ready for bed after dinner one evening when I felt a painful spot on my bottom. My only excuse for what followed is that my mother's first husband died of septicaemia, and all through our lives it had been drummed into us children to be careful about spots and boils. I asked AW to have a look at it. AW, already in bed, said he would in the morning, and in the meantime for God's sake couldn't we just get some sleep? Undeterred, I went into the bathroom and climbed on to the lavatory seat so that I could examine my bottom in the mirror above the basin. I was twisting and turning to get a better look, when my foot slipped down the pan. I flung out my arms frantically, to save myself from falling, and smashed my hand through the small glass window in the bathroom door and cut my wrist.

There are moments in life when something terrible happens because of your own stupidity, and you'd give anything, ANYTHING, to be allowed to re-live the last ten seconds and do them differently. This was definitely one of those moments: my artery was cut and blood was pumping out and poor AW couldn't do a thing until he'd put his contact lenses in, which was difficult with shaking hands.

We had to find a doctor urgently, so he rang reception who told us that there were no doctors you could call – the only thing we could do was go to the Russian aid hospital. AW put a tourniquet round my arm with his tie (unfortunately we didn't know that you have to release a tourniquet every few minutes, so by the time we arrived at the Russians' my hand was blue); he got me into a dressing gown, and we set off. As we left our room, he picked up a pair of my knickers and stuffed them in his pocket in case I might need them later. All I could do was hold my wound together and mutter 'Anaesthetic? Anaesthetic?' to anyone who came near me. Luckily, it's more or less the same word in Russian, so they gave me an injection and stitched me up painlessly. (Thank God, the hotel manager had come with us and was able to pay for this – the doctor wouldn't start until the bill was settled in advance, and AW had forgotten his wallet.)

They decided to keep me in overnight, and we were shown to a room where there were bloodstains on the bedclothes, on the floor, on the walls and even on the ceiling. AW looked around and said, 'Mmm. You know there are rooms with a "lived-in" look? Well, this one has a "died-in" look about it.'

My wound healed into the dramatic white scar across my wrist I have today, and there was only one after-effect. A couple of days later, AW was at an important meeting concerning his project. It was a boiling hot day and halfway through the meeting he pulled out his hanky to mop his brow – only to everyone's astonishment, it wasn't his hanky that came out of his pocket, but my lace knickers that he'd grabbed on the way to the hospital.

It was very soon after this, when we returned to Addis for me to have the stitches out, that the Ethiopian famine came into our lives. In fact, AW had written to me before I left London saying that he'd heard rumours that a disastrous famine was approaching in the north of Ethiopia. Now, travellers in our hotel were telling us of tens of thousands of people who had run out of food, and left their homes and villages to congregate, starving and exhausted, by the one main road going through the area, desperately hoping for help. And not only that, typhoid and cholera epidemics had broken out among them.

All this was told to us in whispers: it was forbidden to speak about the famine or the cholera or typhoid, because Emperor Haile Selassie did not want to admit to the world that he had any problems in his country. Since there was an efficient secret police in the country, everyone obeyed, and neither radio nor newspapers gave the merest hint that something was wrong.

On our second evening in the hotel, I found an anonymous note in our pigeonhole. It asked if I would attend a meeting to be held that evening by missionaries of various denominations, but please, not to mention a word about it to anyone. I discovered when I arrived that the missionaries had asked me because they'd heard I was the only foreign journalist in the country, and they hoped I might be able to write something for my paper so that the Emperor couldn't go on pretending that nothing was happening. I took notes frantically. A distraught young man from UNICEF had been to the north and seen mass graves, but his boss was on holiday and no one at head office was taking him seriously. The situation was completely out of hand, and no help was on its way, for, unless the Emperor requested it, aid agencies could not bring in emergency relief. Without it, the missionaries reckoned, thousands of people were going to die.

A day or two later AW and I were summoned to see the British Ambassador. Rather pathetically, we thought we'd been invited for a drink with him – but when we arrived at the Embassy, we were shown into his office. Somehow he had heard that I had attended the missionaries' meeting and he forbade me to write a story on the famine. AW was astonishingly brave.

'With respect, Sir,' he said, 'you cannot forbid my wife from writing whatever she wants, she is a free person.' The Ambassador had to agree, but warned us 'in the gravest possible terms' that I should not write a story or there would be trouble. As we were shown out, AW said loudly, in a voice that only quavered slightly, 'You'd better get up to the famine area as quickly as possible, Bridge.'

But I worried about AW's career, and thought everything might be easier if I could persuade the *Sunday Times* to send their reporter from Nairobi. I telephoned the foreign desk and explained everything, but the editor I spoke to said, 'Hmm, we've only just run something on the drought in the Sahel, so thanks for ringing, but we've rather done our famine story this year.' I could almost read his mind. 'Oh God, the fashion editor has gone to Africa and seen a beggar and thinks it's a famine . . .' I imagined him saying to his colleagues with his hand over the mouthpiece of the phone as I was talking to him.

I felt hopelessly inadequate. I had never done a proper *news* story from abroad, only stuff from the Paris Collections, for heaven's sake. Now I had the responsibility of getting the famine story to the outside world. I went through the usual torture of thinking how *anyone* would manage this better than me – let alone John Pilger, Jon Swain, John Simpson etc etc. Then, sick with nerves, I put together a story stating the bald facts, along with a quote from the Red Cross saying that the Ethiopian famine was likely to be the century's worst, and sent it by telex. (The *Sunday Times* used part of it, low down on an inside page.)

Then AW and I agreed that this was too important to report on second hand. I must do it properly and go to the famine area to see for myself what was happening. I asked Helen Inkpen, who was a trained nutritionist, to come with me, and we set off in her car, which we stuffed with food because we'd been told that there would be children kneeling in lines across the road, begging for something to eat. There were – and there were other sights so terrible that our trip was like an excursion to hell. We went through

Dessie where a camp had been set up for the starving people coming into the town. They were doing their best, but had very few resources and people were dying: the first person we saw was a skeletal mother carrying her weightless, dead daughter across her arms. The mother's tears had washed two black streaks in the white of her face – for, adding to the horror of the scene, everyone was covered in flea powder to prevent the spread of typhoid.

We drove on north. We put up in a hotel in a town called Mersa, which seemed normal enough, and then someone quietly told us about the hidden famine camp outside the town; there were more than two thousand people without food there, they said.

The camp was down a dirt track and we thought at first that we must have come to the wrong place, because we heard no sound of people at all. And then we saw them – some lying in rows inside a barn-like building, some in the open air – two thousand people, just waiting to die. They had had no food or water for days. An Austrian missionary doctor had been trying to run the camp; he was still there, feverishly darting about the place, but it was obvious the poor man had broken down and couldn't cope any longer. There was no one else in charge, just some sturdy little schoolboys from Mersa, who must have been told at some stage to write the names of the dead in exercise books, and were trying to do their job, though it had now overwhelmed them.

Some of the children in the camp were still just strong enough to be able to go into a field nearby and pick what was left of the grass to eat; some of them were bringing the grass to their dying parents. There were pitiful sights that I can't bring myself to describe, even now. Helen and I wandered around in a state of total shock. This was something outside normal human experience. In a way, I suppose our feelings must have been something like those of the liberators of the concentration camps. But what made it worse was that we were no liberators: we had nothing to offer, we would not be able to bring help here in time to save these people; we were, in a way, just sightseers. I had taken a camera, but nothing could have persuaded me to take photographs – to take anything from these people would have been a gross liberty.

One thing wrenches my heart to this day, and wracks my

conscience. We could have saved someone. We could have taken people to hospital, or tried to give them food and water ourselves. Why didn't we? What on earth came over us that we left that camp, utterly distraught – but not bringing anyone out with us? It's all a daze in my mind now . . . Perhaps we were too shocked to think straight, perhaps it was that we wanted to get back to Mersa as quickly as possible and alert people in Addis to the problem.

We did try very hard to get something done. Helen and I telephoned any contacts we had. We even risked the wrath of the Ambassador by speaking to his wife, who was much more sympathetic. But to save the people in the camp, lorryloads of food and water were needed immediately, not to mention medical personnel. When I got home I tried to explain to AW the horror of what I had seen, but it was no good. I felt that there would always be a gap between us unless he saw something of the terrible situation in the north for himself.

Eight days later we went to Mersa together. The return was surreal: when we found the camp, it was empty apart from a dozen or so children playing under the supervision of two British nurses (the Ethiopian Government had finally requested help from the outside world).

'Where are all the people?' I asked.

'What people?' said the nurse.

I explained.

'Well, there was no one here when we arrived two days ago,' she said.

AW and I concluded that the people must have died and been buried in the mass graves that were being dug on my first visit.

Only one good thing happened: Jonathan Dimbleby, the broadcaster, read something about the famine (I like to believe that it might have been my small piece in the *Sunday Times*). He brought out a film crew and, in the Dessie camp, made a film so moving that it released a flood of compassion and help for the stricken people. Some time after this film was shown on British television, while my friend Meriel was staying (she has loyally visited us in every posting), I had an urgent message from the *Sunday Times Colour Magazine* asking for a long piece on the famine. Meriel and

I wrote it together and they used it as their cover story, but we had no heart in it: too many people – more than a million, it was said – had already died.

We took Meriel up to Addis to catch her plane home. She wanted to buy some presents to take back, so we all went to the Mercato – the market – where she fell for a couple of rather smelly natural camelhair rugs. She needed to change her English pounds to pay for them, so we popped around the corner to a bank, where the man behind the counter looked carefully at each of the notes she had presented and then announced that he couldn't change them unless we had a letter from the Queen. (Presumably this was because the Queen's face was on the notes.) Time was running out and AW didn't have enough cash to buy the rugs, so we came out of the bank, seething with frustration. Then AW had a brilliant idea. In his briefcase, he said, he had some British Government stationery – we could write the letter from the Queen ourselves. We dashed to a nearby café and wrote a letter in elaborate copperplate addressed To Whom It May Concern, giving permission to 'our loyal subject' to change pound notes. We signed it Elizabeth R with lots of curlicues and loopy underlinings, and then, giggling like fools, went back to the bank and handed the letter over with straight faces. To our amazement, without batting an eyelid, the teller agreed to change Meriel's money, and she was able to leave with her rugs. The whole episode could have come out of Evelyn Waugh's *Scoop*.

When I arrived back in Awassa from my first visit to the famine area, AW had had to break the news that my beloved aunt Joan, lively and funny (she was the one who told AW on our wedding day that he had bitten off more than he could chew), had died of cancer, like my sister not long before. Now it seemed to me as if all the-larger-than life personalities in our family had gone, and the world seemed very empty and bleak. To try to fill it up a little we asked my bereaved uncle and young teenage cousins out to stay for Christmas and took them to see hippos wallowing in the Sodare river, and to swim in the delicious hot-spring pool at Nazaret. (When the Italians invaded Ethiopia during the war, the Emperor took refuge at Bath, in Britain, which apparently inspired him to copy Bath Spa in the town of Nazaret, where there was a similar mineral spring.)

We went to the missionaries' church in Awassa for Midnight Mass and everyone sang 'Silent Night' in their own language – we worked out there must have been about eight – and we played charades with Ted Simon, who was passing through Ethiopia on his motorbike journey round the world, and seemed to be suffering no ill-effects from my leg hairs. (Indeed, he went on to write a marvellous book, *Jupiter's Travels*, and I heard recently that he was retracing his tracks to write a sequel – but there'll be no Christmas dinner in Awassa this time round.)

Soon after they left, AW had to go on a field trip to a wonderful wild place in the south called Arbaminch where the local people lived in extraordinary fine-woven cane houses like giant beehives, wore few clothes and carried spears. Some exuberant Irish missionaries had based themselves there, and one of them, Father Mulligan, insisted on taking us out on the river in their little motorboat. Chugging along in the boat was glorious until we suddenly realized that the whole place was crawling with crocodiles. They were lying on the banks, their jaws gaping wide open (apparently that's how crocodiles relax and keep cool) and they were all around us in the water. AW and I were terrified – crocodiles are his worst dread, and my second-worst after sharks. I nervously lit a cigarette and sat in the boat hunched with fear, occasionally stretching out my arm to flick the ash into the water. All of a sudden there was a terrifying whoosh and a splash and the boat wobbled dangerously, and we realized that a crocodile had snapped at the ash, or my hand, when I'd stuck it out over the edge. I have never allowed myself to dwell on would have happened if it hadn't missed . . .

(I told this story to the man sitting next to me at a dinner party in Brussels a couple of years later. Talk about tactless remarks; talk about coincidence – to my horror it turned out that his father had actually been *killed by a crocodile*. The father, a missionary, had swum in Lake Victoria every day for twenty years, until the very last week before he retired when he was seized by a croc on his usual morning dip. His family saw it happening and tried to fight off the crocodile with their bare hands, but it got away with its victim.)

AW decided we should see some of the sights of Ethiopia, so he took a few days' holiday, and we drove Tansy in a big loop round the top of the country to inspect the source of the Blue Nile (which is in Lake Tana, where the fishermen make their boats out of reeds). On the way there, we came to a place in the mountains where a big bend in the road had had to be built out from the cliff-side, on props, over a precipitous valley; beside it was a huge notice saying 'THIS ROAD IS SLIPPING. Travel on it at your own risk.' I couldn't get out of the car fast enough, but AW bravely took Tansy across. (That was thirty years ago; I wonder if it has fallen off the mountain yet?)

We took sardines to eat on our travels, sandwiching them – with a squeeze of lemon – in the soft, slightly sweet, bread rolls which are part of the Italian legacy in Ethiopia (along with restaurants in remote and unlikely places serving *Fegato Veneziana*) and it seemed to me I had never eaten anything more delicious.

In Gondar, where we went to look at the extraordinary castles built by the Portuguese in the seventeenth century (they look just like children's Playmobile castles: nice and square with castellated walls and towers), we bumped into a group of tourists from the very same posh travel company who'd organized the ones on our honeymoon boat in Egypt. The hotel had messed up all our reservations, but AW and I saved the day by taking them to a new hotel we'd been told about, in a beautiful, lonely spot in the Rift Valley not too far away. It was one of the happiest accidents: we were put up in individual thatched Ethiopian *tukuls*, had dinner round a huge campfire in the evening, and all got on famously. (Indeed, the leader of the group, Jane Taylor – now *the* expert on Petra in Jordan – became such a friend that we later asked her to be godmother to our oldest daughter.) Next day, some of the party decided to climb the sheer cliff face from the valley to look at the rock churches carved into the top. This involved ropes, so AW and I gave the outing a miss – our crocodile experience having been enough of an adrenaline rush to be going along with.

We did see other extraordinary churches during our time in

Ethiopia, though. The most beautiful was an enormous round building at a place called Bethlehem, with a thatched roof as big as a hayfield and a ceiling painted with hundreds of cherubs. Another had rocks instead of bells to summon the faithful. These hung on strings from a wooden frame, and when you hit them with a stick, gave off an unexpectedly loud and musical sound. But I have to admit we never got to the famous rock churches at Lalibela – this was all my fault: it would have involved going in a small plane and I couldn't face it.

Back in Awassa, we received one of those messages from the British Embassy: this one said that Lady Tweedsmuir, the Secretary of State, was coming out to inspect the project and we were to organize a picnic for her. Helen, Sue, Jackie and I gathered together to discuss the food. I don't know why, but Helen and I became horribly bossy – Jackie said she would like to make vegetables in aspic, but we told her she couldn't do that because they would melt in the sun, so she'd got to make Cornish pasties. I didn't think any more about this because I was busy wondering how to make a spectacular pizza that would bring tears to Lady Tweedsmuir's eyes (I had suddenly become so overwhelmed by competitiveness that at one moment – which, luckily for Lady T, soon passed – it actually crossed my mind to decorate my pizza with sliced toad-stools, no mushrooms being available in Awassa).

Later that evening our ancient wind-up telephone rang and it was Jackie. I think she'd had a few drinks. 'I'm not going to do pashties for the picnic,' she slurred, 'I'm making veshtables in ashpic, and thatsh that.'

The day arrived and so did Lady T with the Ethiopian Minister for Agriculture, immaculate in a safari suit, and we all set off in Land Rovers for the chosen picnic site – a beautiful crater lake with flamingos that, from a distance, looked like pink pearls scattered over the blue surface. The food was laid out on rugs, and, in the heat, the vegetables in aspic slowly turned into vegetable soup (I was really careful not to look at Jackie) but everyone had a marvellous time. Then Lady T rose from her rug to bring the afternoon to a close. She must have looked around for the Minister and not recognized him, so, in desperation, decided to go for the smartest clothes, rather than the face. For the next thing we knew she was shaking hands with Tradda, our driver, who was looking particularly good that afternoon having only just come out of prison and not touched a drop for days.

'Thank you for a wonderful afternoon,' Lady Tweedsmuir was saying to him in her clear ringing British voice – while all our hearts missed a beat for fear of her being made to look foolish. But: 'Not at all. You are welcome,' said Tradda, as if he were really were the host, and we breathed a collective sigh of relief.

AW had to go back to England for a week or so. I invited Marion, a friend from an American aid project in Addis, to keep me company. Unexpectedly, we were telephoned by a German anthropologist, asking if he could stop by for lunch on his way up to Addis from the south. He arrived with a member of the Hammer tribe whom he was taking back to Germany to appear on television. The Hammer didn't normally wear any clothes except for a skimpy loincloth, but the anthropologist had dressed his tribesman in a Hawaiian shirt and trousers. The only thing was, he still had an enormous pompom made of clipped ostrich feathers on his head.

Halfway through the meal I suddenly had an outsider's view, as it were, of me making polite conversation for all the world as if the man I was speaking to did *not* have a giant pompom on his head, and I nearly exploded with laughter. I knew if I caught Marion's eye I would lose control. The only way to deal with this elephant-in-the-sitting-room situation was to discuss the pompom, so I asked him about it, and he told me how it was made and then everything was all right (though to this day the memory makes me laugh out loud). But I do wonder what happened to the poor Hammer tribesman, and if he ever recovered from the shock of being taken to a television studio in Germany.

A strange restlessness seemed to be building up in Ethiopia. Ever since the famine there had been all sorts of whispers and rumours about the possibilities of a revolution or an army mutiny. Certainly something was brewing: odd things began to happen – Andreas came in a panic and asked if she could hide someone who was in danger in our compound (AW had said yes, so long as we didn't know anything about it, and indeed we never did).

Mulligator took me to Addis to meet AW off his plane from London. On the journey, our car, along with the rest of the traffic, was waved to a halt at the side of the road by motorcycle out-riders for the Emperor's entourage, on its way to the royal retreat at Nazaret. A few tribespeople had stopped to watch, and as the Emperor's Range Rover passed, a window opened and bread rolls were thrown out in their direction. 'He throws bread to his people as if they were dogs,' muttered Mulligator with real rage.

A week or so later, AW had a meeting at the Water Resources department of the government in Addis. Since the meeting was at 3 p.m. we got up early and hurried off. En route for Addis we wondered vaguely why there were so many cars going in the oppo-site direction at breakneck speed, and absolutely none heading towards the capital. But it was only when we got to Mojo, our usual halfway stop where there was a jolly Italian restaurant, that frenzied people rushed up to us and announced that there had been an army coup. The Emperor was under house arrest, for-eigners were fleeing the capital, and no one knew what was going to happen next.

AW explained that we had to go on to Addis since he had a meeting there.

'No, no,' shrieked all the Italians in the restaurant, 'you are crazy. Turn around, get to the Kenyan border, leave now, you may never have another chance.'

But AW was adamant, so we got back into the Land Rover and drove on.

It was eerie. As we drove into the suburbs the streets were empty, the shop shutters all pulled down. Near the Ras Hotel we could hear the sound of distant machine-gun fire. I picked up AW's brief-case and held it in front of my face.

'What are you doing?' he asked.

'Well, this is just in case we are shot at,' I said.

AW explained that a bullet would go straight through the brief-case, so I stopped bothering.

The Ras was a home-from-home for us by now: since my life-

and-death experience there you could say the staff were our blood brothers. In an atmosphere of fear and excitement, we hurried to our room to listen to the World Service on our radio. Within a couple of minutes we heard a gentle knock on the door: it was the Manager with half the staff, wanting to hear what was happening too. And so we learned through the BBC that there had been a revolution. Haile Selassie's reign was over – and AW could assume that the meeting at Water Resources had been cancelled.

All I could think of was that, once again, I was the only foreign journalist in town and here was a scoop if ever there was one. Trembling with fear (fear of actually being asked to write the story) I put in a call to the *Sunday Times*. It took hours, but when I eventually got through and explained what was happening, the girl who answered the phone in the newsroom said 'Don't you know there's an election in Britain today? We're all frantic.'

I put down the phone feeling, as usual, what a hopeless flop I was as a journalist, and that perhaps I should take up macramé instead. (Several times in our lives abroad I have found myself in scoop situations – Ethiopian revolution, invasion of Grenada, mutiny in the Gambia – but I've never yet managed to get a single word about any of them in print. I can feel an anxiety attack coming on now, just thinking about it.)

A curfew was announced – by 6 p.m. everyone had to be off the streets. We met some colleagues from the project in the hotel and they really annoyed me because a) they spent the afternoon arguing about whether this should be called a coup or a revolution, and b) two of them decided it would be fun to break the curfew and go out into the town, as if it were all a bit of a lark. I was quite irritated when they came back alive and unscathed.

Next day everyone in Addis was jubilant – the English language newspaper announced that it would never be censored again, girls gave flowers to soldiers in the city like hippies in San Francisco, and a new, civilian Prime Minister was appointed by the army. We went to his first press conference – he was an urbane, cultured man in a nicely tailored blue suit. But in the distance you could still hear gunfire. After a few days, AW said the revolution was no excuse for not going back to work, so nervously we left the womb of the

Ras. En route to Awassa we had to pass through military check-points where unsmiling soldiers searched the Land Rover each time; once they even checked the glove compartment.

'What are you looking for?' asked AW bravely.

'Ministers,' replied the soldier grimly.

We didn't know any ministers except our landlord, who was Minister of Pensions. He'd recently begun giving us a hard time, threatening that if we didn't pay him a vast sum to compensate for the four holes we'd made in the walls of our bungalow to hang pictures, he would prevent us from getting exit visas to leave the country. We had been wondering how on earth we were going to solve this problem when the revolution happened. They shot our poor landlord soon after we were back in Awassa; we no longer had to worry about his demands – in fact, we were suddenly living rent-free.

About a month after the revolution the wind-up phone rang once again – it was the British Embassy. 'There has been a revolution in the country,' they announced solemnly, 'and we are just checking to make sure you are all right.' Marvellous, we thought.

The revolution developed into a reign of terror far, far harsher than Haile Selassie's rule which poor Ethiopia suffered for nearly twenty years. But that was still to come, and in the meantime AW's and my day-to-day lives went on more or less unchanged, until my sabbatical came to its end. I was going to have to leave AW and the lake and the African bush and the little mission church and go back to London to be a fashion editor.

We bought souvenirs to take home: Ethiopian crosses in silver, Coptic paintings on parchment, and chairs carved out of single blocks of wood. I had also picked up another, less attractive item to take home – a blood parasite, which meant that for months, every time I had diarrhoea, which was about four times a day, I was also sick. I had become so used to this that I automatically picked up a small plastic basin by the bathroom door every time I went to the loo. When it was eventually cured by the Hospital for Tropical Diseases in London, it was ages before I felt secure enough to be parted from my basin. (My parasite was nothing com-pared to my cousin Simon's, which revealed itself at about this time. He went to the bathroom one day and found something thread-like hanging out of his bum; horrified, he gave it a tug and then another and another, until in the end he had about eight feet of what he said looked like unravelled knitting wool in his hands – it was a tape worm. And what's more, by working out its age, and comparing that with Simon's travels, the doctor decided he must have picked it up in Britain, probably eating sausages.)

I'd spent a good deal of the ten months in Ethiopia complaining, but now no house looked more comfy than our bungalow, no way of life looked more attractive than the one I had led in Awassa, and no husband looked more desirable than AW. Worst of all was saying goodbye, for ever, to Andreas, whom I had come to love and respect, and little Solomon. When Meriel came out she had brought Solomon her son's old school blazer and cap, and the day I left he was wearing them over white cotton Y-fronts, with his skinny black legs and bare feet underneath. I cried all the way to Addis. We sent Andreas money from time to time, but when the new authoritarian Communist regime came into power, it was not easy, and we have not been able to find her since. Thousands of Ethiopians died in the subsequent war with Eritrea – I hope to God Solomon was not among them, but twenty years ago he would have been about twenty-five, just the right age to be recruited.

5

Home Alone

Back at the *Sunday Times* Ian Jack, the editor of the *Look!* pages (as the women's pages were called in 1974) wrote a nice piece welcoming me home, but I lay awake every night visualizing my fashion pages being printed blank because I couldn't think of anything to put on them. Eventually I came up with some ideas, and my assistant Margaret and I took clothes along to David Bailey's studio to photograph on the beautiful model Marie Helvin. When we unwrapped the dresses we had selected, I was horrified – they were all so long and dowdy. 'Oh God, Margaret,' I said, 'we're going to have to take these hems up.'

Very gently, without making me feel too much of an idiot, Marie and Margaret explained to me that no, the dresses didn't look frumpy, they were just right. In the ten months I had been away living in the bush in Africa, fashion had completely changed and skirts which had been short when I left were now mid-calf length. Margaret and Marie saved me: my first pages looked great – no reader could have guessed that their fashion editor hadn't a clue. I'll always be grateful.

AW came back a few months later and we bought a little house in Battersea from which he, rather glumly, commuted every day to a tower block in Tolworth, and I went to fashion shows and tried to get my eye back in to what was trendy and chic. (Though I still couldn't understand it when my colleague Michael Roberts, who wore an ankle-length, second-hand tweed coat done up with a piece of string, won a prize for being the Best-Dressed Man in London.)

This comfortable routine was turned on its head when I went to our doctor for a pregnancy test. He seemed strangely lacking in concentration and much more interested in whether AW could speak Farsi than whether I might be going to have a baby. I put this down to the fact that he was deeply involved with the Save the Children Fund, and thought no more about it. Just as I was leaving the surgery, he asked me to get AW to ring him when I got home, which I did. This was a huge mistake. Our doctor's interest in AW's Farsi was, indeed, to do with Save the Children – he was looking for someone to lead a team of doctors and nurses into the mountains of Iran to help Kurdish refugees fleeing there from Iraq. The next thing I knew was not whether I was pregnant (the tests took ages in those days) but that AW was off to Iran in less than a week.

Full of energy, like a recharged battery, AW, with the doctors and nurses from his team, tore round London to unheard-of shops, which specialized in Arctic clothing and sleeping bags and water-purifying tablets, gathering their equipment. I sat in our new house – where I'd looked forward to a cosy pregnancy being cared for by my husband – and felt thoroughly cheesed off. I could have killed my doctor.

Soon AW and the doctors and nurses and zip-up duvet suits and snowboots and the medical supplies left for Iran. Back in Battersea, I found a lodger, a friend called Sally, to keep me company and be there in case of burglars, and I heard from the doctor (to whom I was barely speaking) that I was, indeed, expecting a baby in September. It was now February. If truth be told, Sally was much better at looking after me than AW would have been, and I was reasonably content, but it didn't last long. One day I got home to find her standing on the other side of the road with her suitcase on the pavement beside her. She yelled across: 'Don't come near me. I may have German measles. I can't live with you any more. I'm so sorry. Your supper's in the fridge.'

In my more hormonal, self-pitying moments – which were most of the time – I'd say to myself gloomily that when AW had had to choose between his pregnant wife and a whole lot of Kurds he'd never set eyes on, he'd chosen the Kurds. But to be fair, he didn't know before he left that we were having a baby. (I sent him a telegram when I knew for sure – those were the days when telegrams still existed. I wanted to write something romantic and not too bald or biological, so I put 'In September we will be three'. This was eventually delivered to AW verbally as 'In September we will be free', and from then on the Kurds were more convinced than ever that he was a spy who knew something they didn't.)

AW's mission had become extremely complicated – in fact, he had inadvertently walked into a war. When his team had arrived in the mountains of Iran, they found no Kurdish refugees waiting for help because they had been trapped by bad weather in Iraq. So AW had decided to take his team – illegally – over the border into Iraq to help them *in situ*, as it were. This part was fine, the Iranians were helping the Kurds to fight against their mutual enemy, the Iraqis, and the dreaded Iranian secret police, SAVAK, were extremely helpful to AW and his team with transport and so on. But three months after AW arrived in the mountains with his doctors and nurses, the Iranians made peace with the Iraqis and, overnight, withdrew their anti-aircraft guns and other military equipment, leaving the Kurds defenceless against the enemy, who were now hell-bent on destroying them.

AW and his team, and the Kurds, came under heavy bombardment from Iraqi planes in their base in the Chuman valley. Occasionally I would get a phone call from AW on a crackly line that would be cut off at the crucial moment, telling me the latest horror and urging me to do something to try and get a cease-fire going so that the refugees and everyone else who needed to leave could get away. In the meantime, he said, his team was very active, immunizing the children and taking care of the malnourished and so on – and dodging the bombs.

I became a jittering bag of nerves visualizing AW hiding in caves, being killed in a bombing raid or being captured and tortured as a spy. I made a deal with God that if only he would bring him back safely, I would say my prayers on my knees every night for ever. (And He did, which is why now, I am never in bed before 1 a.m. because I have such a long list of things to pray about. AW gets really ratty about this which is deeply unfair as it all started because of him.)

AW put me in touch with two handsome men working for Kurdish organizations in London, Howar and Jamil, and *Sunday Times* journalists were most helpful about talking to them and writing pieces calling for the cease-fire; Ian Jack even joined my younger sister and me on a march against genocide. I became so obsessed with it all that I decided – with the encouragement of Howar and Jamil – that I should go and join AW in the war zone. The Kurds started planning my journey – it would involve travelling by train from London to somewhere in Iran called Rezayeh, and then making my way over the mountains to the Chuman valley in Iraq on a mule. Why I agreed to go along with all these crazy plans was, I think, because I had developed a bit of a crush on Howar, and was trying to prove that I was not really married and pregnant and terrified but an intrepid adventuress.

I went to see an old politician friend, Ian Sproat, at that time Minister for Sport, who was an expert on Kurdish matters, to pick his brains on the finer points of my journey. I can still remember the look on his face when I told him of my travel plans. 'Er . . .' he began, looking at my swelling stomach.

'Yes, yes,' I said impatiently, 'I'm pregnant, but I'm fine. I'll be perfectly okay.' As a matter of fact, I did feel fine. I felt fitter and more energetic than at any other time in my life.

'Look,' he said gently, 'You've never had a baby before. I don't believe you are thinking clearly about what it really means. You must talk to your doctor.'

My doctor was of course not exactly my number one favourite person at that time, but I did go to see him, and he subtly convinced me that the mule/mountain/war zone parts of my trip were just the teeniest bit risky. But going on a train, why that would be wonderful! Why not go to Istanbul on the Orient Express with AW when he came back? That would be positively good for me. My temporary madness stopped immediately. I sobbed on his shoulder because not having to ride a mule over the mountains, six months pregnant, was such a relief; I could get on with decorating the nursery for my baby.

Eventually a cease-fire was announced, AW and his team came back to England, and apart from a tendency to throw himself on the floor with his arms over his head every time a door banged, AW suffered no ill-effects. And he agreed to the Orient Express trip (he could hardly refuse). Ian Jack, a train buff, decided to join us, and the three of us set off from Victoria Station on our adventure, in two adjoining sleeping cars. It *was* an adventure in those days: the Orient Express was not a tourist attraction, but a proper train that chugged slowly all the way across Europe to Istanbul, taking three nights and four days.

When we came back Ian wrote a piece about the trip called 'Travels With My Fashion Editor', in which he said that every time I opened my mouth I'd squealed, 'Oh do look! Isn't that the *sweetest* farm/horse/sheep/mosque in the whole world!' So I feel no compunction in saying that every morning Ian, most inconsiderately in view of my advanced pregnancy, lit up his pipe. 'Oh Ian,' I'd moan, 'it'll make me ill.' Then he'd go and smoke in the corridor, but on the last day he didn't get out in time and I threw up, all over his feet and the carriage floor.

Apart from that, and the maddening way AW disappeared into strange stations whenever the train stopped, giving me heart failure by hopping back on just as the whistle was blowing, our only misfortune happened in Belgrade. Having eaten our picnic on days one and two, we were suffering quite pitifully from lack of food by that time. There was no restaurant car on the train, but you could buy plastic cups of black coffee. We dreamed of *café au lait*, but there was no milk – until there, on Belgrade station, we spotted a man selling cartons of it. We went to endless lengths to exchange a pound for dinars, and bought one, and I carried it back to the train as if it was the Holy Grail. We ordered three black coffees, and ceremoniously poured in the milk from the carton – which immediately curdled into big lumps. It was yoghurt. We were sick with disappointment.

After Istanbul, AW and I began preparing ourselves for the future. He was going back to Oxford University in order to get an MSc and become the person who thought up aid projects, rather than the poor devil trying to carry them out, and I had to look for a nanny because the baby was due in a matter of weeks.

AW had sold the pale blue Morris Minor he'd had when I first met him and now drove a Robin Reliant fibreglass three-wheeler, which he'd bought off his brother (who had gone to join a religious order in Spain). It had a sticker on the inside of the back windscreen saying ABORTION KILLS. I, on the other hand, had a rather nice Renault. AW persuaded me to swap cars: it would be too dangerous, he convinced me, for him to drive to and from Oxford in the three-wheeler, and I would probably appreciate the convenience of a small, easy-to-manoeuvre vehicle in town. I could see his point about driving to Oxford, but going to the *Sunday Times* every day, hugely pregnant, in the three-wheeler – particularly with the sticker on the back (I couldn't get it off) – was truly embarrassing. What if Michael Roberts saw me? I used to park miles from the office to avoid anyone I knew. Inevitably, though, one morning Michael walked past just as I was heaving my great bulk out of the Reliant – its door was below pavement-level which made this even more ungainly. His face lit up with glee. 'Hmm . . . *glam!*' he said. But we walked together back to the office and became good friends after that – perhaps because he'd seen only too clearly that when it came to *chic*, I was never going to be the smallest threat.

I worked at the paper until the day before our baby was born. This was in order to keep all the maternity leave for afterwards, but it meant that by the time I went into hospital on 30 September I was already so exhausted that I felt like postponing the whole thing. During childbirth classes I'd been quite excited about the birth – the waters breaking and being dashed to hospital in the middle of the night, or having the baby in the back of a London taxi with a kindly, capable driver after whom we'd name the child. But in the event the baby was late and had to be induced, so I just went in for a normal appointment. They gave me an epidural, which was great, except I could feel these cold hard legs in my bed. They were mine of course, but I kept thinking that they'd put the bottom half of a shop-window mannequin in with me, and wondering why. Then in spite of arriving three weeks past the scheduled day, the baby had to be delivered by forceps – you can't get much more reluctant to face the world than that.

There was an embarrassing side to being a fashion editor having a baby in an NHS ward, which had never crossed my mind. I was swamped with flowers. Seriously grand ones. Enormous bouquets arrived from Estée Lauder, from Revlon, from Christian Dior; a five-foot high teddy bear made of daises was heaved in from Yves Saint Laurent. All the other new mums had the normal quota of flowers from husbands and family and friends, but my bed looked as if it were parked in a florist's. I explained that it was only to do with my work, but it was awkward, and in the end I had them diverted to the children's ward. (Three years later, when I had my second daughter in Brussels, this all came back to me rather painfully – I received precisely three bunches of flowers: one from AW, one from my daughter and one from my mother-in-law.)

A week after her birth I carried my beautiful daughter, Hester, home in triumph – and then the worst six months of my life began. I don't know if women now are better prepared for motherhood; but I certainly wasn't. All my life I'd worked, I'd never really been at home in the daytime, and my friends were all working as well. Suddenly I was home alone – no, worse, I was home with a small demanding creature that I had no idea how to placate.

Gloomily I pushed the pram through streets near our house that I'd never been down before, and into parts of Battersea Park that I hadn't realized existed. I wondered if I would ever be allowed to sleep again. I was aiming at a schedule of feeding the baby every 3–4 hours for half an hour, but in fact I seemed to be feeding her every half hour for 3–4 hours. And she was losing weight and coughing all night. Once she did projectile vomiting – a banana-shaped lump of milk shot out of her mouth and across the room. (I'm glad I've seen it once, or I never would have believed it.)

Something was wrong. I was distraught. When AW came home for the first couple of weekends he'd say things like 'Can't you do something?' and I'd scream 'She didn't come with a set of instructions, you know!' I kept taking her to the doctor but he could never find anything wrong. At long last though, one Friday, she was diagnosed as having whooping cough, and all of a sudden had to be rushed off to hospital, where they dressed her in a nylon nightie about ten sizes too big and put her in an isolation ward. I was sent home and told to bring my milk to the hospital later so that they could feed her with it. I sat on the edge of my bed that afternoon, squeezing my breasts until I had managed, drop by drop, to fill half a glass – and then I stood up and knocked it all over the carpet. I cried for hours.

AW didn't know the baby was in hospital. He hadn't rung, and it was almost impossible to get hold of him since he never seemed to be in his digs. I decided to take my revenge. I left a note on the hall table for him to find when he came home that night. It said: 'Hester very ill in hospital. Have left.' And then I went to stay with some friends. I didn't want them to tell AW where I was, but when he eventually telephoned, they said he sounded so distraught that I should give myself up, so I went home to discover that poor old AW now had whooping cough as well.

I don't know how long it takes other women to get out of their dressing-gowns after their babies are born, but I didn't think I would ever again find the time or the energy to get dressed. Then one morning an invitation was sent round by the *Sunday Times* – it was from Harold Wilson, the Prime Minister, inviting me (and my husband) to join other Important Women at 10 Downing Street to celebrate International Women's Year. It was obvious to me that I would have to refuse – how could I hobnob with Important Women? I could only talk about whooping cough, nappies, babies and how tired I was. Then there was the clothing problem – what on earth could I wear? My stomach didn't seem to be any smaller than when I was eight months pregnant. However, AW said that for the sake of my morale we must go, and he helped me decide which of my maternity dresses looked least like one, and off we went. I noticed when the PM greeted us that he had dandruff all over his collar, which made me feel more confident somehow.

In the middle of the party, there was a buzz of excitement – Mrs Thatcher, then Leader of the Opposition, had arrived. Suddenly I found myself being introduced to her. I was supposed to be one of the Important Women, but when she asked me about myself all I could say, with hot ears and a lump in my throat, was that I had just had a baby. 'Well my advice is this,' she said briskly. 'Don't fuss around with au pair girls and so on. Get yourself a nice dependable English nanny and go back to work.'

Work! I nearly cried. I couldn't imagine ever going back to work. Didn't she realize how amazing it was that I wasn't in a dressing-gown? But in the end AW and I had a lot of fun at the Important Women's party, and I was glad he'd made me go. Quite a few people I knew from newspapers and the fashion world were there, and we talked to Mrs Wilson and the PM's detectives, and to Olympic javelin throwers, and actresses and writers (they all asked me when my baby was due) – and AW stuffed his pockets with the cigarettes that had 10 Downing Street printed on them.

Our next outing was even more bizarre. Before I was married I had been sent to India to write an article about the Nizam of Hyderabad, the richest of the Indian Princes. I'd become friendly with his (then) wife, and with her mother, a grand Turkish lady. Now, out of the blue, the grand Turkish lady telephoned us to say that she was in London and would love to meet up with us and inspect the baby – and could we take her to see the famous gardens at Sissinghurst Castle in Kent.

We went to lots of trouble: borrowed a Range Rover from a rich friend, made a picnic, rolled up oriental rugs to sit on, dressed Hester in her prettiest outfit, collected the Turkish lady and set off. AW and I had never been to Sissinghurst and hadn't a clue where to go or what the castle looked like, plus we were seriously over-awed by our guest. So when we passed an imposing entrance through which we could see a stunningly beautiful garden, we drove in, unpacked the picnic on the nearest lawn and began to eat. The Turkish lady was delighted with it all, but I had suddenly noticed people playing tennis in another part of the garden, and the icy hand of fear had gripped my spine . . . we were trespassing in someone's private garden.

Smiling and without moving my lips, like a ventriloquist, I said to AW, 'I think this is a private house, and you'd better go and talk to those people playing tennis before they throw us out.'

AW had already come to the same conclusion, and was halfway on to his feet as I spoke. We'll never know whose garden we were in, but if they ever read this, I'd like to say thank you, for when AW explained to them about Sissinghurst and the grand Turkish lady, they told him not to worry and to finish the picnic at our leisure. So we did and were able to load up and drive away in a dignified fashion.

I dreaded my maternity leave running out; I had settled into a cosy, undemanding routine now that Hester was better, and in any case, as usual, I couldn't think of any ideas for my pages. No, that is not strictly true; I did have one idea, which was to interview Mary Quant about growing older – she was about to turn forty, and, being the fashion designer who, above all others, stood for Youth, I thought this would be a good story. The only trouble was, she didn't want to do it. Since this was the only thing I could think of to write about, I became desperate; I tried sending flowers and a begging letter, I practically became a stalker, but she wouldn't relent and I had to think of something else – I can't now remember what.

We had employed a cheery young Cockney nanny, Sue, to come in every day when I went back to work. She was wonderful, but working on a newspaper meant that I was often late in the evenings, and I'd get back to find her ready to dash out of the door, having written out her notice and left it on the kitchen table. But somehow we both adjusted, and a whole year went by and then, unbelievably, it was Hester's first birthday. Sue and I knew, of course, that children's birthday parties have to be crowned by a cake in the shape of something appropriate – a train, a doll, a Big Hungry Caterpillar, etc, but this was pre-Jane Asher, and cute-shaped cakes were hard to find. We went to the local baker in Battersea and asked him to make a cake in the shape of a teddy bear, and ice it in white. Could I draw it for him he asked, so I did – which probably explains why the cake looked like a small white corpse laid out on a platter. It was quite shocking. Luckily all the mums were more concerned with controlling the big dalmation that Valerie Grove had brought, and which was dashing round the house hoovering up all the sweets hidden away for the older children's Smartie Hunt. (It was very fitting that she later wrote the biography of Dodie Smith, author of *101 Dalmatians*.)

In the meantime, AW had been recruited to go and work in the European Commission in Brussels. (This, or something like it, was exactly what he hoped would happen if he went back to university.) But I had a problem: I had not long been back at work; the Editor had been so kind letting me have a sabbatical in Ethiopia, and then I'd taken maternity leave. I really didn't dare tell him now that I was leaving for good.

We decided that I should stay on in London, and join AW in Brussels when I'd done a decent stint on the paper. I'd also been commissioned to write a book on fashion, called *The Women We Wanted to Look Like*, and knew I'd never get on with that if I made the move to another country. The plan was that AW would commute to London from Brussels at weekends; we'd try this for a year or so and see how it went. The only trouble with it was that AW now hated flying almost as much as I did, so he'd have to have a couple of drinks before he got on the flight, and a couple more on the plane, and would arrive on the doorstep in London every Friday evening swaying and grinning. That would start a quarrel that would last most of the weekend, and then, after he'd gone back to Brussels, we'd spend the week on the phone to each other making up again.

So, for the summer of 1976 – our first since this cross-Channel commuting business had started – we took care to plan a nice relaxed couple of weeks that would bring us close to each other again. As fashion editor, I was obliged to cover the Paris Collections for the paper in July, and AW suggested that the least stressful thing for me would be for him to take the baby down to our little house in France by car, together with our friends Sandy and Adrian, and I could join them there by train, no worries.

Sue, the nanny, left for her holidays and I was packing to leave for Paris the following evening when AW suddenly clapped his hands to his head.

'Oh my God,' he groaned. 'The baby is on your passport. She can't come with me – you'll have to take her with you tomorrow.'

Our well-laid plans suddenly looked as jumbled as the pieces in a kaleidoscope . . . We rang Sue feverishly and implored her to postpone her holiday and come with the baby and me to Paris. She agreed – perhaps it isn't surprising that she later became a double-decker bus driver in London, it must have so much less stressful than working for us. Sue and the baby and I set off on the night train and arrived in Paris next morning with very little time to spare before the first of the dress collections was to be shown, so we decided that Sue should drop me off at the show, take the taxi to the hotel and settle in, and I would follow later.

About halfway through the collection I thought I heard a baby crying in the distance, but I dismissed the idea – a baby at the *haute couture* collections would be as unimaginable as Naomi Campbell with acne. I tried to concentrate on the clothes, but I could still hear the baby, and, what was worse, it was beginning to sound awfully familiar. This wasn't surprising – it *was* my baby, with Sue, who was also crying – she had arrived at the hotel, panicked, and taken the taxi back to find me.

'I don't like foreign,' she sobbed.

After that I had to take them everywhere with me. I have a surreal memory of Hester sitting under a rack of Yves Saint Laurent dresses unravelling the tassels hanging from the ends of the belts, while David Bailey photographed Marie Helvin for my pages in another part of the showroom muttering how much he hated kids. (That was before he had his own.)

After the holidays AW and I went back to work in our different cities. But he seemed to be spending more and more jolly evenings in Brussels pubs and restaurants with his new pals, and I began to worry that he might find this more appealing than his family in London. All his friends seemed to be Irish, and I could visualize only too clearly how a pair of lovely Irish eyes might, one evening, smile into his . . . It was time, I felt, to leave the paper, finish the fashion book, and move to Brussels.

A great chum, Christopher Matthew, lived just up the road and was writing a book too. He suggested that the quickest way to get mine over and done with would be for me to go to his place every day, as though I was going to an office, and work flat out. And what's more he offered to cook me a hand of fish fingers with frozen peas for lunch every day. It was a brilliant idea: with no interruptions – except to gobble down the fish fingers – I was able to finish my book in a couple of months.

6

Babies and Brussels

There were no estate agents in Belgium in those days; house-hunting meant choosing an area you liked and then pounding the pavements until you saw the kind of house you wanted with an À LOUER sign on it.

Lots of Eurocrats lived in the leafy suburbs of Brussels, but AW had taken me to the Place Flagey market in the centre of town, where they sold seven different types of salad greens (this was at a time when you couldn't even buy lettuce in Britain in winter), and I decided I couldn't bear to live more than a hundred yards away from it.

We plodded around the neighbourhood until we found our dream: an elegant terraced house in a pretty street, two minutes' walk from the market. We rushed back to AW's digs to ring the owner, and his son took us around it next day. It was lovely: the huge kitchen opened on to a garden, and an elegant staircase swept in a curve up to a dining room and a sitting room with French windows and a balcony. The downside was that the bedrooms were up a narrow dark staircase on the third and fourth floors, it was all very shabby and run down – full of cracks – and the rent was too high. We decided we'd take it if the landlord, a Monsieur F, agreed to do some work on it. That night we went to meet him, a huge, terrifying old man with one side of his face held up by a piece of tape beside his eye. He was in the church-vestment business and had a grudge against Pope John XXIII, who had abolished elaborate vestments and urged priests into black polo-necks and slacks, and nuns into jumpers and skirts – thereby depriving Monsieur F. of his profitable trade in jewel-encrusted copes and starched linen coifs.

AW cleared his throat nervously to begin our negotiations, but before he'd finished the first sentence, Monsieur F. interrupted.

'Take it as it is,' he boomed, 'or don't take it. But you must decide now, tonight, or I'll rent it to someone else.' Outmanoeuvred – as we have been by all our landlords ever since (as if to make up for the one in Ethiopia being shot) – we took the house.

Actually, we loved living there, though we were always broke because of the rent, and having to fix things that went wrong all the time. And I never slept through a whole night there for fear of fire: the back stairs were made of wood covered with lino, and the electric wiring was pre-war. I'd get up five times to check that the smoke alarm was still blinking, or work out where I would anchor my knotted sheets and how I'd get down them with a baby on my back.

Ever since I was a little girl playing with a dolls' house, I've loved 'doing' houses. I put it down to insecurity – my father was in the Indian army and our family never stayed in one place for more than two years. Lack of funds meant that planning my décor for the house in Brussels really just meant new loose covers for a couple of old armchairs and a sofa, so I called in Mr Bedwell, our local Battersea upholsterer, and he set to work.

Sadly, Sue didn't want to come with us to Brussels after her Paris experience, so AW and I interviewed potential au pair girls in the couple of weekends we had left. AW's technique was very simple – he would ask each applicant if they'd like a drink. Anyone who said yes, and asked for wine, beer or gin-and-tonic, was immediately struck off his list. Eventually we settled for Mandy who'd asked for a Coke, was shy, with nice manners and loved children. Her only fault was that at the very last minute she said she couldn't go to Brussels without her pet rabbit Oreillette (Little Ears). Oreillette (in spite of her name) was enormous, but quite sweet – it was only later that she ate every single plant in our new garden and began growling and snapping at us like a dog. Even Mandy went off her then. (Eventually AW found a new home for Oreillette while we were all in England on a visit. Well, that is what he said, and none of us ever chose to look into the story more deeply.)

When the day of our move dawned Mr Bedwell hadn't quite

finished, so he travelled to Dover in the removal van with the sofa and chairs putting the last stitches in the covers, and took a train back. I was to drive Mandy, the baby and the rabbit to Brussels in my Renault which I'd long since clawed back from AW. Little did I know on that spring day in 1977, as I held the baby up at the rail of the cross-channel ferry to wave goodbye to England, that it really *was* goodbye. We would not return to live in Britain for more than twenty years.

Our first Sunday in Brussels was grey and rainy. We all – even the baby – felt miserable and homesick. AW decided to cheer everyone up by taking us to the dog market. The guidebook said that this was next to the Abbatoir, so we headed off in that direction. (I wonder what the many Belgians who gave us directions must have thought of the little English family desperately searching for the slaughterhouse on a rainy Sunday morning.) In fact, we never found the dog market because when we finally reached the slaughter-house some kind of marvelous cattle fair was going on. We perked up in no time: there were huge, creamy Charolais cows and bulls, so fat they had developed buttocks; adorable calves for Hester to try to pet; hot waffles smelling of vanilla, and masses of food stalls. I bought a whole leg of Parma ham – which was to drag my rela-tionship with the local butcher into a downward spiral and set me on a collision course with every Belgian shopkeeper, but that was still a few days off.

Later that week, while AW was at the office and Mandy had taken Hester for a walk, the landlord came round to see how we were getting on. Suddenly he became very flirty and amorous and began chasing me round the kitchen table. He had told us, when we met to discuss the lease, that he was eighty-two years old, so now I said severely, 'Monsieur, you should be ashamed of yourself. Remember, you are eighty-two years old.' 'Oh no I'm not,' he said, with a triumphant glitter in his eye. 'I am only seventy, but I always pretend I am much older because it makes husbands feel more secure.' (I have to admit that, uprooted and homesick as I was, I couldn't help feeling just the tiniest bit pleased that someone – even if it was just the old landlord – fancied me.)

I managed to shake him off, and went upstairs to clean the bed-rooms, which hadn't been done since we'd moved in. We had a very pretty Persian rug (bought with wedding present money) on the horrible nylon carpet in our room; I hung it on the rail of the balcony while I hoovered the rooms, and only some time later did I notice it had gone – blown off by the wind. I leapt on to the balcony and looked down – the street was empty of Persian rugs. Someone had stolen it. Naturally, it was not insured. In the five years we lived in Brussels, I never passed a carpet shop without checking whether it was in the window – though quite what I would have done if I'd seen it, I have no idea. Especially because it was not long before I could hardly set foot in a Belgian store without having a major row.

The shopkeepers were so unhelpful and rude after London. In fact, they were positively obstructive – before you'd even asked a question, they'd be getting their lips pursed ready to form the word '*Non*'. So the butcher wouldn't slice my Parma ham for me, even though I was a good customer. The travel agency wouldn't refund the supplement that AW had to pay to get on a flight because they'd made the wrong booking. The bicycle shop wouldn't put the pram wheel back on the pram when it suddenly rolled off one day. The supermarket wouldn't change the tin of crabmeat, which was so bad it was black. The babies' shoe shop wouldn't replace the expensive little shoes I'd bought for Hester, which fell to bits after a week. (I made a total fool of myself there, saying in French, 'I warn you, this is not the end of the story – I am a journalist known throughout the world . . .' before being led away past smirking attendants.) And when Hester tripped over in Dujardin, the posh children's clothes shop in Avenue Louise, and cut her cheek on the sharp corner of a table, they bustled us out into the street without a word of help or apology, desperate to get rid of us before their rich Belgian customers saw the blood.

Looking back, I think it might all have been to do with the fact that in those days I used to dress in hippy style – lots of scarves and coloured stocking and embroideries and dangly necklaces. They probably didn't realize that the Ethnic Look was (quite) fashion-able in London, and thought I was a genuine gypsy. (I stopped dressing in this way when the *Daily Telegraph* did an article about me in their 'Me and My Clothes' column some time afterwards. For the photograph, I decided to wear an unusual Indian hat and I arranged a bulky shawl over one shoulder. When the picture appeared in black and white, head and shoulders only and seemingly taken with a fisheye lens, I looked like a deranged hunchback. I moved into tailored black, and have never worn anything remotely ethnic since.)

Dog mess was the other thing that drove us mad in Brussels. It was everywhere: on the pavements, in the parks – you couldn't throw a ball in any open space for fear of what it would roll in. (Having a child makes you extra aware of the dangers of dog poo.) And the dog owners were totally shameless – they'd hold the lead and wait while their pet did its business on our doorstep. AW and I used to lurk in the playroom next to our front door, ready to rush out shouting abuse the moment we saw a dog approaching.

People accuse the British of being obsessed by their pets, but honestly, across the Channel they leave us standing. Hester and I peeped into a pram one day in the Place Flagey, ready to go 'Aaah . . .' but there on the pillow was a dachshund's head instead of a baby's; we almost shrieked in horror. We saw dogs in cardigans, dogs in gumboots – up the road from where we lived there was a dogs' outfitters selling dogs' evening dresses, dogs' sheepskin coats, dogs' jewellery and dogs' luggage. All this said, going back to Brussels two decades later I found the shopkeepers had had a blanket personality change: they were all charming, even helpful – in fact they made London shops seem boorish – and I went round in a state of pleasant shock. But the dog poo problem was as bad as it had ever been, maybe worse.

Being a lady of leisure in Brussels felt very odd. In Ethiopia, and on maternity leave, I had known that my time off was limited, and I would soon be going back to my job. Now I realized that this was probably going to go on for ever. I had, in effect, retired. Soon after we arrived the man next to me at a dinner party asked what I did. This was exactly what I had been wondering myself, but instead of bursting into tears and sobbing, 'I don't know, please

help me, I used to be a fashion editor, but now . . . what am I?',
I said, with a false little smile, 'Well, I suppose I am a housewife.'
Whereupon he hitched his chair just a little bit away from me, and
talked to the woman on his other side for the rest of the evening.

I agonized about my role and identity for months, until I slowly
came round to the idea that perhaps I had the best of all worlds.
I was at home with my baby, and yet I had help; I didn't have to
drive through traffic to be anywhere at 9 a.m., but I had some
work to do. I had been commissioned to write a biography of
Christian Dior; and I had managed to persuade the local English-
language magazine, the *Bulletin*, to use me as a freelance contrib-
utor, as well as lining up some pieces about Brits in Brussels for
the *Evening Standard*. (I still smile when I think of the *Standard*
because once when they rang little Hester got there first. 'Gaga
dooda, sloopoop,' I found her saying into the mouthpiece. I seized
the phone from her, too late – the caller had put the phone down.
A short while later it rang again; it was a woman from the *Standard*.
'I'm sorry,' she said, 'I rang earlier but got your secretary. I think
she must have been speaking Flemish, and I didn't understand, so
I hung up.')

I set up my office on the dining-room table and decided I would
work every morning and spend the afternoon with the baby. This
became, more or less, my routine for the next decade or so. The
only thing I'd do differently now, is that I wouldn't use the dining
table as my desk – simply because clearing it all away is such a
effort that you never eat off it again.)

In those days, Brussels was a fusty kind of place, old-fashioned and
politically incorrect, with a seemingly higher-than-average elderly
population. At the height of the anti-fur frenzy in the rest of the
world, you could still see women in Brussels dressed from head to
toe in real leopardskin. And once a year, the kind of animal circus
we no longer had in Britain would pitch its big top in Place Flagey,
just round the corner from our house. We would be kept awake
by the lions roaring and elephants trumpeting and once a neighbour of ours, looking out of his dining-room window, saw an
escaped kangaroo bouncing along the road.

In Belgian high society, manners seemed to belong to another century – men wore silk stockings and shoes with little pompoms on the front, and Brussels was the only place I could imagine where a dinner jacket might need to go to the cleaners regularly – where it might even wear out. I can't remember now how on earth AW and I found ourselves taken up by the aristocratic set, but I do remember an awful evening when I went to sit next to one of the men with pompoms, in some grand drawing room before dinner, and he told me bluntly not to sit there – the place was reserved for his '*soupeuse*' (dinner companion). There was nowhere else, and I had to go and stand alone with my drink in a corner. AW, who found himself similarly place-less, came up and whispered 'Sod 'em all Bridge, is what I say.'

(That was just a small foretaste of what happened to poor AW at the Lord Mayor of London's banquet for the President of the Gambia. This involved hundreds of people and liveries and traditional English ritual, culminating in everyone sitting down at their tables at exactly the same time – everyone, that is, except AW. Everyone had a seat to sit on except him. To avoid sticking up like a sore thumb in the middle of the room he adopted a sitting position, held by tremendous effort of thigh muscles, until a waiter could get to him with a chair.)

Those Brussels dinner parties were fearfully grand with butlers and fantastic food (oysters, lobsters, fillet of roebuck) and elaborate table decorations – I knew a woman who used to have her candles specially dyed to match her table linen. I interviewed one of Brussels' most popular freelance butlers for the *Bulletin* and he told me that at an immaculate dinner I'd been to myself a couple of weeks before, someone had dropped the gravy in the kitchen and they'd had to scoop it up and serve it anyway. I learned a curious detail about Brussels high society before it dropped us: this was that the worst social blunder you could make was to ask to go to the loo in your host's house. 'It would be better to squat down in the driveway before going inside,' said my informant earnestly. I never knew if this was true, or just her own personal obsession.

The best thing that came out of our short spell of high living was that one of our grand acquaintances knew Hergé, the creator of Tintin, and very sweetly asked him for his autograph for our daughter. Hergé did a little pen and ink drawing of Tintin with Snowy the dog, and signed it for Hester. It was our most prized possession – it was going to keep us in our old age – until Hester decided to colour it in with lurid felt-tips.

Any entertaining on our part was done humbly round the kitchen table, but one day we decided to be incredibly brave and invite the British Ambassador and his wife and some friends for a proper dinner party in the dining room. I spent a day clearing the table, and about two weeks hyperventilating about the menu. Our dining room was on the first floor, but there was a dumb waiter – a small wooden lift on ropes that you could pull up and down a shaft leading to the kitchen.

As the dinner got under way, Marga, our au pair of the time, loaded and unloaded the lift at the kitchen end, while I pulled things up at the top. Everything went perfectly, until it was time to clear the table after the main course, send the dirty plates down, and haul up the pudding. I don't know why, but as I loaded the last dirty dish into the lift, I said gaily to the guests, 'I expect the ropes will break now and everything will go crashing to the ground.' Which is exactly what happened. The ropes snapped and a second later there was the most almighty crash as our entire dinner service hit the floor of the cellar below the kitchen. All I could do was visualize the look of shock on Marga's face as the lift shot past her on its way down, and this gave me almost-uncontrollable giggles. We only ever had one other dinner in the dining room – that time we carried it all up and down by hand.

Looking back, I think it must have been Julia who was our key to high society in Brussels. Julia's husband was one of the Commissioners in Brussels, and though he was far, far senior to AW, whose feet were still on the bottom rung, we had mutual friends in London. As if sent by a guardian angel, Julia had turned up on my doorstep when we'd been there only a few days, and we immediately became partners in discovering what life in Brussels was all about. Very often our guide was Carole, a frantically energetic American who had lived there for years and knew all the tips and short-cuts. Julia was – is, because she became a life-long friend – the kind of warm, wacky, irrepressible Englishwoman on whom Evelyn Waugh modelled his great character, Julia Stitch. She probably saved her husband's life. They came out of their house one morning and Julia couldn't remember where she'd parked the car the night before. As they both craned their necks to look up the street to the left of their house, an IRA bullet shot past her husband's right ear and embedded itself in the front door.

I loved her from the moment she told me about her Roy Jenkins experience. Roy, who had just become President of the Commission then, invited Julia and her husband to a party. When they arrived he greeted them and asked Julia what she'd like to drink. Julia, who didn't know him at that stage, told me she was so nervous that her mind went blank. 'Um,' she replied, frantically trying to remember the name of a drink – *any* drink – to ask for. 'I'd love an um, er . . . an um . . .'

'Come on, Julia,' said Roy, 'what will you have?'

'Oh, I'd like an um . . . er . . .'. She was getting really desperate when suddenly a drink came into her mind. 'I'd love a *Ribena*,' she said.

'Ribena?' said Roy, taken aback. 'We don't have any of that. How about a sherry?'

'Yes, yes, I'd absolutely love a sherry,' said Julia with relief.

Julia and I found a mission in Brussels. We had become intrigued by the Art Nouveau and Art Deco architecture for which the city is famous (though less so in those days – they had only just stopped demolishing masterpieces) and in our enthusiasm had gone knocking on the door of the hotel Solvay. This was a house on the Avenue Louise, built by the great Belgian architect, Victor Horta, for the industrialist, Solvay, at the end of the nineteenth century, and it was rumoured to be the most perfect example of Art Nouveau that existed in Brussels. It was never open to the public, but Julia and I thought we'd give it a go.

The owner, Monsieur Wittamer, a courteous old gentleman, opened up and took us around. The house was spectacular. A huge Art Nouveau stained-glass window glowed in the stairwell above an enormous wall-painting by van Rysselberg, a renowned artist of Horta's time; the curvy banisters matched the pattern in the parquet floor, which matched the carpets, which matched the painted walls, which matched the furniture – and everything was golden or ochre or pale yellow so that the place seemed bathed in sunshine. But then M. Wittamer told us that parts of the house were in danger of falling down, and he was going to have to sell some of Horta's specially-designed furniture to pay for the restoration. That sounded terrible, and Julia and I promised to go home and think of a way of helping him to keep the house and its contents intact.

After much debate, we decided that our only hope was to write to the King. We composed a diplomatic letter and sent it off and, next thing, we were summoned to the Palace for a formal meeting with the Lord Chamberlain. The end result was that the Belgian electricity company was persuaded to rent the hotel Solvay for use as a prestigious venue for their official entertainment, and to restore it. Everyone, including Monsieur Wittamer, was happy, and I look back on the Saving of the hotel Solvay as one of my proudest achievements.

In the autumn of 1977 I was pregnant again. We'd hoped this would happen because Hester was now more than two, I wasn't working very hard, and there was no reason on earth to postpone it. (It's a fact that the birth rate among ex-pats is much higher than that of 'normal' women living and working in their own countries; when you can't have a career and are living away from home, family life is the only way to go.)

I went to childbirth classes in French, where they taught me to *respirer* and *souffler*. One day when the class was talking about pain, I said rather smugly that I, personally, wasn't expecting pain, as I would be having an epidural. The teacher looked at me pityingly. 'Having a baby usually involves some pain,' she said, 'that is what we believe here.' Silly old thing, I thought, I'll talk to the doctor about it.

My obstetrician had the uncannily appropriate name of Dr Poulain, which means Dr Foal, and he was one of the nicest people I'd ever met. So I told him all about how I'd had an epidural for the whole eleven hours of my first delivery in London, and would be grateful if we could do the same again. 'How was it?' he asked.

'Well, I don't know,' I said, 'I was terribly sick and uncomfortable and frightened and it was a forceps delivery, *but I felt no pain.*'

To my horror, Dr Poulain said he would allow only one single epidural injection (none of that business of leaving a tube in your back to be topped up); he wanted me to help push the baby out. I went back to the classes and paid close attention.

AW came with me to the hospital (like the first one, this baby was late and had to be induced). We spent the morning doing the crossword. Then I experienced my first contraction – it was really exciting because I hadn't felt a thing when Hester was born. But as the contractions got closer and fiercer, I got less and less excited and more and more worried about when, exactly, they were going to put in this epidural . . . or perhaps they weren't, and it had all been a trick?

Then an extraordinary thing happened. I've never been able to do crosswords. I am hopelessly stupid about them; I can't even manage the easy one in the *Evening Standard*. But in labour, I was suddenly brilliant. 'Amphibian found river in thick mist?' AW asked.

'Frog!' I shouted triumphantly, and so on. It has never happened again since.

In the late afternoon I asked Dr Poulain, now gowned-up and in blue clogs with white daisies painted on them, if I could have the epidural. He agreed, and I was taken to the delivery room where he examined me and then said in French with a sad smile: 'Oh dear, this baby is not going to be born for another hour or two, which is very annoying because I was planning to have *canard à l'orange* for dinner, washed down with a little Burgundy . . .'

AW interrupted. 'If the baby is not coming yet,' he said, 'could I go and collect my mother who is coming on the coach from London? I could be back within an hour.'

'With your mother?' Dr Poulain looked appalled.

'No, no,' said AW, 'I'll take my mother home and come back by myself.'

Dr Poulain agreed there was plenty of time. But as the sound of AW's footsteps faded down the corridor, I felt the urge to push.

'Dr Poulain,' I piped up in my best French, 'I have the sensation that I must push . . .'

'Impossible!' he said, 'But I'll check . . .'

When he did – *Wow*! Everyone rushed into action, especially me, and the next thing I knew, I had a baby daughter. AW, meanwhile, was only just arriving at the bus station.

They tidied me up and put swaddling bandages around the baby and me so we were like two cocoons. (Though it sounds a little out of date – like 2,000 years – I must say swaddling feels very cosy and secure.) Ages later, when I'd been moved back to my room, AW reappeared and, as I heard him at the door, I called out, 'You've got another lovely baby daughter.'

'Oh wonderful,' he said – but I glimpsed in the mirror across the room his mouth turning down as he realized there'd be no young buck in our family for him to clash antlers with one day. Of course, when he held her, a minute later, it was love at first sight. For me, almost the best part of the whole thing was showing the new baby to Hester who came toddling in next day with my mother-in-law, both of them clutching little posies. It didn't *really* matter that there was no teddy bear made of daisies from Yves Saint Laurent, or orchids from Christian Dior (though I must admit I did think about them).

I just felt like the luckiest, happiest person in the world.

Apart from the dog mess, Brussels was a most unstressful and easy city in which to bring up a family. There was something for all of us: parks and woods to play in, lakes with ducks to feed, cinemas with the latest films, opera and ballet (though I think we only went once), marvellous food markets, no traffic jams and easy illegal parking. (I did get a *contrevention* – a parking ticket – in the Place Flagey, on a day when everything seemed to be going wrong. I accosted the policeman, waving the ticket. 'How could you do this to me? You can see I have a small child and lots of shopping and I'm in a terrible hurry . . .' I was almost crying. Suddenly he burst into tears. 'I am sorry,' he said, 'but I too am having a terrible day. I am not feeling well at all. My wife has left me . . .' We ended up sobbing in each other's arms in the middle of the Place, and he tore up my ticket.)

Apart from the flea market in the Place du Jeu de Balle, my passion was the auction houses. They were far cheaper than English ones, and full of unusual and curious things (oh, the treasures I could have bought in Brussels in the 1970s if only we'd had the money). AW and I got quite hooked on the monthly viewings, and once I sneaked off on my own and without really meaning to, bought an enormous dining table for ten, and a hideous sideboard/cupboard thing. AW could see the point of the dining table but not the sideboard.

'Look at it more carefully,' I said, trying to convince him how clever I'd been, 'It's verging on the Arts and Crafts movement.'

'It's verging on the crap,' said AW. We've still got it in storage in Brussels.

Another perk to living in Brussels was that all medical treatment was private, paid by insurance, according to the Belgian system, so no queuing from dawn in a surgery full of people with colds, or waiting with bored children for appointments. And, unlike the people in the shops, the medical personnel seemed, like Dr Poulain, to be charming. We were especially thrilled with the dentist – the most gentle, caring one that either AW or I had ever revealed the insides of our mouths to. All my fear of having teeth drilled vanished – until one day as I lay, totally relaxed, in the chair in his surgery, he suddenly said, 'I really think you should have your tongue shortened.'

'*What*?' I shrieked, sitting up abruptly.

'Well,' he said, 'Your tongue is just a little bit too big for your mouth, so I think I'll just trim off a few millimetres here and there.'

At first I thought this must be some sort of joke dreamed up by AW in the waiting room, because I always talk too much, but he was deadly serious. I was out of there in a split second, and none of us ever went near him again. (Not long ago I met someone who'd lived in Brussels at that time, and when we got to talking about the old days, he said, 'There was a marvellous dentist there, I can't remember his name, but he was always nagging at me to have my tongue shortened . . .')

But Brussels, as we ex-pats were fond of saying, was also – still is – a wonderful town to get out of: all Europe was on our doorstep.

We used to spend odd weekends in the pearly grey luminous light of the Dutch islands, where we rented a house from a friend who worked in the glue industry – 'it's a sticky business' he used to quip. (Once, at a rather formal dinner, he nipped my thigh with an empty lobster claw. The hostess was not amused.) We'd rent bicycles with baby seats and idly pedal around the empty, flat roads, stopping for mussels and chips at lunchtime. Those weekends were my favourite treat.

Antwerp Zoo was another popular outing – though I feared for a time that our last experience there might have damaged Hester for life. She and I were walking peacefully hand in hand past various cages with different animals in them, until we came to an enclosure where we saw nothing except a large pool of water.

'I wonder what lives in here?' I said cheerily. 'Perhaps it's a baby seal or a green froggie.'

'P'raps it's a little fishie,' Hester was just saying helpfully, when there was a tremendous, breathtaking whoosh, and a roar, and a huge dark slug-like creature about forty foot high, with eyes like black hardboiled eggs, rose up from the depths and towered over us. We screamed, and Hester went on screaming for about a week. It was, apparently, a sea elephant – and for me, another reason (besides sharks, jellyfish, sting rays etc) for not feeling comfortable about swimming in the ocean.

In September 1978, a month after Claudia was born, we decided to send Hester to a little Montessori school that was just opening. This was a giant leap of faith, because, apart from having a husband called Elvis, the young American woman running the school had found only one other pupil. I was so worried about there being just the two of them – but then, when others began to crowd in, I felt quite put out.

Suddenly, we were out of babyhood, and into school friends coming to play. I'd very much like to know what happened to one of them, an English boy called Christopher Gossage. He came to lunch one day and, halfway through the meal, picked up the spaghetti bolognese from his plate and dumped it all on his head. Another afternoon, when his father came to collect him, Christopher somehow managed to whack his dad in the crotch so hard that his father hopped round our kitchen clutching himself. Then little Christopher started hopping about with anxiety. My friend Christopher Matthew, who was staying at the time, witnessed this extraordinary scene and has referred to them ever since as The Dancing Gossages.

It was Christopher Gossage who led a rebellion at Hester's sixth birthday party (the first indication that my daughters and their friends would be Trouble one day). By that time I'd become expert at birthday parties and always had them planned in advance, with exciting games to play, and prizes. That particular day, we went to the park and I assembled all the children.

'Right,' I said, 'now Hester and Christopher are going to pick teams and then we'll start some races.'

I beamed at the group who all nodded and agreed, when a voice – Christopher's – said, 'No we're not. We're going to play in the woods.'

In a second it was mob rule – all the children ganged up behind Christopher and went peeling off to the woods, shrieking and whooping, drunk with anarchy and power. The rather bossy mother who had volunteered to help me with the party was horrified – 'We must re-establish control,' she said. 'Do you mind if I take over?'

The only good part about the rest of the afternoon was watching her running round the woods like a deranged sheepdog, calling 'Children, come back now, come at once,' and no one taking a blind bit of notice.

AW had to travel quite often in his job – Africa mostly, but sometimes the Pacific. And I would usually choose these times to visit all the grandparents in England which, given my lack of organizational skills, meant five years of scope for travel disasters. I would get Claudia, Hester, the au pair, and myself, all safely tucked into the car, and set off – then discover later that I'd forgotten the nappies or the picnic or the passports. I don't think I ever left the house without coming back ten minutes later to collect something.

My personal worst was driving three hours to Dunkirk to catch the hovercraft, then remembering, just as we got there, that I had left the croissants heating up in the oven in Brussels. I did a three-point turn and drove all the way back to Brussels, only to realize, as we entered the city, that I had turned the gas off at the mains so it didn't matter about the oven.

In the summer of 1979 AW decided to take us all to Kashmir for a holiday. This was partly a reward to the family for having tried – and mostly succeeded – to settle down in Brussels, and partly to cheer me up because I still occasionally felt like a displaced person. He chose Kashmir because, for years, I had collected Kashmiri lacquer-work, and had always wanted to find out more about it.

We set off, AW, Sue (the current au pair), Hester, Claudia, me, a folding cot, toys, crayons, drawing books, and a mountain of nappies, and spent a month living on a houseboat on Dal Lake. (To keep Claudia quiet on the plane, I fed her for the whole nine-hour flight, so that when we arrived in Delhi my breasts were like two pitta breads hanging off my chest.) It was all wonderful – the only flaw was that we knew very little about Kashmir, and there were no guidebooks then to tell us about the history of the place, or the sights we saw, let alone about the lacquer-work. I decided that when we got back I would try to write one myself – I didn't realize it at the time, but this was a project that was to stand me in good stead for the next few years.

In the early summer of 1981, unknown to us, of course, our pleasant lives in Brussels were about to come to an unexpected and abrupt end. It started with AW getting restive. He was finding work at the European Commission increasingly stressful – partly to do with the weight of bureaucracy that made decisions agonizingly slow, partly to do with the competitiveness and back-stabbing between rival nations, and partly to do with the fact that Britain did not seem to take Europe seriously enough and was missing opportunities all the time. He decided he needed a break, and applied for a job as a Deputy Director of UNWRA – the UN agency that takes care of the Palestinian refugees – in Beirut. When, to his surprise, he was offered the post, he arranged with the European Commission to give him two years' unpaid leave.

The weeks before he was to due to leave were a most peculiar time. At first the children and I were supposed to be going to Beirut with him, then the UN said it was too dangerous for families and we should live in Cyprus, and then, just to complicate things, AW said we should live in Turkish Cyprus rather than Greek Cyprus because he's always liked the Turks. I went along with all this in a zombie-like way, and began, through friends who knew the commander of the Turkish forces in Cyprus, to look for a house to rent there. But it all seemed unreal somehow – I should have been feeling as anxious about the future as my darling mother, Doomwatch, but I was coasting along in neutral as if, subconsciously, I believed that none of it was really going to happen.

My subconscious was right. (How did it know? I often wonder.) One Monday morning, about three weeks before AW was to take up his new job, he woke with a terrible pain in his arm. Since AW has the highest threshold of pain known to medical science, alarm bells rang, but neither of us knew at that time that a pain in the arm can be a heart attack. AW thought it must be caused by his suit being too tight; I recommended that he should have a hot bath, then we both decided that his best course of action was for him to see the office doctor when he arrived at work.

I was still pottering round in my dressing gown with the children when he telephoned to say the office doctor was on leave, so he was going round the corner to our normal doctor. Next thing, the normal doctor rang, sounding completely abnormal, to say that AW had something called an *infarctus*; he must get to hospital as soon as possible, but was refusing to go by ambulance because he wanted me to take him, so could I come immediately? I didn't know what an *infarctus* was, but I could tell that this was urgent so I drove AW to hospital. When we arrived he was rushed into the intensive care unit and I was pushed out to wait in the corridor.

I sat there for hours, every now and again plucking up courage to knock on the door and ask what was happening, but each time I was simply told to wait. Then – a miracle! – who should I see coming out of the lift but Dr Poulain. I flung myself at him, weeping, and begged him to find out what was going on. He discovered that AW was having a massive heart attack, told me that they were doing everything they could, and that they thought he had a reasonable chance. I should go home, he said, because I would not be allowed to see him until later, but I would be kept informed.

I went home in a dream and rang his and my parents and Julia and our friends Sandy and Adrian very, very calmly. Afterwards they told me that, having broken the news of AW's heart attack, I kept saying, 'Now that's enough about us, how are *you*?' and they all thought I'd lost my wits. I also rang UNWRA in Vienna and told them AW would not be able to take up the job in Beirut. (Years later, we heard the unbelievable news that the man who took AW's job had been killed in the Israeli bombing of Beirut. So what had seemed like very bad luck had in fact saved AW's life.)

When at long last I was summoned to the hospital and allowed to see AW, they told me he was probably going to be all right. In the bed next to his was a man with a bald head and thick black hair all over his body, who had also had a heart attack. He and AW started competing over which of them was the most ill.

'My heart attack was more serious than yours,' the bald man would say.

'Yes, but I am younger,' AW would reply proudly (he was thirty-five at the time).

AW was eventually allowed home, but instructed that he must not consider going back to work for six months or longer, so we decided to go and live in Somerset with AW's parents who had a small cottage attached to their house. AW's father came over to take him home, and I packed up the things we needed, locked the house and drove Marga, the au pair, Hester and Claudia home. I didn't forget anything this time.

The heart doctor in London decided that if AW lost weight and got very fit there would be no need for a bypass, yet. So AW bought a bike and spent his days in Somerset cycling up and down hills until he was ruddy and skinny and fitter than an Olympic athlete. Hester went to the local primary school, and Claudia to a playgroup, and we all settled in nicely. But there was a question mark over our future. The doctor said that AW must never go back to his job in Brussels – he should, in fact, change as many things about his life as possible, because clearly, the way he'd been living did not suit him. (For a wild moment I wondered if I'd have to go . . .) So AW transferred to the overseas service of the European Commission so that he could be posted to one of their Delegations abroad – far away from the stress of day-to-day office life in Brussels. And that is why we found ourselves, in 1982, *en route* for Port of Spain in Trinidad.

7

Jumblies and Flying Freemasons

Our second evening in Port of Spain set the tone for the next two years. I often wonder how life in Trinidad might have worked out had we *not* been invited out to dinner that night . . .

As it was, a kindly middle-aged English couple who had lived in Trinidad for years and were friends of AW's new boss, asked us to come for a family supper and meet a few of their friends. Unfortunately, that very day someone called Dolores, whom they all knew, had been viciously attacked by an intruder with a cutlass (a *cutlass*! – our eyes were on stalks, not knowing that in Trinidad everyone has a cutlass; it's like owning a penknife). First they discussed this ghastly attack in minute detail and then they moved on to all the other attacks (rapes, killings, dismemberments and mutilations) that had ever happened to white people in Port of Spain, in spite of burglar bars ('Oh, with modern American bolt cutters anyone can get through them in a trice') and alarm systems ('The police won't come because they don't have enough vehicles; you have to go and collect them yourself if you want them'). When the time came to leave I was almost too scared to go home, and this fear never left me the whole time we were there.

It was such a beautiful tropical island, with steep, forested hills, every kind of glorious flowering tree from jacaranda to flame-of-the-forest, and – growing wild all over the place and twenty foot tall – the kind of 'indoor plants' that cost £15 in pots in Marks & Spencer. In our own garden we had avocados the size of footballs and tiny bananas. I should have revelled in it, but every time I managed to conquer my terror, some frightful new thing would happen to bring it flooding back. An Englishwoman we knew was raped at gunpoint in her house by someone who stopped her at her gate pretending to ask for directions to the local doctor. He was, in fact, a notorious gangster and the police cornered him and shot him dead as he tried to get away. (She told me later that this was the only thing that made her nightmare survivable.) Then there was the night when, at a very anti-social hour, AW and I heard terrific hammering and banging coming from a neighbour's garden. How extremely inconsiderate, we thought, to be doing building work at this hour. Next morning we discovered the noise had been burglars smashing down their reinforced front door.

AW had to go to regular meetings between the European embassies to discuss security, and what 'incidents' their nationals had suffered. After one of these, he rather foolishly told me that four rapes had been reported – one victim being a *man* who had had the extreme misfortune to wake up when there were burglars in his house. Then AW made the further mistake of telling me the saga of his predecessor, an Italian called Alberto, who sacked his odd-job man, but then, feeling sorry for him, allowed him to stay on until he found other work. One night the man came into Alberto's room and threw boiling water over his head when he was asleep. Although horribly scalded and shocked, Alberto had the presence of mind to realize that the man would come back to finish him off. He tried to lock the bedroom door but the key wouldn't turn; so he had somehow to wedge himself between the door and a wall to prevent the man getting at him. The struggle to keep the door closed lasted all night. When daylight came the man fled, leaving behind the thick wooden truncheon he had carved specially for the purpose of killing Alberto. And all this had happened in what was now AW's and my bedroom.

I hated our new home from then on, though it was a perfectly pleasant suburban house in a street called Eagle Crescent; part of an American-style development in Maraval, the 'posh' residential area of Port of Spain. It was a bungalow, but it was built on the side of a hill so that though the living room was on the ground floor the bedrooms were on the first floor. This may sound like an insignificant detail, but it is very important to what came later.

Our household consisted of AW and me, Hester, who was now seven, and Claudia, four, plus a South African au pair girl called Lin who was going to help us settle in for a few months. It had been almost impossible to get Lin, from apartheid South Africa, a visa for Trinidad, and I can't remember how AW achieved it in the end. I certainly wish that I *didn't* remember quite so clearly the phone call I made before he did – to a powerful friend who worked in the Home Office, begging him (I may even have tried to bribe him) to give Lin a British passport so that she could come with us to Trinidad without any complications. He was absolutely astonished at my request.

'Of course I can't, Bridge,' he said, 'you know that.'

'But you've just given one to Zola Budd,' I said surlily – referring to the South African barefoot runner whom Britain wanted in our Olympic team. But it made no difference to my case.

And then there was Carmelita, our maid, whom AW had hired just before the rest of us arrived. Carmo, as she came to be known, was an illegal immigrant from the island of St Vincent, which meant that she had to run and hide in her room every time someone rang the doorbell. Her family were very poor: she had barely worn shoes before she came to us, and the nearest she'd got to eating chicken, she told me, was to chew the claws. She was a fervent Baptist and used to sing hymns in a screechy voice as she went about her work. We loved her. She told us that her father was so good at dancing and singing in church in St Vincent that he was known locally as 'Moshun'. (Later, when we heard that he'd gone a bit mad, AW said to me quietly, 'I suppose he's Loco-Moshun now.')

Like most people in the Caribbean – and often the newspapers – Carmo spoke in patois. She was steeped in superstition: only Jesus stood between her and the terrifying, ever-present threat of jumbies (the Caribbean name for zombies) and *maljo* (evil eye) and *obeah* (voodoo). Once out of the blue she asked if I realized that freemasons could fly. No, I told her gently, I hadn't heard that before, and I wasn't sure it was true. 'Oh yes it is, Mum' (she always called me Mum), 'my cousin was on a plane to St Vincen' an' a freemason got on in de air and sat down right nex' to him.'

That was in the early days of my four-year campaign to try and help Carmo to distinguish between truth and fiction, and before we hit the brick wall of *Planet of the Apes*. Carmo had seen it on TV and was convinced it was real: 'Mum, have you been to dat place ruled by apes?' she asked.

'It doesn't exist Carmo, it's a made-up film.'

'No Mum, you can see deir faces – dem faces real.'

'No Carmo, that's very clever makeup.'

She never believed me, and would sometimes spring a question on AW or me to catch us out – 'Did we know anyone who'd visited the country ruled by apes?' or 'What was the weather like there?'

Carmo's other unshakeable belief was that certain death would follow if you opened the fridge door or put your hands in cold water within a few hours of doing the ironing. This was obviously a hangover from the days when flat-irons were heated on fires and the person doing the ironing got extremely hot, and had to avoid catching a chill. I tried explaining to Carmo that this didn't apply with an electric iron, but it was no use. Then she went home for a few days on family business, and when she returned I said, 'Carmo, when you were not here, I did the ironing every day, and then I opened the fridge to get the milk for my coffee, and then I peeled potatoes in cold water and nothing happened to me.'

Carmo was unmoved: 'I know Mum,' she said understandingly, 'it because white people have differen' blood.'

In Brussels days, AW and I had started a routine of playing games with Hester and Claudia – snakes and ladders, ludo, pelmanism – for an hour before their bedtime. In Trinidad we asked Carmo to join the group, and these sessions became her passion; she had not had the luxury of a childhood. 'Playin' tonight, Mum?' she'd ask me in an undertone each morning, as though I ran some kind of dodgy casino.

AW's new office was just up the road in an attractive old Trinidadian house, and his boss, Gerald Waterson, was elegant and charming. (There was a rumour, I don't know how it started, that he was the illegitimate son of Edward VIII. AW and I were absolutely convinced of it, because everything fitted: first of all he looked *exactly* like him and secondly, he had been brought up in Switzerland which is just what you'd expect, somehow, for the illegitimate son of an English king.) His wife was nice too; she gave me the recipe for a delicious cocktail snack made of rice that was her speciality, though I think she may have done that thing of leaving out the vital ingredient, as they've never worked for me.

We found our local Catholic church and went to Mass there. I was really shocked by the rudeness of the congregation: most of them seemed to be reading the Sunday paper – and then it dawned on me that the order of service was printed in it. Hester and Claudia were booked into St Andrew's school which was just round the corner from our house; they learned the Trinidadian National Anthem – 'Every creed and race has an equal place and may God bless our Nayshun' – and seemed to be happy there.

And so, after three weeks in Port of Spain, apart from my obsession about intruders, life seemed set fair. Then disaster struck. The whole terrible drama that followed was all my fault, but to show what a hero AW is, he has never once brought it up in all the many rows we have had over the years since then.

AW went to bed one night leaving Lin and me chatting in the living room. A couple of minutes later we followed him into the bedroom area, which was separated from the living room by a huge iron burglar gate. This was locked with a padlock, which I, being anxious to seal off the world of rapists and murderers as quickly as possible, snapped shut without thinking – only remembering as the click of the lock registered in my brain that the key was still the other side of the door, on the living-room table. My stomach turned over. We were now all locked into the bedroom quarters on the first floor with no escape – what if there was a fire? It was another of those awful moments when I wished that I could be allowed to relive the last few seconds of my life – I'd have wished it even harder had I known what was going to happen next. I confessed to AW what I'd done; he was furious, but said let's go to bed and deal with this in the morning.

I was woken at crack of dawn by the sound of AW unscrewing the burglar bars on our bedroom windows with the screwdriver tool on his Swiss army penknife. (Oh, if Swiss army penknives were not so efficient. Or if he hadn't been given one for Christmas.)

'What on earth are you doing?' I asked.

'I'm unscrewing the bars so that I can jump out of the window and get into the living room to unlock the padlock,' he said grumpily.

'It's awfully high,' I pleaded, 'I don't think you should do it. Let's phone someone for help.'

But who to phone? We didn't really know anyone except AW's boss and we didn't want to admit to him what a stupid thing I'd done. I'd got the number of English neighbours at the back of our house (in case of burglars) but we didn't really know them.

'I'll hang from the windowsill and drop down so there won't be too much of a gap,' said AW.

He climbed out, hung from the sill and then let go. His feet came into collision with a plank of wood that the gardener had left on the cement border round the house – and which, peering out of the window in the half-light of dawn, neither of us had seen. He lay on the cement, groaning. 'I think I've sprained my ankles,' he said, but he couldn't get up and walk.

What on earth to do? AW was lying in the garden in agony and I was locked inside the house. Praying that the telephone would work (it usually didn't), I rang the English neighbours. They were marvellous. I never knew, and forgot to ask, how they got into our house, but they did, and found the key and unlocked the padlock and got AW on to the sofa. The phone miraculously worked a second time when I rang the doctor who had been recommended to us on our arrival, a wonderful Trinidadian called Wilma Hoyt, who came immediately. X-rays were the priority, then we could decide what to do, she said.

Somehow we got AW into the car, and to the radiologist, whose pictures revealed that both his ankles were shattered. There was no question of flying back to London for treatment; there was internal bleeding and something had to be done immediately. Wilma called a surgeon friend of hers, Buster Robertson, who was retired, but agreed to do the operation. Taking the X-rays, I dashed off to see him. A huge, kindly black ex-rugby player, he told me that he would have to 'fix' AW's ankles; they were too badly broken to do save the joints. 'I am afraid he will have difficulty walking afterwards.'

I wept; this was too big a decision to make on my own, but AW was not in a condition to decide anything himself.

'If my husband was your own son, what would you do?' I asked.

'I would do this operation,' he said, 'it is the only thing there is to do.'

An anaesthetist was found, nurses were hired (everyone seemed to be freelance). The team assembled at the clinic and Buster Robertson began the operation. I sat on the verandah of the building and prayed. Suddenly all the lights went out: there was a power cut, or outage as they are known in Trinidad. I waited to hear the rumble of the generator coming on, but there was silence – it had no fuel. The operation came to a halt while someone was sent to fetch diesel, and then Buster Robertson went back to his work.

Ages later he came out on to the verandah. He had not 'fixed' AW's ankles, he had managed to patch them up. It might work and it might not, he said, but he was smiling. I hugged him with gratitude. Months later when AW saw a British specialist, he admired Buster Robertson's work, but assured AW that he would have to have his ankles 'fixed' within the next few years. It's twenty years on now, and they are still more or less okay – I put it down to my prayers on the verandah.

AW slowly got better, graduating from bed to wheelchair, and then to crutches. During the wheelchair phase, our wonderful neighbours invited us to lunch one day, and with some difficulty we manoeuvred AW through the hedge between the gardens. Afterwards Lin and I took the girls home via the hedge, but Peter and Paul, fellow guests at the lunch, said they'd drive AW and his wheelchair back in the car. It would be far easier, they said, and would only take a minute. I didn't see them again for eight hours.

Lin, Carmo, Hester, Claudia and I were soon frantic with worry. What on earth could have happened to them? We walked the route;

there were no accidents. We realized they must have gone on a pub crawl. I could imagine the scene: vulnerable white man in wheelchair in a black bar, everyone getting drunk; vulnerable white man in wheelchair being smashed over the head with a beer bottle, never getting out of wheelchair again. Looking back, I don't know how I had the nerve, but I got into the car and drove downtown to check in obvious bars, but there was no sign of them. They eventually turned up at midnight; I could hear them singing drunkenly as Peter and Paul wheeled AW into our garden, and when I saw their silly sheepish grins, I stood on the front steps and screamed words of abuse I didn't even know I knew. I didn't speak to AW for days.

But this escapade led me to what *Reader's Digest* used to call 'the most unforgettable character I ever met'. (Except in this case it would be more truthful to say 'the most unforgettable *possessions* of a character I met.') Peter felt so guilty about leading AW astray, that he took me to meet Dallas Doxford, an elderly Englishman who lived on a run-down plantation in the Central Ranges of Trinidad.

Peter told me a little background: Dallas was a son of the Doxford family of Sunderland which had made a fortune out of inventing a marine engine. Because he was gay, his family had funded him to live outside England so he would not be an embarrassment to them. He had spent years in Paris in the 1920s, moved to California during the war, and then on to Trinidad.

We arrived at a decrepit Art Deco house, overgrown with tropical vegetation, and Dallas greeted us. My shoulder brushed against a picture hanging on the hall wall; I turned to straighten it – and saw that it was signed *Cezanne*. Peter noticed my surprise and gave me a proud little now-haven't-I-made-it-up-to-you smile. As we were taken through the house I was flabbergasted – all the pictures were by famous artists: Picasso, Gauguin, Paul Nash, you name it, and the antique furniture was the sort that most of us only ever get to see in photographs.

Dallas took us to look at his Hepplewhite four-poster-bed – and then I noticed that the bottoms of its legs were completely eaten away. The whole house was stuffed with priceless objects –

but everything was decaying, faded, bleached, eaten by ants or termites. Later, when AW and I knew Dallas better, he told us indignantly that people were always urging him to put his things into museums where they could be looked after, but why should he? He had bought the paintings because he liked them, in many cases he'd known the artists in Paris – and he wanted them around him. We saw his point, but at the same time, it did seem a terrible waste. Dallas must have died long ago; AW and I often wonder what on earth happened to all his extraordinary possessions.

AW being helpless in a wheelchair or on crutches did nothing for my sense of security. I decided we must have burglar bars on the living-room windows, which is how we came to know Cosmos, the metal man. Cosmos was a mixture of African, European, Indian and Chinese, which somehow made him look exactly like a wilder version of Anthony Quinn in *Zorba the Greek*. He was a buccaneer – things in Trinidad often smacked of pirate days – and always keen for a jump-up (party) or an adventure. When AW was better Cosmos asked him to make a trip to Venezuela with him in a fishing boat, over a long weekend. AW had too much work in the office and couldn't go – which was just as well as Cosmos was arrested by the Venezuelan coast guard and didn't come home for six weeks. It was at Cosmos's house that we heard a parrot really speak. It was hopping around on the floor among a group of children who were all calling it from different directions: 'Come here, Polly', 'No, come to me Polly', 'No, to *me*' . . . when the parrot suddenly said 'I don't know what to do, I really don't know what to do.' It's true, we all heard it. Meanwhile, no sooner were the burglar bars fitted than our Indian landlady gave us notice, and a huge row developed because she said she wouldn't pay for them, in spite of the fact that they were to stay on her windows. We won this battle in the end, so it wasn't necessary for me to implement my last-resort revenge plan which was to spray F★★K MRS PENCO in weedkiller on the lawn. I was quite disappointed.

We moved to a big, shabby old house with an enormous garden just below the British High Commission residence and opposite the children's school. In my memory, it is as if our time in Trinidad was spent in two entirely different islands: the island of the painful, nightmare months in Eagle Crescent, and the island of happy days (though still with a strong undercurrent of fear for me) in the big shabby house. It was there that we actually began to *live* in Trinidad.

I set up my typewriter in an alcove by the dining room and researched my Kashmir book, writing endless letters to the India Office and London libraries. The children walked down the hill to school, and when they came back in the afternoon, we'd go to the run-down Country Club nearby (a relic of British colonial days). The swings in the playground were broken, the lavatories barely usable, the garden a jungle, but, thankfully, the pool was kept in reasonable condition. (Not that Trinidadians actually ever swam – wearing the latest in sexy swimsuits, they'd get into the shallow end and stand in the water, gossiping, all afternoon.) At weekends (when the horrid stinging sandflies were not in season) we'd follow the trail of litter left along the road by the locals to Maracas beach to play in the sea and eat Shark 'n' Bake – a delicious bun filled with fried shark and hot sauce. I could see why whole calypsos are written about Trinidadian street food.

One day on Maracas beach we had a curious little insight into the picky ways of ants. I had taken a plastic box of coleslaw as part of our picnic and forgot to close it when we all went for a swim. We came back to see a piece of shredded carrot about fifty feet long moving slowly across the sand away from our rug. It was ants marching head to tail, each one with a piece of carrot slung over its shoulder. The cabbage was left untouched. Occasionally we would make excursions into the forest to a nature sanctuary called Asa Wright – a slightly sinister place where everything smelt of rotting vegetation, but the children loved it because you could swim in a natural pool with a waterfall in the undergrowth, and if you were lucky, see the huge blue butterflies – each wing as big as a small hand – called Emperor Morpho, flapping through the gloom. It was an isolated place, and I always felt extra-vulnerable there, expecting drug-crazed brigands with cutlasses to emerge from the forest and cut our group to pieces.

I made a playroom for the children in the garage – Cosmos created wrought-iron gates for it which stopped anyone getting in or out illegally, but made it feel like part of the garden. A bit too much like part of the garden in fact. One evening I was tidying up the toys and muttering under my breath: 'Why don't you girls ever put anything away – these dolls go in this box, the painting things should be on the shelf, and this plastic snake should go . . .' My hand was almost closing on the large plastic snake (which somewhere in the back of my mind I knew I hadn't seen before) when it shot off at the speed of light and my screams could have been heard in Caracas.

We somehow acquired a pack of dogs. It all began at our first house when some people asked if we'd like to see their puppy. 'Now, Hester and Claudia, we are definitely not going to get this puppy, we are just going to *look* at it,' I warned before we set out. Of course the puppy came home with us, and I named it Tabitha, which was what I had wanted to call Hester, but AW wouldn't let me. Tabitha was pale and leggy (there was some Weimeraner in her) with grey eyes that completely spooked Carmo – 'Why dat dog have white man's eyes?' she would ask, shuddering. Then someone enquired if we'd take their Doberman puppy, and we thought, oh well, since we've got one dog we might as well have another. AW called it Hinza. Then Hester left the gate open when Tabitha came on heat and we suddenly found ourselves with eight puppies. We found homes for all except one, Sylvia, and the next thing *she* had puppies. Overnight, Tabitha turned into the Mr Hyde of the dog world: first she attacked the puppies and killed one, and then, a couple of days later, she bit a friend of Hester's who came to play. I had to take her to the vet to be put down.

In the meantime, Hinza had finished digging up all the seeds AW had planted, and acquired the habit of pulling the washing off the line and eating it. (Possibly the most disgusting thing I have seen in the course of my life was the sight of one of AW's best socks hanging out of Hinza's bum.) And then one awful morning I ran over and injured one of Sylvia's surviving puppies. Thank God my cousin Frances was staying at that time, and kept her head when I completely lost mine, and we managed to get the pup to the vet. It survived.

Actually, I seemed to spend more time with the vet, Dr Rahman, than I did with AW at that time; the wretched dogs had taken over my life. I think my darkest hour was when they all got ticks, which somehow migrated off the dogs and began crawling all over the kitchen walls. The morning they appeared Carmo and I stared at them with horror. 'Dem tings warp my blood,' she said.

As if our own dogs were not enough of a problem, someone had to run over a huge stray just outside our gate. The authorities in Trinidad never removed dead dogs, they were just left to rot where they lay; the sickly-sweet smell of dead things seemed an integral part of the island – but I didn't want it on my doorstep.

AW was away, Carmo was out, and old George, the gardener, wasn't there, so I decided I would have to move the dead dog myself, before it began to decay – which would be almost immediately in that climate. Wearing rubber gloves, I managed to heave the dog into a big box so that I could take it to Dr Rahman's incinerator, but I couldn't lift the box into the car. Hester and Claudia had some little English boys for tea that day and I asked them rather sheepishly, hoping they wouldn't tell their parents, if they would help Hester and Claudia and me get the box into the car. They were all thrilled and demanded to come to the vet's, and to look in the incinerator: 'Oh look, there's a lovely dead dog with curly white fur in there ...' one of them said happily. The boys went home saying it was the best tea party they'd been to – I never dared enquire what their mother felt about the type of entertainment to be found at our house.

Then there was the night that the elegant Gerald Waterson, AW's boss, came to supper; he had been very kind to us all during AW's recuperation. We polished the silver, lit the candles and set the table on the verandah. Suddenly Sylvia and Hinza appeared in the dark garden having a great game, tugging and pulling and bouncing at either end of something elastic. 'I wonder what they are playing with?' asked our immaculate guest. AW went to find out and came back, acutely embarrassed, with one of my bras, in holes and covered with mud. Luckily, just at that moment, my friend Meriel arrived in a taxi from the airport that needed paying and created a diversion.

When we left Trinidad we found homes for Hinza and Sylvia.

Hinza flourished, but Mrs Mayani, the woman who'd taken Sylvia, rang me to say that she was so sorry, but Sylvia had been poisoned. Months later, I happened to see Dr Rahman far, far from the West Indies, at Heathrow airport. I dashed up to say hello, and mentioned how sad I was that Sylvia had died of poison. 'She didn't die of poison,' said Dr Rahman, 'Mrs Mayani ran her over' – proving that lies will always be found out.

School-age children are the key to a social life in any overseas posting – you meet all your new friends through them. I soon found two women I came to love among the other mothers of kids at St Andrew's: Marie-Pierre, whom I first spotted waiting to collect her child, so blonde and elegant in linen shorts and shirt that she could only have been French; and Wendy, a young English woman, who had married a son of one of Trinidad's leading families.

All Wendy's in-laws looked as if they'd stepped straight off the set of *Dynasty*: the men were uniformly tall, dark and dashing, the women all high heels and sexy clothes and big hair and glamour. They used to invite us on to their huge motor launch to go on picnics 'down the islands' where Trinidadian high society had their beach houses, and where the sea was so full of silt from the Orinoco river in Venezuela that it was black as pitch, and menacing. (Occasionally, as you swam, your leg would bump against something man-sized under the water and you'd automatically say sorry – then realize with horror that the nearest human swimmer was several yards away.) Wendy's husband had a maddening way of saying, 'I not axing you, I *tellin'* you', meaning you were not allowed to argue with him. One Sunday, down the islands, I heard him call out to her, as he lolled back in a comfy chair with a glass in his hand: 'Wendy! My father needs a drink – bring some beers.'

Through Wilma, the doctor, we met a well-known Trinidadian painter, Bosco Holder. He used to call me 'peaches and cream', and I was wildly excited to be chosen as the friend of someone so flamboyantly camp and exotic – until one day he suddenly said: 'You know, I thought you were so amusing when we first met, but now you seem to have become rather dull.' But in the short time that it lasted, Hester and Claudia were very impressed by my friendship with Bosco – because his brother, Geoffrey, played a big part in the film *Annie*.

Society in Trinidad seemed entirely colour-blind – when you went to a dinner party you never knew whether the people next to you would be black, yellow, brown or white (and the white ones might be French Creoles or of Spanish or British descent). Among our favourites were a charming older couple, Joan and Gerald Furness-Smith (of British origin), who lived in a lovely house on Fort St George Hill, overlooking the sea. They invited us to a grand lunch one day, during which someone described how they had water-skied over a manta ray and clearly seen its huge wings spreading out under the water beneath his skis.

'Oh my God,' I exclaimed, horrified. '*How* big was it?'

I threw out my arms to indicate potential size, and walloped the maid, Stella, who had just arrived on my left to serve a dish of roast potatoes, in the solar plexus. The potatoes were flung all over the floor. Mortified, I helped pick them up and put them back into the silver serving-dish, and then Joan said calmly, 'Stella, please bring the other potatoes from the kitchen.' Stella came back a minute later with the 'other' potatoes, but we all knew they were the same ones with the dog hairs picked off.

Somewhere along the line we became friends with the British High Commissioner, David Lane, and his wife Sara. They lived on the hill above us, and their daughter, Victoria, was best pals with Hester and Claudia. Our friendship was sealed over a tarantula. David rang us early one morning to say that they had just spotted one in the drawing room of the Residence, and would we like to see it. We all trooped up excitedly, and huddled in the middle of the room while David swiped at the shockingly big and black tarantula, perched high up on the white wall, with the swimming-pool skimmer. He knocked it down on to the floor and then it disappeared. We looked around nervously, but it was nowhere to be seen – then suddenly, like a scene in a horror film, we saw its thick legs climbing over the top of the piano. We all shrieked and David whacked it on to the floor and then stood on it, making a horrible crunch. I collected the body and dried it out and put it in a box, which is still sitting on the dresser in our kitchen in Somerset.

Our friendship with the Lanes survived a testing time. This was when they discovered that little Hester had signed the official Visitors' Book in the Residence over and over again – each time she'd been to play with Victoria, in fact, which was almost every day. Worse, her childish writing appeared above and below and opposite the formal signature of The Right Reverend Robert Runcie, Archbishop of Canterbury, who had been on an official visit to Trinidad. The book had to be sent to London to have Hester eradicated.

The Lanes showed us the most beautiful beach in Trinidad, Mitchell Trace – a secret sandy cove at the bottom of a long flight of steps which was empty except for a group of pelicans. We never joined the hordes at Maracas again. But Trinidad so often had a dark side: once we found all the pelicans lying dead on the beach – they had obviously been killed for their meat, as only the big beaks and wings and skins had been left. To try and save the day, the grown-ups swam out to sea, dragging the sad remains to the next cove so we could all pretend we had never seen the horrible sight. As I towed a dead pelican out into the bay, I decided that to live successfully in Trinidad you had to be a mixture of Ernest Hemingway, Florence Nightingale, *Jim'll Fix It* and James Herriot.

In fact we'd already heard about the Trinidadian tendency to kill anything that moved from Mr Boos who ran the zoo (and let Hester and Claudia play with the baby boa constrictors which he kept in ice cream cartons in his fridge). His main problem, he told us, was people breaking into the zoo at night, killing the animals and taking them off to eat, or to sell as 'wild meat', which was apparently considered a delicacy in Trinidad. He'd arrive for work some mornings and find half the cages empty.

We could believe this; in our own garden we had a large iguana, which lived in a drain. Old George, our gardener, told us that the next-door gardener's mouth watered every time he saw it, and that we must be extra vigilant in case he got in and killed it. (The children composed a song: 'We don't want to eat an iguaaaaana/We'd rather tackle a banaaaaana . . .', and so on for several verses.)

The row over the iguana simmered on until one day the gardener next door threatened to go to the police about 'George's crops', which he'd spotted over the fence. George had a marijuana plantation hidden between the rows of peas (Caribbean for beans) he'd planted at the back of our garden. In fact, AW knew about it, but feeling sorry for the old man, had turned a blind eye. But now, as the tenants on the land, we risked getting into trouble if the next-door gardener carried out his threat, so AW told old George to harvest his crop immediately. Next day it had all gone – and the iguana was still living happily in its drain when we eventually left Port of Spain.

Gradually we were learning about life in the West Indies: that two people yelling murderously at each other were actually having a casual chat; that you just had to accept that most nights you would be kept awake by barking dogs and whistling frogs, and all your neighbours' ghettoblasters pumping out calypso: 'PUSH, PUSH PUSH', 'HOT HOT HOT', 'BOOTS BOOTS BOOTS BOOTS' (I didn't mind this last one, an anti-war song by the Barbadian Mighty Gabby).

We learned that you could not possibly *ever* hope to have electricity, telephone, gas and water all functioning at once. One of them – usually the telephone – would not be working. We discovered that the most priceless thing you could possess in Trinidad was a telephone engineer's phone number. (We managed to get one when AW spotted a repair man up a telegraph pole and bribed him with a bottle of whisky to come down and mend our phone which had been lifeless for four weeks; he became a firm friend.) We learned to keep the baths full, so that when the water went off you would have some saved. But there wasn't much you could do about the electricity outages. Once when the power went off for three days and our deep freeze melted, I had to cook a pound of shrimp, three pounds of fish, four packs of chicken breasts, a pound of steak, a bag of home-made fish balls and a packet of fish fingers, and take them all to Mr Waterson's house where the power was still on.

I never really came to grips with cooking the local dishes in Trinidad. Down in the HiLo supermarket you could find beef clods, boneless goat, cow heels, pig tails, beef tripe, hearts, livers and tongues: I didn't want to get involved with any of them – especially not the pig tails. These go into lots of Trinidadian recipes, particularly the national dish, slimy green callalloo soup. In the deep freeze at HiLo were polystyrene trays of pig tails packed together with something that looked to me suspiciously like pig's willies. I never dared ask. But I did enquire of a rasta at the checkout one afternoon, where in the supermarket he had found the bunch of parsley in his trolley. 'Hey man, it's all around you,' was his curious reply. I didn't press the point.

What AW and I did take to in a big way was rum punch – the most delicious concoction that had ever passed our lips. We learned the local recipe: 'One of sour, two of sweet, three of strong and four of weak' (measures of lime juice, sugar syrup, rum and water). We thought we'd never drink anything else again, but somehow it never tasted the same outside the West Indies. In the meantime, though, we made the astounding discovery that in Trinidad a bottle of Angostura Bitters – normally the only thing in your drinks cupboard that hangs around unused for years – lasted only a couple of weeks; a dash of bitters being the finishing touch for a good rum punch.

Gradually we learned the language of Trinidad, with its outages and jump-ups, and *bobol* (corruption). 'I vex' meant I'm annoyed; 'kicksin' or 'hecklin' meant teasing; 'humbugging' meant annoying ('don't humbug me, man'); 'hold strain' meant keep calm; 'heavy manners' meant punishment, 'one-time' meant immediately; 'hurt your head' meant worrying ('don't hurt my head with dat'); 'hot lashes' meant a hard smack – as in Carmo promising to give Hester and Claudia 'one hot lash' if they didn't obey her, a terrifying-sounding threat which we all knew had no chance of being implemented. I discovered that 'carry' could mean 'bring' at a ladies' lunch when a plump black lady in a fancy hat told me the unlikely story that she had carried her husband to Port of Spain from Jamaica. A tray was called a 'waiter', which could lead to the surreal request for someone to 'carry in the waiter' instead of 'bring in the tray'; and 'walk with' meant 'take' as in, 'Are you going to walk with your car to Barbados?' To this day my family often finds a West Indian phrase more expressive than an English one: it's hard to beat 'That kills my spirit' when you want to say that something has depressed you.

White people in Trinidad were good-naturedly called honkies, after the noise that pigs make – pigs being pale pink like us. (An English friend in Jamaica couldn't understand why people shouted out 'Trenton' when he passed, until he discovered it was the name of the local bacon factory.) AW loved the Trini humour. Again and again he chortled – still does in fact – over the joke about a man who goes to the dentist in Port of Spain; the dentist looks into his mouth and says 'Teet okay, gums gotta go.' What *I* liked was that in Trinidad flu epidemics, like hurricanes, were always given names. When we were there, 'Rambo' swept the island – which meant that when you got ill, you could ring up all your friends and say that you were in bed with Rambo.

Our first Christmas in Trinidad was a cosy family one, spent with AW's parents and his sister and her children who all came out to stay. (Claudia insisted on making five Baby Jesuses for the crib, otherwise, she said, he'd feel lonely.) It was just what we needed in our still-frail state after AW's accident.

Then, in February, my parents decided to come for the Carnival. The two of them had spent their whole lives travelling by boat to and from India when my father was in the Indian army, but their flight to Trinidad was only the second time they'd been in a plane. Mum was now seventy-seven, and Dad eighty-two. Shortly after they left London, their pilot announced that they were flying over Plymouth Hoe. My mother looked out of the window and saw a long brown strip of land pointing out to sea – Goodness! she thought, you can see the Hoe very clearly. An hour later she looked out again and saw it was still there – trying not to panic, she asked the air hostess why they were still flying over Plymouth Hoe. The air hostess looked out and explained that it wasn't Plymouth Hoe, it was the wing of the plane.

In spite of her age and all her fears, my mother was a gallant guest – you could say, 'Mum, tomorrow we are going to spend eight hours in the burning sun climbing up a mountain,' and she would say. 'That sounds lovely, darling.'

We took them for picnics and drives around the island, and in the early evenings, overtaken by joggers in silver shellsuits, we'd stroll with the children on the Savannah – the grassy open space in the centre of town – buy baby coconuts from the vendors to drink their milk through a straw, and look at the last of Port of Spain's picturesque old gingerbread houses. Mum and Dad revelled in the tropical heat and in Trinidad's mixture of races – but especially they loved the Carnival.

As it approached, Trinidad grew noisier and noisier and more and more hectic – and the island became obsessed. No one could talk about anything else. If the Third World War had broken out, it would have made a short paragraph somewhere inside the local papers, while 'DE MAS' HEAT IS ON' would still have been the banner headlines across the front page.

If you were going to 'play mas" (i.e. join the thousands taking part in the Carnival Parade) all your time now had to be spent in costume fittings. But even if, like us, you weren't, you had to support a band, like supporting a football team in other countries. We supported Peter Minshall, whose band that year was called 'River', and told the story – through hundreds and hundreds of people dressed in astonishing, unbelievable, *brilliant* costumes – of the clash between man and nature. We were not surprised, years later, to find that Minshall had been chosen to design the opening spectacles for the Olympic Games in Barcelona and then in Atlanta.

But the Trinidad Carnival wasn't as simple as just watching a fancy dress parade. We discovered that the day *before* the bands and their thousands of costumed followers made their way across the Savannah in front of the judges (which is the climax of the Carnival on Shrove Tuesday), everyone who can move in Trinidad turns out at crack of dawn to celebrate the opening of the two-day carnival festivities. This is called 'J'Ouvert' (pronounced Jouvé) – short for *jeu ouvert*, or 'game open', in French – and involves dancing along, or 'chippin', behind steel drum groups as they tour the town.

AW and I got up at 3.30 a.m. and joined the dense throng of people 'pushin' band' in a fog of marijuana smoke and rum fumes. I've never felt so awkward and British: Trinidadians know how to 'chip' from birth – their bodies just move seamlessly with the rhythm of the music. My dancing neighbour could see that I wasn't doing it right – 'Hey girl, jus' let your hips go and de rest will follow,' he advised – and it almost did, especially when I had swallowed a few squirts of rum from his leather '*bota*'. AW entered the spirit of it much better than me, possibly because every time I looked at him he seemed to be puffing from the same dancing neighbour's foot-long reefer. By mid-morning we were exhausted, so we chickened out and went home, but most of the crowd, we were told, would probably keep going for the next thirty-six hours.

Next day we took Mum and Dad to watch the Carnival parade from the stands in the Savannah and then, when all the bands had passed, we went home to collect the children and spent the rest of the afternoon happily collecting up bits of costume that the revellers had discarded once they'd passed the judges' stand. Our dressing up box in Trinidad suddenly became the best in the world.

We had arrived in Trinidad at around the same time as an intruder was found inside Buckingham Palace, and the hit calypso of that first Carnival was Mighty Sparrow's song, 'Philip My Dear', based on this incident, in which the Queen apologizes to Prince Philip for having made love to the intruder, mistaking him for her husband. Everywhere we went people were singing:

> There was a man in me bedroom,
> Tryin' on royal costumes,
> Dippin' in royal perfume,
> Wearin' your shoooooes . . .
> He came on de bed, doo-doo (darling),
> and I took him for you.

The words were very saucy – Carmo said 'Dat Sparrow better watch out when de Queen hear his song'. I asked David Lane if Sparrow could get into trouble – *lèse majesté* or something – and

he said, 'Why should he worry? He's not exactly in line for a
KCMG is he?' I wrote a little piece about the calypso for Atticus,
the gossip page of the *Sunday Times*. Needless to say, they didn't
use it.

My career as a freelance journalist never achieved lift-off in Trinidad,
not even when the American invasion of Grenada happened almost
under our very eyes. For some unaccountable reason, our phone
– when it worked – was one of the few that could get through
to Grenada before, during and directly after the American invasion, and AW would speak several times a day to his EC colleague
there, who spent some terrified days crouching with his family
behind the back wall of his house, overlooking the very beach
where the Americans landed. I probably had more information
about what was going on than almost anyone, so I wrote a piece,
sent it off to the *Spectator* and never heard another word.

My only achievement in Port of Spain, apart from researching
my book on Kashmir and being a wife and mother, was to put up
a plaque commemorating the death of a nineteenth-century but-
terfly collector. Just before going to Trinidad I had read a charming
book called *Love Among the Butterflies* by an ex-*Sunday Times* colleague of mine, Bill Cater. This was the edited diary of Margaret
Fountaine, a Victorian woman who had travelled the world collecting butterflies with her Syrian 'dragoman' (who was really her
lover). A sequel came out when we were in Trinidad, and to my
amazement I found that Miss Fountaine had died in the monastery
on top of Mount St Benedict, about an hour's drive from Port of
Spain. I went to the monastery (where there were always queues
of people waiting for Brother Bruno to take the evil eye off them)
to find out more, and discovered that though the old lady had died
there, she had been buried in Port of Spain.

Sara Lane and I went to the cemetery, and, through the records,
found her unmarked grave. A gravedigger told us that she was not
alone in it; a number of people had been buried on top of her in
the years since she died.

Perhaps because I often felt homesick myself, it seemed sad to
me that this indomitable old lady should die in Trinidad and lie in

a grave that didn't even bear her name, so I decided to try and raise some money to put up a plaque in her memory at the monastery. I gave a fundraising lecture on Margaret Fountaine to the members of the UK Women's Club, and we raised enough to pay for a plaque engraved by a local sculptor, Ken Morris. The Abbot agreed that it could be displayed on the monastery wall, and David Lane said he would officially unveil it. But, he warned, 'This has got to be done properly, Brigid. I don't want any sort of chaos when I arrive at the monastery.'

'*Of course not,* David,' I pledged.

Ken and I set off very early on the day of the unveiling with the plaque, a drill, screws and hundreds of yards of electric flex. But at the monastery we found the flex was not long enough to reach from the nearest plug to the wall where the plaque was to be fixed. The monks didn't have an extension lead. How in heaven's name were we going to put up the plaque? I was in a complete panic. Then Ken said he could make holes for the screws in the stone wall by hand with a hammer and chisel, but that would take some time.

'What can I do to help?' I babbled.

'Stay as far away from me as possible,' said Ken.

I looked over the monastery wall down to the plain below and to my horror saw David Lane's shiny official limo turning into the first hairpin bend of the climb up to the mountain top. I wished I could throw tin-tacks down to puncture its tyres. Ken banged away feverishly with his hammer while I sat on a stone and tried to stave off a nervous breakdown. But the last screw was tightened as David's car swung into the monastery complex. There was no chaos (at least as far as anyone knew). David Lane unveiled it; the Abbot blessed it. I felt very proud. I'd love to know if it is still there.

Hester and Claudia each came home from school with a type-written note which said: 'Your child is found to have lice and eggs in her hair.' The good news was that 'and eggs' had been crossed out.

The school had a sports day with mothers' and fathers' events.

In the sack race, I jumped past a large, perspiring mother looking just like a well-filled sausage come to life; she was having the greatest difficulty getting further than a foot from the starting line, but called out to me cheerily, 'De trouble is de sack too tight.'

At a school Open Evening I watched a huge row erupt between two parents. Several of us, waiting to see teachers, were sitting in a big classroom decorated with posters made by the children. These showed a family doing various things under the titles: WE GO SHOPPING TOGETHER; WE GO TO THE BEACH TOGETHER; WE PLAY TOGETHER. Gazing at them, the mother suddenly hissed at her husband. 'We never do anything together,' she said. 'You never come shopping, you go out playing golf; you never play with the children, you are too busy watching television. And you never come to the beach, you go to the office instead . . .' I knew how she felt because I was at the school Open Evening by myself. In fact, come to think of it, I can't remember AW being with me at any Open Evenings, at any school, in any country. (Nor has he ever had to make yule logs for the PTA Christmas bazaar.)

I was there to discuss Hester's curriculum. At school she seemed to be learning: 'Ed has a big dog. The big dog bit Mary'; at home she was reading *Lord of the Rings*. But she and Claudia seemed settled and happy, and life went on in as humdrum a way as it ever could in Trinidad (finding killer bees in the garden . . . watching scarlet ibis in the Caroni swamp . . . seeing the President picking his nose at a party, etc, etc) and suddenly it was New Year again.

AW and I thought it would be romantic to spend New Year's Eve together at home. The first thing that went wrong was the surprise phone call we'd planned to Sandy and Adrian who, we knew, were celebrating at the home of other friends of ours. At midnight their time, eight o'clock ours, all excited we rang their number. A child answered the telephone but forgot to tell anyone we were on the line; minutes (and dollars) ticked by while we listened to the sound of distant revelry all the way from Somerset – glasses tinkling, people talking, merry cries and laughter. We whistled, we bellowed, we screamed, we even hung up from time to time, but when we picked up the receiver again, there they were, still at it. By the time someone noticed that the telephone was off the hook all we felt like saying was goodbye.

Then after supper, at about 10.30 p.m., AW suggested that we should open our bottle of champagne so we didn't have to knock it all back after midnight. Somehow we finished it by eleven o'clock and then AW lay down on the bed 'for just five minutes' and promptly fell into a deep sleep, or possibly a coma.

At midnight I was at our bedroom window looking down over the lights of Port of Spain, alone, with tears in my eyes, listening to the haunting sound of all the ships in the harbour hooting to celebrate the arrival of the New Year – and to the less haunting sound of AW's snores, which sounded like something heavy being dragged over gravel. I woke him up to wish him a happy New Year, and tell him how much I hated him.

Soon after that, Marie-Pierre and her husband were posted to the USA. I was heartbroken; she was a wonderful person and I didn't know how I would manage in Trinidad without her. Not that we didn't have lots of other friends by then – Trinidadians being the most hospitable, upbeat, party people on earth. But Marie-Pierre was the one I went to when I felt depressed or had what I called Caribbean Collapse – days when for some reason (the heat? the humidity?) the only way I could get out of bed in the morning was to think of the siesta I could have in the afternoon.

Then AW came home from the office one day with astounding news – we were being moved to Barbados. BARBADOS! We were going to be *paid* to live in the dream holiday island of Barbados! The glamorous *Dynasty* family gave us a lavish farewell party. It was obvious everyone felt a bit sorry for us. Trinidadians considered Barbados to be a dreary, stick-in-the-mud kind of place, Little England they called it; they warned us that we'd find the people cold and snobbish, and that there was a huge divide between black and white.

I didn't know if I was sad or happy to be leaving. Trinidad was an extraordinary place where every creed and race *did* seem to have an equal place, and what's more, they had come together to form one distinct national identity. A Trinidadian could be any colour or mix of colours, but he/she shared a common humour and language. That was impressive. But it was also an anarchic place – there was a feeling it could all fall apart in undisciplined chaos when the potholes in the roads became too big to drive over; when the services stopped altogether; when the violence got out of control. Perhaps it was because my father was an army officer who believed in order and duty, or perhaps because I am so chaotic myself, but somehow in fun-loving, laid-back Trinidad I never dared to join wholeheartedly in what they called the 'baccanale', and *really* let my hips go . . .

8

Worth It for the Twiglets

When AW's new driver, Ken, met us at the airport in Barbardos, I was astonished to hear him speaking in a strong Somerset accent. Then the receptionist at the hotel where we stayed while our house was being repainted did the same, and then the waiters . . . Was this some elaborate scheme that AW had prepared to make me feel at home? It took me a while to discover that everyone on the island spoke like this because it had been Britain's earliest penal colony, and among the first 'criminals' sent there were the Monmouth rebels, from Somerset.

In the meantime, AW was puzzled to be asked by someone in his office how his mistress was settling down, but it turned out that they meant no one more exciting than me. 'Mistress' meant Mrs, 'four-roads' meant crossroads, 'vista' was view, 'almanac' meant calendar – we had another whole new language to learn: Shakespearean English, perfectly preserved for centuries on the little island of Barbados.

Our new house was spread out around a big verandah that looked over the garden, and beyond, to the sea. It was built on the edge of a golf course (which was a bit of a waste since AW and I don't play) behind the Sandy Lane Hotel, which was the most expensive in Barbados – not that we ever went inside its marble halls, but we were allowed to use the beach.

It seemed too good to be true. My only complaint was the numbers of lizards and geckos who shared our house (as well as huge fat centipede things called congerees, not to mention whistling frogs and slugs in the rainy season). The problem was that you couldn't guarantee the lizards and geckos would stay quietly on the wall minding their own business – occasionally there would be the quiet 'plop' of one falling on the floor or – horrors! – on to the bed, and once I came across the remains of a lizard fight – a mangled heap of bits of leg and tail, very like a small version of the crocodile fight in *Little Black Mingo*. One day I was having a quiet coffee with a friend on the verandah when she suddenly said, 'I don't know what you feel about lizards, but the huge one over there looks as if it's going to jump on you.' I quickly moved out of range.

Before my sister Tessa – who can't *stand* creepy-crawlies – came to stay, I went round the guest room and knocked all the geckos and lizards into a waste-paper basket and released them at the bottom of the garden – but a day later they were all back again. Strangely, our children didn't seem to mind them at all; in fact Hester called the big lizards in her room William and Tony, and worried about them being bored.

Hester and Claudia were booked into St Winifred's school in Bridgetown and we shared the school run of about half an hour into the town with Val and Richard Richings, a British couple with a young family who had also just arrived on the island. They ran a restaurant called Bagatelle in a lovely old plantation house. I never thought a daily school run could be such a treat: as I bowled along through the sugar-cane fields, over the gentle hills to and from Bridgetown, with the bougainvillea blooming all around and the sky blue overhead, my heart used to sing. I was even quite patient with Paul, the Richings' eight-year-old son, who used to ask what have become known in our family as 'Richings questions' – i.e. totally unanswerable ones such as: 'Bri-gid, how long would it take a snail climbing up a long piece of string to reach the moon?' There were five children plus me in the car; we listened to pop music on the radio or chattered away, and I discovered that they had all learned the Pledge that they had to make every day at school assembly, touchingly wrong. 'I pledge allegiance to Barbados . . .' was what they were supposed to recite, but they were all saying 'I pledge *our legions* to Barbados . . .'

The oldest Riching, Rachel, turned thirteen at this time and I asked the local radio station to play her favourite pop song, 'All

Night Long', as a school-run surprise. To my amazement they wouldn't – they said it was an unsuitable song for a thirteen-year-old. In Trinidad they would have complained that it was too tame, man.

Carmo came with the family to Barbados – she was now two stones heavier than when she had first come to work for us (in fact when Wilma, the doctor, came to say goodbye in Port of Spain she didn't recognize Carmo, and thought we must have hired someone new).

Our luggage was getting heavier too. We brought our car from Trinidad, as well as the bamboo three-piece suite we'd taken there from England. Now there were my trophies from Port of Spain as well: an iron four-poster bed made in Birmingham for the tropical market (it had a rail for a mosquito net) and some fretwork arches I'd bought from workmen demolishing an old gingerbread house. My plan was to glue them together to make a little gazebo, but they are still in worm-eaten pieces in the garage in Somerset.

Our landlords were a black Barbadian lady called Mrs Hayes and her son, Trevor. We thought Trevor must be some kind of businessman as he seemed to live part of the time in Canada and always looked so smart, but it turned out that he was actually a water-ski instructor.

New additions to our household were Wilmont, the gardener, a young giant who pushed our little hand-mower over the humps and bumps of the big rough lawn with one arm as if it were a well-sprung pram on a smooth pavement. He was mad about cricket and during matches wore a transistor radio strapped to his ear with masking tape.

Then there was Eiffel, the nightwatchman. Every evening as we went to bed I'd call out 'Good night, Eiffel, sleep tight,' and then shriek 'No, no, I don't mean that! Stay awake, please!' Late one night I stalked Eiffel to see what he really did when he thought we were asleep – I found him snoring on a beach lounger he'd set up in the garage. We heard that when AW's new boss, Johan, a forceful Dutchman, caught his nightwatchman asleep he picked him up and threw him into the swimming pool, but we didn't really have the stomach for that kind of confrontation – and anyway we didn't have a pool.

It seemed ironic that in Trinidad, where it would have soothed my nightly fears to have a watchman, we didn't have one, but in Barbados, where I felt much calmer, we did. But then again, perhaps I felt calmer just because he was there, even if asleep in the garage.

There were no burglar bars on our house in Barbados; in fact, there was no glass in most of the windows, just thin wooden louvres, but everyone talked about violent crime being on the increase, and one of the first stories I read in the local paper was about twelve guests who had been tied up and robbed at a dinner party (I secretly thought that I would have been only too thankful if it had happened in my house, since it would have taken everyone's minds off the food). The only burglary we knew of first-hand happened to Richard Riching's friend, an Englishman with a glass eye, who was staying in a holiday flat near the beach. He woke in the night to see a thief crawling through his bedroom window. This gave him such a fright that his eye fell out and bounced across the floor, which in turn freaked the burglar so badly that he shot back through the window again, and ran screaming down the road.

Our first social event was an invitation to 'welcome' drinks from one of AW's new colleagues. They were English, and were really nice about it when Hester, for some reason, crawled under the flimsy table where all the bottles and glasses were laid out, and then tried to stand up. The party (as well as the table) rather fell apart, then, with most of us crawling around picking up peanuts and shards of glass. I can't say it wasn't hideously embarrassing, as it all happened in front of AW's boss, the dynamic Dutchman, on whom we had been hoping to make a really good impression.

AW started his day so early that we were able to go to the beach together after the children were finished with school and homework, and I'd done my regulation number of hours on the Kashmir book. We always pitched our camp on the sand in the same place and watched the world go by. Everything happened on the beach – gossip and news was exchanged, famous people spotted, friendships made. There were so many celebs in Barbados that Hester and Claudia decided to buy autograph books – but naturally they didn't have them on the beach the day Keith Richard, the Rolling Stone, ambled past in pixie boots. When they asked for his signature he wrote KEITH RICHARD on the sand in letters four foot high, but then took pity on them and did proper autographs on hastily-found bits of paper.

Since we saw them every day, we got to know all the fruit and bead sellers and the afro hair plaiters, and the handsome beach bums in revealing pouches who strolled the sand introducing themselves by their nicknames: our favourites among them were 'Good Times', and two others who came with slogans: 'De Man in Green is on the Scene', chanted one every time he came by, while the other would say, 'De Man in Brown is Hangin' Aroun''. (One afternoon when my sister Tessa and her husband Malcolm were staying with us, I joined them, late, on the beach; Malcolm looked up from his book as I arrived, and said '"Good Times" just passed me by.' It still makes me laugh.)

The concept of 'sex tourism' didn't exist then, but we saw it happening under our eyes – the beach studs chatting up the white women, or vice versa. Later, when we came to know the manager of the Sandy Lane Hotel, he told us that one night he'd seen a beach bum sneaking into a guest's room through the ground floor window. This was strictly forbidden, so he burst into the room and found them naked on the bed. They leapt up; the guest was furious.

'How dare you,' she said, 'this is my visitor.'

'Yeah,' said the manager, 'I know. I can see his visiting card.'

Hester and Claudia were learning to water-ski. One day, after her lesson, Claudia looked very strange – all her freckles were standing out in three dimensions, because her face was so pale. I kept asking if she was okay and she said she was fine – but when we got home she told Hester that the instructor had shown her his willy in the ski shed and told her to touch it. Hester told Carmo who said Claudia must be scrubbed with bleach, but luckily decided that AW and I should be told first. We were appalled – how could such a thing have happened? We had been sitting on the beach all afternoon, two yards from the ski shed. AW went to the beach to confront the instructor and then called the police; I talked to Claudia and tried to make it all right.

This type of thing always seemed to happen to Claudia – still does in fact. She must have inherited it from me – I was inevitably the one who got exposed at or groped when I was growing up. In Trinidad she was invited to a friend's house to watch a video of *Swan Lake*. The mother was out when Claudia arrived and so, rather than wait for her, the two little girls put what they thought was the ballet video into the machine – it turned out to be a porn movie, but thank God the mother came home before they'd seen too much. I was furious – I remember yelling at her that it was no use apologizing, nothing could eradicate the images in Claudia's mind. And now, on top of that, there was the water-ski instructor . . . Between us, AW and I and Hester and Carmo managed to turn the incident into something the family could talk and joke about together; and Claudia was fine. It helped that not long afterwards she made her First Communion and was distracted by all the excitement involved in that.

Even though the priest asked us every Sunday how we were enjoying our holiday, and we told him, every Sunday, that we were not visitors but *living* in the island, we all liked going to church in Barbados – mostly because of the brave little black girl with pigtails who, all alone, sang the 'Our Father' every week. I could never concentrate fully on the service though, as a large part of my mind was taken up with wondering when the rickety ceiling fans were going to break away from their moorings and spin round, slicing off all our heads.

Once the priest asked us to pray for the Pope 'who has to walk the tightrope between the spiritual and material worlds'. Not long afterwards we heard that our dear friends, the Lanes in Trinidad, were being posted to the Vatican. I told Hester and Claudia that the Lanes would be seeing the Pope, and Claudia got very excited: 'Will they see him walking the tightrope?'

One day when Hester and Claudia and I were driving along the west coast on our way to a birthday party, we noticed some kind of drama taking place at the side of the road ahead. An elderly white man seemed to have collapsed, and a white woman was bending over him. As we approached she waved at me to stop – 'I think he's having heart trouble,' she said, 'could you take him to hospital in your car?'

I looked at him – he had green snot all over his face. If there is one thing I have never been able to deal with, it is what comes out of people's noses; it makes me physically sick. I could feel my stomach heave.

'I'm so sorry,' I said, hurrying back to the car, retching. 'I can't cope . . . you'll have to find someone else'. I was sick twice before we got to the party, but I felt terrible about what I'd done. So later that week, when a shabby old man waved me down in Bridgetown after the school run, I was so anxious to atone for my previous lapse that I stopped and offered him a lift. He climbed into the back, and round and round Bridgetown we drove for hours while my passenger tried to decide where he wanted to get out.

'Shall I drop you here?' I'd say gently, or, a few miles later, 'Here?' Eventually he came to a decision, and I let him out, gave him a little money, and went home where I discovered he'd pee-ed all over the back seat.

But apart from the water-ski instructor, and the pee on the seat, Barbados continued to be like heaven. It passed the dead dog test (corpse removed from road within twenty-four hours) and the pot-hole test (hole filled in within one week) – though we did have an outage on our first Christmas Day when Sandy and Adrian and their family were staying, and had to eat sandwiches instead of turkey.

And then, as though life wasn't good enough already, I discovered the Barbados auctions I went to them regularly in the hope of finding some priceless treasure hidden amongst all the strange stuff that came up for sale. Of course I never did, but I bought a silver-topped cane which had once belonged to the Barclay's bank manager in Bridgetown, a stick rack for putting it on, and a sideboard that turned out to be just hollow paint – the termites had eaten all the wood underneath. However, my best purchase in Barbados was not at an auction, but from an antique shop in Bridgetown: two matching Victorian urns which should have been covered with shells, but were mostly bald. It took me the next fif-teen years to restore them.

Career-wise things seemed to be looking up too. I had nearly finished my book on Kashmir and had heard that a publisher, Collins, was interested. I was taking photographs of the charming little wooden chattel houses of Barbados for a picture spread in the *Sunday Times*. (Their name comes from the fact that these houses can be dismantled and moved, and are therefore considered to be part of a person's goods and chattels.) And I had arranged to interview King Dyal, the eccentric self-appointed mascot of Barbados cricket who would turn up at every important match at the Kensington Oval dressed immaculately in lime green suit, shocking pink shirt and purple hat (or some such outlandish com-bination) and take a bow to the amusement – and applause – of the crowd.

Life was pretty full, if rather solitary – writing and photography being things you do alone. And then one morning the British High Commissioner's wife telephoned, asking me to help raise funds for a day care centre for handicapped children. To be honest, I wasn't particularly keen on the idea, but I agreed to visit the centre and meet some of the children. Of course, I was bewitched by them – Clarence, Andrea, Cinnamon and the rest of the gang. They and their mothers and the other fund-raisers instantly won me over, and I became completely caught up in the project, writing pieces for the local paper about the individual children, and then helping to make a series of short TV fundraising 'commercials' about them. Barbados was full of very rich people, especially the Americans, Canadians and British 'snowbirds' who came to escape the winters in their own countries, and money began to roll in.

We sold fund-raising Christmas cards and a car sticker (Hester and Claudia designed that), held painting exhibitions and a raffle. The top prize was a cricket bat signed by the England and West Indian teams which I had at home for 'safe keeping'. It nearly didn't make it to the raffle: AW took it into his head to whack a cricket ball across the garden with it, which made a dent in its pristine surface that had to be patched up hurriedly with varnish.

Becoming more adventurous we decided to make a Christmas

record. For a brief moment of glory I was the Bob Geldof of the Caribbean, hobnobbing with the stars: having tea with the calypsonian, Mighty Gabby, and Eddie Grant, the rasta singer, who wore his long dreadlocks in an amazing waist-length hat. To crown it all, one of my new charity friends took me to my first cricket match and I got priceless autographs from Ian Botham, David Gower and Viv Richards for Hester's and Claudia's books.

It was one of the happiest times of my life ... which was just as well, because, very soon, I heard that Collins no longer wanted to publish my book, that the *Sunday Times* didn't think my 108 photographs of chattel houses were good enough, that no one was interested in my story on King Dyal, and that AW had applied for a job in the EC office in Algeria. I was plunged into gloom and felt a miserable failure: friends in London seemed to be doing so well, and here I was, clutching at straws ...

But in the end, months later, the *Sunday Times* relented and published my pictures, *GQ* magazine found a space for King Dyal, and AW heard that he had not got the job in Algeria.

When Trinidadians had called Barbados 'Little England' they did not mean it as a compliment – to them, it was shorthand for boring and dull. It was true that the island lacked the fizz and sparkle and fun of Trinidad. The food was pretty English too, of the type now known as pre-Elizabeth David (i.e. sliced white bread, salad cream, etc) and completely lacking the tasty input of the big Indian and Chinese communities that lived in Trinidad.

There'd been onion and sugar shortages when we lived in Port of Spain, which seemed to us extraordinary, but in Barbados – incredibly – there was a shortage of fish: Japanese crews had trawled their seas empty. The contact to have if you wanted some was a Mrs Nurse – I don't know if her husband or son was a fisherman, but she seemed to be able to get fresh fish when no one else could, and so it was important to stay in her good books, which meant never refusing what she offered. One day she rang to ask if I'd like a king fish which had come her way. 'Oh yes of *course*, Mrs Nurse,' I said, but when it arrived it was taller than me and looked like something out of Ernest Hemingway's photo album. It took Carmo and me most of the day to cut it into about two thousand steaks for the freezer.

The children definitely did not take to the local West Indian food – I remember a huge row over a dish of salt fish, green bananas and breadfruit cooked by Carmo.

'When the Third World War comes,' I remember saying dramatically, 'this may be the only food available.'

'Okay,' said Hester logically, 'we'll eat it then, but we are not eating it now.'

As for me, for some unaccountable reason the only thing I could think of to cook most of the time was hummus, the Middle Eastern paste made of chickpeas, lemon and garlic. The first time I made it in Barbados I didn't realize that the chickpeas were full of weevils, so when I took the paste out of the blender it was speckled black with their mashed up bodies. I sprinkled the hummus with cumin seeds and no one noticed.

In Trinidad we'd plucked up our courage and invited AW's boss to a quiet supper; now we got really ambitious and decided to have a dinner party. I think it was a success, but I can't remember much past the guests arriving: I was so nervous that I knocked back about ten rum punches in rapid succession beforehand and ended the evening – happily, after everyone had gone – groaning, and throwing up in front of Claudia who had crept into our bed. To my shame, she reminds me of it from time to time.

Trinidadians had warned us about the big divide between the black Barbadians, who had the political power in the island, and the whites, who controlled most of the money (and were also paranoid about security – we once glimpsed a pistol strapped to a man's calf when he crossed his legs at a dinner party). The two groups did not socialize together and we missed the multi-racial society we'd got used to in Trinidad, but Barbados was reassuringly ordered and cosy, and I was happy to settle for those. It also felt incredibly British, with a National Trust to protect the plantation houses and other historic buildings, as well as a State Opening of Parliament almost identical to Westminster (except that most of the faces were black). The State Opening was almost the cause of a divorce between AW and me. He was delayed at work the day it took place, and rang to ask me to bring his dark suit from home so that he could change in the office. Running late, and in a panic, I grabbed his dinner jacket by mistake and he had no option but to wear it with an ordinary shirt and tie. He was furious, but no one seemed to notice AW's unusual outfit except Richard Richings who saw it on television, and rang to offer him a job as a bouncer at his restaurant.

Our second autumn, as if to make us feel even more at home, we had a state visit from the Queen. Before reaching Barbados, the Royal Yacht cruised round the smaller Caribbean islands, and in each one Her Majesty gave a reception on board ship. AW's boss was on leave, so AW had to fly to all the different islands in order to represent Europe at each one of these parties. He was exhausted, but said that it was worth it for the Twiglets that were served with the drinks.

The grand finale of the Queen's tour was a garden party at Government House in Barbados. Women guests were told that hats and white gloves should be worn. I didn't have a hat (I dreamt that I wore one made out of an egg carton) but at least hats could be bought in Barbados. More difficult was the white gloves instruction: there were none to be had on the island. By luck, rummaging through all my things, I found two odd left hands, so I wore one and held the other.

AW, the party boy, was flying in from the last of the Queen's island receptions that evening, and the plan was that Ken, the driver, and I (dressed in my hat and gloves) would meet him at the airport and take him straight to the garden party. But a typhoon blew up, and his flight was cancelled, so Ken had to take me to the party by myself. As we drove through Bridgetown with the flag flying on the car, and me sitting alone in the back, quite a few people waiting at the side of the road thought I was the Queen and started cheering and waving their flags. For the Queen's sake (so that they didn't think her rude), I waved royally with the back of my hand – and then I felt guilty. What if, having waved at me, and got a wave back, they all went home leaving empty streets to greet the real Queen?

I wasn't presented to the Queen at the garden party, but since I knew her face so well, it seemed impossible to me that she didn't know mine, and I expected her at any moment to rush over saying 'Good Lord! Bridge! Fancy seeing you here.' But better than the Queen for me were the British journalists covering her tour – I was so excited to be among my own, as it were, that I dashed up with verbal diarrhoea about how-I-myself-was-once-a-member-of-the-Press-actually-quite-senior-on-the-*Sunday-Times*-but-was-now-a-humble-ex-patriate-housewife etc.

One of the journalists was Simon Hoggart who was famous even then. To capture his interest I told him every Barbadian political scandal I could think of, but when he rang next day to hear more, I was suddenly afraid that the phone might be bugged and was reduced to monosyllables in case I got AW into trouble. (In fact, there was a huge scandal in Barbados at the time – a murder trial that involved politicians and drugs. I can't remember much about it now, except that when I read the list of exhibits shown as evidence – bits of intestine, brain and lung – I thought they sounded like the ingredients for the Barbadian national dish of souse.)

Carmo had always had a very peculiar sense of humour, and one of the first things she did in Barbados was to hide in the cupboard in Hester and Claudia's room one afternoon and jump out at them when they were getting ready for bed. They got the fright of their lives, and Carmo laughed until she cried. But soon afterwards she changed completely and entered a new phase of being really hostile to us all. My conclusion was that perhaps her new pastor in Barbados had given her the idea that she was an exploited victim, rather than a beloved member of the family.

The first sign of her new mood was when she said angrily one morning in the course of a mild argument, 'I know you hate me because I am black.' She no longer wanted to play games with us in the evenings, and she wouldn't even eat her favourite roast chicken any more – it was now known as 'white man's food'. She stopped wearing her hair in neat braids, and began frizzing it out in an afro; even her skin began to look darker.

When Sandy and Adrian came for Christmas they felt quite nervous of her – and the day that Sandy (alone in the house for some reason) found a 'fetish' doll in the hall and heard the sound of African drumming coming from Carmo's room, she was so frightened that she hid in the hedge of the drive to wait for us to come home. In actual fact, the fetish was a doll that Hester had made to give Claudia for Christmas, and the drumming turned out to be water-hammer in the plumbing, but with Carmo in such a dark mood, it was easy to imagine all kinds of voodoo at work. There seemed to be an anti-white feeling across the whole island at that time. AW took the children and me out for a drive one day, and we passed some workers at the edge of a cane field. Normally, in Barbados, you'd wave and call out 'Orrrrright?' as you went by, and the people you were passing, would reply, 'Orrrrright,' but this time when we called 'Orrrright?' they shouted back, 'Pig shit.'

Carmo's hostile mood didn't last for long – perhaps another preacher came to the church – and after a month or so, she was back to her usual self. I knew everything was all right again when one morning she said, in her old, friendly fashion, 'Mum, you know dem birds roun' dis house? Well, dey not birds, Mum.'

'What do you mean Carmo?' I asked, thinking she was going to tell me they were jumbies or flying freemasons or something.

'No Mum,' she said, 'Dem's not birds, dem's pigeons.'

Visitors came thick and fast to Barbados, as you might imagine. One of them was a friend who ran a prestigious polo club at Windsor.

'Do you play polo?' he asked AW.

'No,' replied AW, 'I suck them.'

AW has a very peculiar sense of humour, and though he is witty, he is hopeless at telling funny stories. (He also has a curious lateral mind, which works in baffling ways – once he said to us all at supper: 'Mondays will be Wednesdays next month.' Oh yes? Keeping very calm, I asked him how he had reached this conclusion. It turned out that he was thinking of the new airline schedule he'd been looking at in the office.) There was an old joke we knew from my father's days in the Indian Army, which went: 'The Indian Army was a great white elephant with black privates' (privates being non-officers). AW found this hilarious, and one night he decided to tell the joke at a dinner party. My heart sank. 'Have you heard about how the Indian Army was a great white elephant with black balls,' he said, missing the whole point and rather shocking his audience, who had no idea what he was talking about.

My friend Meriel came to stay. Punk had hit fashion then and Meriel, always up to the mark, appeared one day in a very expensive T-shirt with rips in it held together by safety pins. Carmo took me aside and asked if I couldn't lend Meriel some money so that she didn't have to go round in rags. In fact Carmo was distinctly unimpressed by our clothes. One evening as we left for a cocktail party she looked at us, both smartly dressed in black (the devil's colour), and said, 'Oh Mum, de people surely going to run from you tonight.'

The Lanes came for a last visit to Barbados before they left the Caribbean for Rome. There was huge excitement the day we spent together on the beach – the Leatherback turtle eggs that no one even knew were buried in the sand started hatching out, and dozens of tiny turtles scrambled along trying to get to the safety of the sea before they were plucked up by seagulls. Hester had a special interest: she had been taken to see the Leatherback turtles laying their eggs at night on a beach in Trinidad (a fearful scene apparently, with some people trying to kill the turtles for meat and others trying to protect them). She was desperate to save the little turtles, and ran up and down the beach ferrying them to the sea. David Lane tried to stop her on the grounds that this was interfering with nature, and a furious argument broke out, but nothing could have stopped Hester – or, indeed, any of us – on this rescue mission.

Hester was growing up. She went on a school trip to Caracas and came back wearing an entirely new outfit of clothes. She tells me now that she and Claudia knew they were the worst dressed children in the Caribbean and used to dread 'mufti' day at school. Looking back at photographs, I have to admit that while all their friends were wearing jeans and T-shirts, H and C seemed to be in lime green towelling jumpsuits, so she is probably right. How could I have dressed them that way?

Hester was mad about Madonna, and kept asking me what name

I thought Madonna would use if she were staying at the Sandy Lane Hotel (a Richings question if ever there was one). One morning she used up all AW's disposable razors shaving a tennis ball. It was very annoying for AW, but we thought it showed imagination. Hester and her friend Judith used to pretend to play 'families' with Claudia. 'You are the baby,' they'd say, 'now you have to go to sleep. Hush baby . . .' Poor Claudia would spend days 'sleeping' – while Judith and Hester would run off and play some entirely different game on their own.

My parents came – and, like Trinidadians, found the island rather tame, even though our house was less 'white' than most because of the fund-raising and the children's school friends. Then AW's mother, sadly now a widow, booked herself in for a month over Christmas. I was a bit apprehensive about entertaining my mother-in-law for whole four weeks, but I loved her dearly, and Hester and Claudia were over the moon with happiness. The day of her arrival was the first of the new dry season: the colour of the sea had changed from grey to turquoise overnight, the sky was clear and there was a sparkle in the air like the beginning of spring in England. Her flight was due in the early evening so we went to a happy lunch party at Nicholas Abbey, an old plantation house, and drove home in time to prepare WELCOME banners. Oddly, our neighbour came round to tell us that British Airways had been trying to contact us. Then the telephone rang; it was British Airways, who broke the shocking news to AW that his mother had died on the plane. One moment we'd been so happy and excited and full of schemes and plans for her visit, and the next we were plunged into grief and emptiness. Claudia had a fit of uncontrollable shaking. AW went alone – he wanted to go alone – to the airport to meet the plane. It was terrible for him.

We all travelled home with AW's mother's body and buried her in the Somerset village that was her home. It was desperately sad and seemed so unfair: she never had that month in the sun with her granddaughters which she, and they, would have loved so much.

Not very long after this terrible time, AW heard that we were to be posted to India at the end of the summer. I couldn't believe it,

I had spent the past four years in the Caribbean trying to research my book on Kashmir by post – and now we were going to live in New Delhi where I could have done it all in a few months. None of us wanted to leave Barbados, or our house, or our garden which thanks to AW's planting had turned into a Douanier Rousseau jungle. And it meant saying goodbye to Carmo. She decided to try to get a job in Canada. AW gave her a terrific reference and I gave her the bamboo three-piece suite we'd brought from Trinidad. She and I took it on a truck down to the Careenage in Bridgetown to load on to a sailing schooner for St Vincent, the island that was her home. In that little corner of the port the scene had probably not changed for hundreds of years – the men working on the wooden ships that sailed between the islands wore pony-tails and trousers cut off below the knee and looked just like pirates. We corresponded with Carmo for years; the last we heard (a long time ago now) was that she had become a Canadian citizen and married a Canadian. AW and I were so pleased for her.

Our own baggage was packed in separate loads: one for India, one for the UK, and we caught the plane home, where I noticed that my skin, all smooth and plumped up with tropical humidity, immediately began to crease up in wrinkles in the dryer English climate. I felt like the portrait of Dorian Gray.

9

The Trouble with Hari

When AW's office sends families off to a new country, it provides them with a report on the place. These are meant to be helpful, but usually, by the time you reach the fourth paragraph, you are looking for a gas oven to put your head in. The briefing for New Delhi told us that it was the second most polluted city in the world, had a miserable climate, was extremely stressful to live in and not to be recommended under any circumstances for those with weak hearts either physically or emotionally (which covered both AW and me) – and of course the diseases you could get there . . . well, you'd be lucky to survive to see another posting.

That August, the list for my annual shop at our local chemist to stock up on all the things the family could possibly need over the next months abroad was even longer and more revolting than usual.

'Good morning Mr Coldman,' I said brightly. 'Could I possibly have some worm tablets – yes, that is for round, thread *and* tape worms; and some athlete's foot powder please, and something for mouth ulcers, and some lotion for head lice, and a tube of Anusol for piles, and some wart remover, oh yes, and verrucca treatment, and a box of pessaries for thrush, and some prickly heat powder, and several boxes of diarrhoea tablets, and something for amoeba, and something for giardia, and some nose drops, eye drops and ear drops, and some broad spectrum antibiotics, and some ointment for styes. . . .' I was quite surprised that Mr Coldman didn't pull on a pair of rubber gloves before handling my money.

We arrived in all the confusion of Delhi airport in the middle of the night, tired and disorientated, and nervous about the new life we were embarking on. No one was there to meet us. AW and

I tried to put on brave faces for the children, saying things like: 'Mmmmm – the exotic smell of India,' and 'Look at all the pretty ladies in saris, girls,' but our upper lips were losing their starch, and when Claudia burst into tears and said she wanted to go home with the British Airways hostess we all secretly felt the same.

New postings are usually organized so that you arrive in September, in time for your children to start the new school year. We had asked our office in Delhi for advice and they told us there was a British school in Delhi, so we had booked places for Hester and Claudia – only to discover when we arrived that there were no British children in the British school. British children all attended the American school. The British school was patronized by mostly Indians, plus the children of non-aligned or even enemy countries – North Korea, Albania, Iraq, and so on, who wouldn't dream of setting foot through the door of an American school.

Nor was there a house available for us in Delhi, so we were booked into Claridges Hotel (no relation to *the* Claridges), where we ended up living for two months while AW and I house-hunted. I cried a lot in Claridges, especially when AW had to go on business to Nepal almost immediately after our arrival, leaving the three of us sick with some tummy bug. I remember lying with Hester and Claudia on the double bed in our hotel room, and wondering weakly whether there was any point in getting better.

We knew no one, but somehow heard that there was to be a Hallowe'en party at the American Embassy compound a couple of weeks later. AW was away yet again, so I took Hester and Claudia along and we stood nervously at the edge of the crowd. No one spoke to us, but at one stage I noticed an English-looking woman of my age with two boys leaving the main group and setting off across the football pitch. I ran after her – 'Hullo . . . Hullo!' I cried, 'Can I introduce myself – we have just arrived in India . . .' 'No, not now,' she called out brusquely as though I was an unwanted salesman, 'we are late for an appointment,' and she strode off. Hester said, 'You are never to speak to that lady again, even if she comes crawling on her knees,' and I thought exactly the same. In fact, she became quite a good friend later.

AW returned from his travels, sized up the situation (not too difficult with my red eyes) and took us all off on a wonderful trip to the Pushkar Camel Fair in Rajasthan. We stayed in a canvas town in the desert, ate and washed in huge communal tents, and wandered around in the dust among the camels and horses and traders, food sellers, snake charmers, holy men and musicians. It was a perfect introduction to the other, magical side of India.

Our lives in Delhi were saved by two things, or rather, people: one was that *The Times* correspondent turned out to be Michael Hamlyn, whom I knew from *Sunday Times* days, and who was married to Claire, the nicest and most hospitable person you could ever meet. The second was that in order to overcome my misery, I had managed to stir my stumps and organize an interview for the *International Herald Tribune* with someone called Faith Singh, who, with her husband, ran Anokhi, a clothing company that was big in London then. It was as if Faith and I recognized each other from another life, we became such good friends. In fact, when the day came for us to move into the ground-floor flat we eventually found in Poorvi Marg in the Delhi suburbs, it was Faith who organized it all with AW because I had collapsed into bed in a depression, completely unable to cope with leaving the womb of the hotel to face the great subcontinent on my own.

AW always complained that our apartment was too small, and it was; but it was cosy and had a little garden and the landlady who was supposed to live upstairs was always away, so it was like having the house to ourselves. It was on the flight path to the airport, opposite a low-cost housing estate for Indian Airlines employees, and near some quarries, so besides the general non-stop Indian hubbub outside there was also the scream of aircraft and the earth-shaking boom of quarry explosives from time to time. But we were on the very edge of Delhi and there were patches of countryside where we could walk in the evenings – at 'cow dust time', as they called dusk in India. We even discovered the ruins of an old town to explore nearby – and I liked it.

Now we had to find staff. There was very little accommodation to offer, just a converted garage, so we decided to go for a couple. Claire told us that the American Embassy ran an employment bureau, so I went along and found a sort of slave market in progress. Outside the Embassy compound, squatting on the grass verge, were dozens of Indians looking for jobs. When you registered your name at an office inside, the American girl in charge would go to the gate and yell out your requirements to the crowd of Indians outside.

'Are there any couples here today?' she shouted out on my behalf, and Hari and Meena stepped forward to be vetted.

I hadn't a clue how to interview a cook, but it seemed sensible to ask him what dishes he could make.

'I make good Korean beef,' said Hari, wobbling his head nervously.

This sounded rather exotic and impressive. 'Anything else?' I asked.

'Oh yes, Madame,' said Hari, 'Korean chicken.'

I should have been suspicious: in fact Hari couldn't cook much at all because he'd worked for American families who'd eaten everything out of tins. But he was nice, and his wife Meena, who was to be our cleaner, was gentle and sweet and adored Hester and Claudia and spoiled them terribly, even sponging them in the bath (they were twelve and nine now). Meena would spend hours playing Scrabble with them, which can't have been a bundle of fun for her since she couldn't read or write. H and C dictated what to put when it came to her turn.

Unexpectedly, Hari and Meena brought along their sons, Paul and Alex; how they all fitted into the garage I will never know. Alex was still at school, but we decided to employ Paul and train him as a bearer (which is what butlers are called in India). The trouble was that he was so shy he couldn't speak. One day I drove back from the market, swung the car through the gate, and waved cheerily to Paul who was standing on the edge of the drive. I was just prising myself out from behind the steering wheel, when I heard a quiet little voice asking if it would be too much trouble for me to move the car a few inches. It turned out that I had parked *on Paul's foot*. Luckily the wheel had trapped only the toe of his shoe, but it was a nasty moment. I wished I could send Paul on an assertiveness course.

Before we found Hari and Meena, the Indian grapevine had somehow produced a man called Gangaram, who turned up at our house to apply for the job of bearer. He was nice, but halfway through the interview I noticed that he had two thumbs on his right hand. My mind went into overdrive, imagining the Queen coming to dinner and having to order specially made white gloves with three thumbs, or guests fainting when they saw two thumbs on the plates as he removed them from the table – and I could just hear AW saying, 'Gangaram, you seem to be all thumbs today.' In fact we wouldn't have hired Gangaram, because we'd already decided that we had to employ a couple, but I do regret that I didn't offer to help him have an operation on his hand.

On Monday mornings, after the school run, Hari would appear by my side at the breakfast table with his Book. In this, I was sup-posed to write down what I'd like him to cook for the whole week's meals. It was a nightmare. 'Hari,' I'd start decisively, 'Tonight we will have macaroni cheese with tomato salad.' Then I would remember that he was supposed to be working his way through Madhur Jaffrey, because he didn't know any Indian dishes, so I'd say, 'No, sorry, not macaroni. Try the Moghlai Chicken Braised with Almonds and Raisins on page 39.' Then I'd remember that Hester and Claudia were sick of Indian food after two months of it in the hotel, so I'd say, 'No Hari, we will have sausages and chips.' Then I'd remember that we were out of English sausages and we couldn't have the local ones for fear of pork-brain worm, and so I'd fall back on the macaroni cheese. I wasn't as scared of Hari as I often was of Carmo, but I did sympathize when I heard of a young Englishman in Delhi who'd never had staff before and was so nervous of his cook that he used to introduce his guests to him: 'Ram Lal, I don't believe you've met Professor Simkins and Sir Nigel Parkes . . .'

Following the Monday morning scene with The Book, I would move into the garden to discuss estate management with the *mali* (gardener). Our garden was only about thirty feet square, but it was a little oasis in the dust, and we took it very seriously. One day, not long after we'd taken him on, the *mali* told me that he would have some celery ready at the end of the month. I was hugely impressed that he could grow it in only three weeks; I know nothing about gardening, and presumed this was some mysterious, miraculous thing to do with the Indian climate, so I enthused about how much we liked fresh vegetables and how pleased I was that he was growing celery etc, etc. He looked more and more confused. Eventually it dawned on me that he had been asking for his *salary* at the end of the month.

After our dog experiences in the West Indies, pets were barred in India, but there was a cat lurking round the garden. AW called it Lucky – ironically, because it was missing an ear, a paw, half its tail and about a third of its fur. Hari used to feed it and we rather liked seeing it around.

Behind our house ran a narrow lane where the garbage was put out. When Hari accidentally threw out one of our knives, I had to go through the garbage in the lane and discovered what happened to it every day. It was amazingly efficient: first the rag pickers would come through taking out plastic bags, tins, and anything that could be sold or re-used (including the knife apparently, because I never found it), and then the animals – cows and pigs – would amble through scoffing anything edible. Very little was left for the dustbin men to take away.

Our garden gate, guarded by Paul and the *mali*, was like a safety curtain between us and the 800 million Indians outside. Kashmiri carpet salesmen, lace vendors, snake charmers, and men offering camel-rides were constantly trying to penetrate it without much success, but soon after the celery business a woman appeared holding out an empty dish. 'We cannot turn away any person asking for food,' I announced with my Mother Teresa face on, and asked Hari to find something to fill her bowl. He reappeared with a saucepan of *dhal*, but to my amazement the woman was furious. It turned out that she was *selling* the bowl and the last thing she wanted was to have it messed up by food.

My nephew Perry was staying when two snake charmers happened to come to the gate one day – he'd never been to India before, so of course he had to see their act. Perry was young and cool and watched quite impassively as the cobras swayed (and the other snakes tried to escape into our garden). Then when all the snakes were tucked back into their baskets, he asked if he could buy the charmers' musical instruments. I was seriously worried about this: after all, it would deprive them of their means of livelihood; but Hari said it was all right and undertook the negotiation. Then I fretted that Perry had paid too little, and that in revenge the charmers would post a deadly viper or two under the gate, but far from it: snake charmers came in charabanc loads to sit on the pavement outside our house playing their weird music and waving their musical instruments (bigger and better ones than Perry had bought) at us over the gate.

I was told by an old hand that the only way I'd ever get the telephone line to our new apartment connected was to go to the main telephone office with a bribe tucked into the application papers. Afterwards I wondered why I'd bothered, since the new line almost never functioned. AW reported it out of order, and for days it rang every ten minutes with telephone engineers on the line yelling at us in Hindi. Finally it began to work – until our first Christmas a few weeks later, when fifteen people claiming to be telephone engineers turned up asking for a Christmas box. We didn't believe them, and told Hari to send them away – a big mistake. The telephone went dead the next day, and stayed dead for about a month. I can feel myself getting agitated about this, even now, seventeen years later. In Delhi I used to try not to think about the telephone for fear of ending up like the Indian Government Minister who placed a long-distance call and when it hadn't come through *three days later* went berserk and stormed into his local telephone exchange brandishing a revolver. The worst part of the story was that he *still* didn't get his call – all that happened was that the telephone operators went on strike.

The next crisis that Christmas came when I went to collect my chestnut order from the Simla Fruit Mart and found they had given it away to someone else, but I discovered that sweet potato made an excellent substitute in the stuffing. (I was a bit startled when I looked up stuffing in the index of my Constance Spry cookbook to find 'See also FARCES'. For a wild moment I thought this might be some sort of prophecy about how my stuffing, or perhaps the whole Christmas meal, was going to turn out.)

What *did* almost ruin that festive season was me – *Me*! the social incompetent – suddenly having a rush of blood to the head and inviting twenty-six people to lunch one Saturday. I regretted it instantly and lay awake at nights visualizing our friends thinking how boring our other friends were. Then I would fall asleep and dream that AW was carving one chicken leg to make it feed twenty-six people. An additional worry was that since we had never entertained more than about ten, we didn't have cooking pots or serving dishes that were big enough. First I thought I'd borrow some from Claire, but three days before the lunch I decided it would be much more practical to buy some of the lovely big brass cooking-pots called *deksis* that Indians use, then we could both cook and serve the meal in them, and we'd have them for ever. I asked Hari what he thought of my plan. He said, 'As Madame wishes,' which was his standard reply when he thought I was embarking on something foolhardy. But he loyally trudged the streets of Old Delhi bazaar with me for hours, looking for the brass street (I wondered if this could have been the origin of the expression 'brassed off'). It was hard going, there were so many people and vehicles. Without a word of a lie, at one stage the only way we could cross the street was by climbing into someone's rickshaw and out the other side.

We found the *deksis* in the end – they were sold by weight – and struggled home with them. Then I discovered from Hari, who hadn't thought of mentioning it before, that you couldn't cook in them until they had been tinned inside. As it happened, a tinner had been sitting outside our gate lining all Poorvi Marg's pots and pans for weeks, but naturally he had now disappeared, and we had to lug the pots to a tinning place, miles away across the other side of town.

However, when the time came for the party, the gleaming row of *deksis* looked wonderful, and Hari had managed to master some Madhur Jaffrey dishes to put in them (indeed, Hari looked so smart and pleased with himself that quite a few people thought he was the host), and I needn't have worried about the guest list as half the people didn't turn up anyway. Margie, then wife of the *Financial Times* correspondent, told me that in India, if you want twenty-six people to come to a party you have to ask sixty

– but then you run the risk that all sixty will come, bringing friends.

After all that stress and tension, we left Delhi and went to Kerala for a week's holiday with Meriel. It was wonderful, though it might have been marginally easier if, on Day One, I hadn't found an antique shop in Jewtown, Cochin, selling a whole lot of beautiful old painted Dutch plates. I was able to convince AW that we needed them for our new life of glamorous entertaining, but even so, he said they were to be entirely my responsibility. The plates were packed up into two boxes which were too big to fit into any normal taxi and so, on our journey south, we could only take taxis with roof racks which were far rarer than the normal type. I was definitely not popular with the rest of the party but it was worth it – the plates are now hanging on the walls of our kitchen in Somerset.

Thanks to AW and his work connections, we stayed for part of our holiday in the State Guest House at Kovalam beach. This was a ravishing place on top of a cliff, looking out over miles of blue sea and beaches and palm trees. But the first night we were there Meriel had a nightmare that she was being eaten alive, and woke up to find that it was true: there was an ants' nest in her mattress. AW opened his eyes and found himself gazing into those of a four-inch long cockroach sitting on his cheek, and I discovered that ants had eaten my knickers.

On the beach were a few genuine Sixties hippies with leathery brown skin who did yoga at sunset, and lots of German and Italian men who'd swapped their normal swimming trunks for lewd-looking pouches tied on with string (our children called them 'willy bags') which were sold by beach vendors. What with them and their topless girls, our modestly dressed group agreed, it was no wonder that droves of office workers from the nearby town of Trivandrum came out by bus after office hours to stare at the tourists.

We did the standard boat trip round the waterways of Kerala and I worried a bit about us all being bitten by mosquitoes . . . 'Is there any danger of malaria here?' I asked the guide, who replied rather wistfully, 'No, we have had malaria eradication programmes here.' Then he perked up and said 'Elephantiasis is available.'

In the evenings in Kovalam we ate fish curries in the garden of an old hotel called Blue Seas, where the tables were cosily grouped around the owner's grandfather's grave. He was a Mr Panicker who had died, according to the epitaph, 'while aged ninety'. I wondered if he could have been the founder of Panicker's Travels back in Delhi, an agency I always smiled at when I passed, thinking my mother should have been one of its clients.

But my tenderest memory of Kovalam was hearing AW's very English voice in the lobby of the Guest House one evening. Loudly and slowly he was saying: 'Two days ago I asked for lavatory paper, but nothing has happened. The situation is now serious – please bring lavatory paper to rooms 4 and 5. Do you understand? Lavatory paper, toilet paper, to our rooms now please.'

At the beginning of the New Year a Delhi astrologer predicted that some time during the following twelve months an insect would crawl or fly into Fidel Castro's mouth while he was making a long speech and choke him. Talk about going out on a limb. My own Indian newspaper horoscope was not nearly so detailed; it simply said that the following year would be one of the very best of my life . . . Within eight weeks I had had my wallet nicked, my bag stolen, had nearly been electrocuted twice by the light switches in our house, and then I measured my length on the stone floor of the veranda after Paul polished it, and cricked my neck.

In our early days in India, when we were still living in Claridges Hotel, I hurt my back, and a house agent (they were the only people I knew in those days) took me to see an old man in Shankar Market with (he said) an extraordinary knack for getting spines in order. I waited in the taxi while the house agent disappeared into a hardware shop to fetch the old man, who told me that, yes, he could cure me, but only if the treatment was done at a crossroads at sunrise or sunset, and in the meantime, he'd start preparing some sacred powders. I am all for giving people a chance (in Trinidad I actually had my neck manipulated by a chiropractor with a broken arm in plaster), but somehow I couldn't envisage anything happening to me at a crossroads in Delhi, except being run over or asphyxiated by exhaust fumes. But I was probably wrong not to try it. An Indian friend I met later told me that when she lost a piece of jewellery she consulted her astrologer about it. He told her that if she went home and gave some yoghurt to a black dog, he (the astrologer, not the dog) would be able to tell her where it was. She did what he said, and the astrologer then drew a map showing her where she would find the lost piece of jewellery – it was in her safe deposite box in the bank.

In Claridges, our rooms had been only a couple of doors from the resident astrologer, and one day Claire and I plucked up our courage and made an appointment to have our fortunes told. We turned up at the agreed time of 10.30 a.m. to find the astrologer's office locked; he had not yet arrived for work. Later that day we met him in the corridor and he apologized for missing the appointment, explaining that he had been caught in a traffic jam. 'Well, *you* obviously can't see very far into the future,' said Claire cruelly.

The same sort of thing happened the following summer in a hotel in Jaipur – I walked out of the astrologer's booth in the garden, barefoot, straight on to an upside-down drawing pin lying in the grass. I hopped around clutching my foot, wanting to go back and yell at him for not being able to predict something so painful lying in wait for me only a few seconds away. What he had told me was that I liked organizing people – i.e. was bossy – and that although people never complained to my 'face-side', they were constantly slagging me off around my 'backside'. That was disturbing, but not as much as discovering later that while the fortune-teller had assured me that I would have a contented, trouble-free middle age with a husband who had a 'soft corner' in his heart for me, he'd told AW that he would fall in love with someone else and start a whole new family.

But after six months in India, I had friends other than estate agents to advise me where to take my newly-cricked neck for treatment, and the general opinion seemed to be that Mrs Natrajan's physiotherapy clinic was the best place. Mrs Natrajan's did not look promising: packed into one small room were between eight and ten men and women in various stages of undress strapped to a selection of grim-looking appliances. It looked like some kind of torture-chamber, but in fact it was rather jolly. In between theatrical groans and hisses of pain (there was not much stiff upper lip among Indian patients, I noticed) we would chat away on all sorts of topics from Rajiv Gandhi to cricket, while glamorous Mrs N bustled around, hitching her sari on to her shoulder, and moving us from massage bed to machine or vice versa. I confided to my fellow patients that I would love to have a proper horoscope done in India, but the problem was that my mother couldn't remember the time of my birth – she could only dimly recall hearing the noise of the Frontier Mail express train passing Ambala in the Punjab, where I was born. One of the other patients turned out to be a train buff – he could easily find out what time that was, he said, by consulting his old timetables. He would tell me at our next session. Sure enough, at our next appointment he turned up with everything written down – only one question remained, was the train going up or down? I rang my mother that evening; she tried and tried, but couldn't remember, so that was the end of the accurate horoscope for ever.

Once, at the clinic, from behind a screen, I heard a curious exchange between Mrs N. and an Indian gentleman.

'I can't help thinking this is a little bit rude,' said the gentleman skittishly.

'Rude? What is rude?' asked Mrs N. briskly.

'When you help me take my trousers down,' the gentleman faltered, sounding as though he rather regretted starting this conversation.

'That is not *rude*,' snapped Mrs N., dispelling any little fantasies he may have had, 'that is kind.'

Soon it was time for the annual Sports Day at the British school. This always took place in the winter because the summer was too hot. Usually, at Hester's and Claudia's school functions abroad, I spent most of the time sobbing into my hanky because I was so moved by the mixture of colours and nationalities among the children – the Great Family of Man as I thought of it – but that day, after the parents' lime-and-spoon race had to be re-run because so many parents had cheated by holding the lime on with their fingers, I forgot all about that, and concentrated on winning the Mothers' Race. In fact I came second (the woman who won actually changed into professional running shoes), and had to stand on the podium in front of everyone to have the silver medal put round my neck by the Headmaster. I was desperately embarrassed but I thought the children would be so proud and pleased. I looked around for them from my great height on the podium, but I couldn't spot them anywhere. It turned out they'd gone into hiding in case someone worked out that we were related. Afterwards they made me promise that I would never enter the Mothers' Race again, never come to school wearing any sort of Indian outfit, and whatever I did I was never again to wear toe rings in front of their friends (I had run in bare feet).

They were right: I *had* gone a bit overboard on the ethnic outfits, but I was just living through the standard phases that every new person in India experiences. These are: One. You fall totally in love with it all, you actually want to *be* Indian, and you start burning incense, oiling your hair at night (AW said it was like going to bed with a fried poppadum) and wearing Indian clothes and toe rings. Two. You begin to loathe and hate everything about it – the beggars, the climate, the dirt, the staggering gap between rich and poor, the corruption, the telephone; you can't wait to go home. Three. You go into neutral and get on with living there as though it were any other country, but with rather more exotic things to see. (I would have given up the toe rings anyway, because when the decorated bits swivelled under my foot, it was like being the Little Mermaid and walking on knives.)

I hired a tailor to come and sit on our verandah and make clothes for us all. The first thing he did when he arrived was to take off his trousers, which gave me a fright, but this turned out to be for no more sinister a reason than wanting to put on a looser pair in which he could sit cross-legged more comfortably. I never took to him; he used to spend just that little bit too long smoothing the bust darts. Once, when I complained that the front of a dress he'd made for me was bulging out a bit, he said 'Yes Madame, that is because you are a little fatty.'

In India nearly everyone had a tailoring disaster story to tell, the same way they all had cooking and dinner-party disaster stories. Michael Hamlyn, *The Times* man, had a safari suit made which came out with one breast pocket down near his waist and the other up towards his shoulder. He could only wear it, he said, if he stood with one hand on his head. AW decided to have a summer suit made in the Khan market (the tailor on our verandah couldn't do suits). We chose a nice innocuous-looking beige cotton, not realizing that we were looking at the back of the cloth. On the other side it was shiny cotton satin and when AW went for his fitting he was presented with something that Elvis might have worn.

Nothing in India ever quite worked out how it was intended. At a craft fair, I found a man making the most beautiful embroidered shoes. I ordered a pair, and since the shoemaker lived hundreds of miles from Delhi, near Jodhpur, I asked for them to be sent by post, but a few weeks later, the shoemaker himself turned up at the gate with my order. The shoes were absolutely exquisite – but enormous. Why did he make them so big, I asked him, when he had actually drawn round my foot on a piece of paper? He explained that he thought my feet might have grown in the few weeks since he'd seen me.

This, the human error factor, was what drove you bananas in Delhi, but it was also precisely the most endearing thing about the place, because it meant that you never knew what was going to happen next. In India truth was always stranger than fiction.

I was brought up to believe that reading novels before lunch was decadent (chores had to be done first). For this reason I always felt slightly guilty reading the Indian newspapers at breakfast – the stories were better than any book. MAN BITES SNAKE TO DEATH; STRAY DOG STEALS NEW BORN BABY FROM HOSPITAL; YOUNG GIRL KIDNAPPED FROM HER HOME TWELVE YEARS BEFORE TURNS UP ON DOORSTEP AS A BLIND BEGGAR AND IS RECOGNIZED BY AN OLD SERVANT AND SAVED.

The story that gripped us most in all the time we were there was the one headlined 'NOTED NAD EXPONENT BEHEADED'. The murder victim was, apparently, in the *Guinness Book of Records* because of his moustache, which was six foot long and worn coiled up on his cheeks like two giant Catherine wheels. At the time we read the story in the paper, the police had not yet found his killer, and AW suggested that perhaps they should be looking for the man with the 5 foot 11 1/2 inch moustache who wanted to get into the *Guinness Book of Records*. As for being a 'nad exponent', the paper did not reveal what a nad was, but we discovered later that it was a musical instrument, which solved the arguments we'd been having about whether or not you could use the word 'nad' in Scrabble.

With its vast population, events in India were always over the top – we once read a newspaper story about a car accident, which read '. . . of the 33 people travelling in the jeep, 16 died immediately', etc. etc. *Thirty-three people travelling in a jeep.* How was this possible? When you saw the word 'mishap' in an Indian newspaper, you had to brace yourself for something terrible. A mishap in Britain might mean knocking over a cup of tea at the vicar's party, but in India it meant disaster, as in FERRY MISHAP KILLS 250. There was also a tendency to describe organizations as 'bodies', which lead to some gruesome headlines: NEW HEAD FOR BODY, FARMERS TO OPEN BODY. Once we saw a headline that said BODY TO HELP MEDICAL VICTIMS – but, as AW pointed out, medical victims were likely to be bodies themselves. You had to adopt an Indian way of thinking, or you could find yourself on the wrong wavelength, as I did when I saw PULSES RISE IN DELHI and thought it must be a tale of passion and romance, only to find the price of lentils had gone up, or when I read OUTLOOK GRIM FOR PADDY IN ORISSA – which was, of course, about the danger facing the rice crop, not a lone Irish traveller.

Indians had a passion for sending notes – *chits* they are called. Hari once sent me a note at the start of a dinner party we were giving. 'MADAM COME IN KICHEN QUICK' it said. I excused myself and dashed to the kitchen expecting to find that it was on fire, or that Hari had accidentally severed his artery with the carving knife and was unconscious on the floor breathing his last, or, at the very least, that the *lunch* was on the floor, but he was just standing there calmly. 'Oh Madame,' he said when I appeared, 'should I serve toast with the pâté?'

The saddest *chit* was the one presented by a little boy at the gate. It was typed and said: 'I cannot Speak, I have no Tongue, therefore, make this Humble Request in writing. I am without parents and house less. Nobody awaits me on the surface of the earth.' This was heartbreaking, and over time we gave him lots of rupees – until the day Paul saw him chatting away happily with a gaggle of boys at the end of our road. (That happened the very same week I saw the leper outside church unfolding ten good fingers from the apparent stumps of his hands – I longed to sit down beside him and learn how he had concealed them so cleverly.)

There were so many things to cry about in India – the desperate poverty, the deliberately mutilated child beggars, the perishing cold in winter for those living on the streets (the cold had really surprised us all – Delhi airport was probably closed by fog more often than Heathrow). But there were many things to smile about too – the surgery up the road from us, run by Doctors Nag, Nag and Nag; the fact that you could while away the time spent queuing in the Post Office reading the list of standard telegrams pinned up on the wall. In India you could order your telegrams like a Chinese meal: I'll have a number 7 ('Congratulations on the Distinctions Conferred on You') and a number 16 ('May Heaven's Blessings be heaped upon the Happy Couple') plus one number 13 ('Many thanks for your Good Wishes which I/we Reciprocate').

After the bitter winter in Delhi, the hot weather comes all of a sudden – before you know where you are it is the end of April and too hot to do anything at all. In summer Delhi hotel swimming pools are *chilled*, and if you go out in the sun you feel like a pork chop under the grill. With this in mind, friends of ours organized an early spring excursion to a wildlife adventure camp near the city, where they arranged a mini-safari on camels. When the moment came to climb on to my camel, I changed my mind and decided that with my head for heights I'd be happier sitting with Deborah, a young mother with a baby, on the front of a camel cart. Deborah and I discovered the hard way that camels pee backwards . . . The driver of our cart kept leering at us, saying 'Camels very sexy.' Deborah and I decided that everyone was entitled to his own opinion – but he was only trying to explain that it was the camel mating season, which apparently accounted for why the camels were blowing huge pink bubbles, exactly like chewing gum, with some bit of their mouths that other animals don't have.

There was never a shortage of things to do. We took a very English friend, Camilla, who had come out to stay, to a Game Reserve hoping to see tigers. We didn't see a tiger but we saw peacocks and lots of quails 'Look look! Dear little birds . . .' said the children.

'Delicious!' boomed Camilla, 'just ten minutes in a hot oven.'

I asked a passing game warden if there were any bears in the reserve, and he replied that I could probably pick one up later. Pick up a bear? We wondered what on earth he meant. Perhaps there was an orphaned cub being looked after somewhere . . . Ages later when no one showed up with a cub or spoke to us again, it dawned on us that he must have thought I asked for a *beer*. It still mortifies me to think that for ever and ever that warden will be convinced there was an alcoholic Englishwoman desperately scouring the jungle for a beer.

Back in Delhi, AW's boss invited us to a grand dinner in his garden. There were Rajahs and Maharajahs and it was a wonderful evening until AW decided to pour water on to a clump of candles that were spluttering dangerously near the table decorations – the whole centre of the table then went up in a whoosh of flames. We were never asked again. But to tell the truth I was more upset by my Indian neighbour who, right at the beginning of the evening, told me that I reminded him very much of someone, but he couldn't quite put his finger on who it was . . . Mmmm, I thought, rather pleased, who could it be? – imagining some sort of glamorous film star – when he suddenly turned to me and said 'I've got it! You look just like Tiny Rowlands!' Tiny Rowlands was a well-known business tycoon of the time; he had a long face and white hair and was about sixty-five. I felt miserable for days.

It was in Delhi that we first came across the British Foreign Office handshake. This is used by officials in receiving lines at receptions, and is designed to prevent anyone lingering for a chat. As the Foreign Office official shakes your hand, he/she simultaneously moves it forward firmly, propelling you on to the next person in line or into the reception. AW and I wondered if it was actually part of a British diplomat's training, or just something they pick up along the way.

AW's office in Delhi was in the same building as Oxford University Press, India, and one week, without saying a word to anyone, he secretly took the rejected manuscript of my book on Kashmir, cause of so much heartache, out of my desk drawer, and gave it to the editor there to read. At the same time, in London, my old friend Christopher Matthew had shown some of my letters to the editor of *Punch* magazine. So one marvellous, memorable day, out of the blue, I had a call from Rukun Advani, the Editor at OUP India, to say that they would like to publish my book on Kashmir, *and* a long-distance call from *Punch* asking if I'd like to try my hand at doing a funny column about living in India. The Indian horoscope was right all along – that year *did* turn out to be one of the best of my life.

Hester and Claudia made good friends at the British School; they were doing well there, and enjoying it, but a cloud was hanging over us – GCSEs. If Hester was ever going to attend a British university, she had to do GCSEs and A-levels – and in order to do those, she had to be at school in Britain by the age of twelve or thirteen in time to start the course. I was desperate not to send Hester away – I had so hated my own years at boarding school – but there didn't seem to be an alternative. No school in Delhi did the British GCSE course. Hester herself was quite keen on the idea, so we booked her into the school in Somerset where AW's father had taught. (With hindsight, this made precious little sense, since he had died two years earlier.) She would start the following September, and I promised her that if she hated it we would take her out after a year.

In the meantime, every day on the school run we used to pass a family of beggars at the main traffic lights on our route: there were five children of all sizes, with a particularly bright looking eleven- or twelve-year-old girl as leader of the group. Each morning we waved to them, and Hester and Claudia would say, 'If only we could take them home and give them a nice bath and comb their hair and give them new clothes . . .' I felt the same but I didn't think we could abduct them from the traffic lights and take them home without causing trouble. But then, extraordinarily, one boiling hot Sunday morning in May they appeared at our gate – how they knew where we lived was a mystery. It suddenly looked as though the school-run fantasy might come true.

By chance we had one of Hester and Claudia's Indian school friends staying for the weekend, and she acted as interpreter. Would the children like to bathe and wash their hair? she asked them. The bright girl said yes, they would, but only if there were no men around, so AW, Paul and Hari went inside to do something else, while the rest of us set up two huge plastic tubs in the garden, filled them with water from the garden hose, and then let the children bathe in them with shower gel and shampoos and conditioners. They spent all morning splashing about and had a great time, and then we combed their hair, dressed them in new clothes and dropped them back at the traffic lights.

I worried about it – had we done the wrong thing? What if they caught cold? What if they got into serious trouble? Next day we looked out for them at the lights, but there was no one there, nor the next day. I began to panic . . . but on the third day they were back – looking dirtier than ever. We asked them what had happened: the bright little girl told us they *had* got into trouble, but not too seriously, and they had loved their morning with us.

Five years later, AW and I, on a visit back to Delhi stopped at the traffic lights to see if they were still there – they were, and the bright girl, now grown up, recognized us and rushed up, waving and laughing. We gave her some money and drove off again, feeling very sad. I still do; she haunts me.

Soon it was time for Hester and Claudia and me to go home for the holidays; the heat was terrible, people in Delhi talked about nothing else, and knowing the precise temperature in degrees became obsessive. Just before we left India, we visited a museum in Alwar, Rajasthan, and to give ourselves an idea of how hot it was (there was no thermometer), we felt the forehead of a bronze bust of Queen Victoria in the museum. Her temperature was so high that we agreed that had she been alive, she would have been dead.

Suddenly, it seemed, it was time to start sewing name tapes into Hester's clothes and getting her ready for boarding school. The terrible day of parting dawned – she had hardly ever been away from us before – and we drove her off to her new school, trying desperately to be brave about it. AW carried her cases up to the dorm; we met her housemistress and some of the other girls, and then said goodbye. It was agony, and the tearful phone calls started that night. I decided not to go straight back to India, but to hang around in Somerset so that I could see Hester at the weekends for a while – that would also give me time to have a strange mole on my leg checked out, and my permanently upset stomach investigated.

The upset tummy, it turned out, was caused by a huge round-worm – the doc thought it could be *several feet long* – which was easily disposed of (I still wish I'd kept an egg or two, though, to re-grow the worm when needed, like Maria Callas, because I immediately began to put on weight). The mole was more serious – it was a melanoma and had to be removed as soon as possible. Emergency plans had to be made: Claudia was enrolled as a day girl at Hester's school, and my sister Tessa came down from Cumbria to look after us while I was in hospital having a chunk taken out of my leg. AW rang every day to tell me lovingly that it would ALL BE ALL RIGHT. Since this was/is his standard response to any crisis, I never believed it, but, as he pointed out the other day, so far it's always been true. I recovered from the operation in only a few days, but for a while I was consumed with panic at the thought that the cancer would come back, and would find myself crying in Marks & Spencer or in the middle of a dinner party.

I thought Hari in India would be worried about us not coming back for so long, so I called him. AW would have gone berserk if he'd heard the conversation: 'Hello, Hari,' I said through the crackling on the line, 'this is Madame in England.'

'Yes,' said Hari, 'Madame is in England.

'No Hari,' I said, 'This *is* Madame. I am telephoning from England'.

'Yes, yes,' replied Hari, 'Madame has gone to England.'

'*Hari, listen to me!*' I shrieked, '*I am Madame. I am in England.*'

'Madame will be in England until the end of September,' replied Hari.

This went on for about half an hour, but in the end Hari understood and said, 'Oh! You are *my Madame*,' so tenderly that I cried again.

Eventually Claudia and I went back to Delhi leaving Hester at school, and the telephone bills began to soar to new, unprecedented levels – they have never returned to what you might call a normal average since.

Back in India after the Christmas holidays I worked on my *Punch* column and on revising my Kashmir book for publication, and the weeks passed calmly (for a change), until the following Easter when Hester and three friends came out for the holidays. Since that made five children, and our house was very small, we decided to take them on a tour. We all kept diaries, and this is mine:

Day One

Set off in Land Rover, taking our pillows. It is the most peculiar thing that millions and millions of chickens are eaten in India every year, and yet no one seems to use their feathers. Hotel pillows are either so tightly stuffed with kapok that you knock yourself out when you lie down, or they are carved out of rubber foam so that your head bounces up and down every time you turn over.

We had also packed cartons of medical supplies, Indian mineral water (in spite of the advertisements around Delhi that said: Beware! Mineral Water May be Spurious), mosquito repellents of various sorts, a picnic hamper and tinned foods. Quite a few of these, in fact, got left in the hall, and we never opened the tinned stuff because there was always a lorry drivers' pull-in near to hand, where we could indulge our new craving for hot chapattis spread with (our own) peanut butter and honey, rolled up and eaten longways. By the end of the trip we must have entertained more people in India than a popular film. At one stop Hester counted a crowd of more than a hundred people pressing round watching us drip melted peanut butter and honey all over our clothes. (The Indian stare is a truly amazing thing – an unabashed, open-mouthed, un-blinking *gawp*, done as close to the victim as the starer can get. The problem is that it is catching, I used to find myself doing it in church in England.)

Arrived at posh hotel in Agra at 4.30 p.m. after five and a half hours' travelling, hot and dirty and tired, to be told by manager than he had given our rooms away as we had not checked in before 4 p.m. He picked on the wrong family. Once – in Brussels days – I would have claimed to be a travel writer of international fame who would blacken the name of the hotel for ever, but that doesn't seem to work – positive action is what is called for. So the children unloaded all the pillows from the Land Rover, and we explained firmly that since we had nowhere else to go, we'd sleep on the lobby floor. A couple of seconds later, we got our rooms back.

Day Two

Set off to see the Taj Mahal. It was 100 degrees, which may not sound much, but it's a lot to be seeing sights in, especially when they are made of white marble and reflect the sun back at you like those silver-paper screens that dedicated suntanners prop round themselves on the beach.

At the entrance to the Taj, you must either take your shoes off and go barefoot, or pay an extra rupee to have cotton bags tied over your shoes. Some French tourists in front of us loudly declined the bags on the grounds that they were a rip-off, and removed their sandals instead, while the shoe-bag man smiled to himself. Three sizzling steps across the burning marble and the French were hobbling back with lightly fried soles, begging for shoe-bags.

AW and I made the children hide their eyes until we were right opposite the Taj itself, and then they looked, and gasped. It was wonderful; I felt so happy . . . and then a man came up to me out of the blue and said: 'Hullo. You are very old. You have grey hair and five children. Please give me some rupees.' I was utterly taken aback – all I could think of to say, pathetically, was, 'My hair is blonde not grey.'

Day Three

Drove to Jaipur and arrived at hotel feeling hot and dirty and tired, to be told by manager that he had no double rooms left – *but* would it be too much trouble for us to choose between the Maharajah Suite and the Princess Suite, one of which he would like to give us for the price of a normal room. The Princess Suite had a fountain in the middle of its sitting room so obviously we had to have that one. After the porter had dumped the luggage and disappeared, AW showed the children how, by blocking four outlets in the fountain with your fingers, you could make the remaining jet eight feet high. Decided not to do any sightseeing in Jaipur, but to play with our suite instead.

On our way out of Jaipur we saw an elephant and its *mahout* turn off the main road and go down a track to a lake. AW pointed this out. We will wait and watch, he said, and see a truly wonderful Indian sight. We will see the *mahout* bathing his elephant in the lake water. So we waited and watched and what we saw was the *mahout* getting off his elephant and squatting down to go to the lavatory, and getting back on to the elephant again. We agreed it was a truly Indian sight.

Day Four

Drove to tiger reserve at Rantambore. There were two places to stay: a Government Rest House outside the reserve, or a

Moghul pavilion, with no electricity, but a romantic atmosphere, in the middle of the reserve. We were booked into the pavilion, but naturally when we arrived, found that an Indian Air Force officer had turned up that morning and commandeered the whole place. Eventually we were given two tiny rooms, but AW and I had to sleep on mattresses on the verandah.

I was just dozing off when it occurred to me that there was absolutely nothing at all to prevent a tiger strolling on to the verandah and dragging AW or me off for dinner. Woke AW to ask him what we should do. Turned out AW not asleep as the same thought had occurred to him. So we got up and built a barrier around our mattress with the cane verandah chairs. Of course, as we said to sneering people next morning, we knew our barrier wouldn't *stop* a tiger, but it might give us more warning than being woken by the warmth of its breath on our cheeks. Did I say woken? What a joke, neither of us slept a wink. All night long we could hear a tiger roaring, to the accompaniment of a Tarzan Jungle Noises soundtrack, all eerie hootings and whistlings and gurglings and sudden spine-chilling yelps and barks.

Day Five

Spent day travelling to Samode Palace Hotel, near Jaipur: a rambling princely palace-turned-hotel with five courtyards and painted rooms. All of us in seventh heaven.

Day Six

Woken by unfamiliar sounds. Opened eyes to see room crowded with big grey monkeys who had formed a chain and were passing all our picnic supplies and recently-bought fruit out of the window to their chums in the garden. Children ecstatic – not so much at the sight of the monkeys, I suspect, as at seeing the last of my picnic. (I have a thing about throwing away food, and was still dishing out the Delhi sand-

wiches – in fact, the day before, I overheard one of the visiting children saying he hadn't liked the sandwiches when
fresh, let alone five days later.)

The children went on a camel ride, while AW and I
sweated along on foot beside them, accompanied by half the
town. Passed a newborn donkey – all white and fluffy with
long ears – exactly like an expensive toy in Harrods. Rushed
up to pet it and in enthusiasm did not notice mother donkey
manoeuvring herself into position until I was kicked, really
painfully, in thigh. Villagers clapped and cheered.

Day Seven.

Back in Delhi, visiting children and Hester are leaving soon.
There is a heatwave. Milk is now rationed and water and
electricity very dodgy.

It was just as well that we'd seen something of India on this
holiday, for only a few weeks later the rug was pulled out from
under our feet: AW was to be posted to the Gambia, West
Africa. In theory, postings are supposed to be for four years, but
we'd spent only two in Trinidad, two in Barbados, and now only
two in India.

AW was pleased because he was being promoted to Head of
Mission – Ambassador – but we hadn't seen a quarter of the things
in India that we'd meant to: we hadn't been to Calcutta or to
Gwalior, or the temples with rude carvings at Khajuraho, and it
was only quite recently that I'd discovered that the place called
Varanasi where friends were always going at weekends was the same
as Benares. We'd never got round to hanging the last picture in our
house in Poorvi Marg, and we hadn't so much as glanced at the
box of junk we'd been lugging round the world for years and were
definitely going to sort out in Delhi.

The worst part of it was breaking the news to Hari and his
family – they wouldn't go to church for a week because they were
angry with God. But we found Hari a job with the incoming
Reuter correspondent and his wife, and Hari was pleased because

his new house had twenty-three rooms as opposed to ours which had only eleven, counting lavatories.

The moment I heard we were leaving, I was seized by a shopping mania; you'd have thought there was nothing to be bought in any other country. It was obviously something to do with the insecurity of moving, and I wasn't the only one affected. I had a Canadian friend, also changing posts, who spent an extraordinary amount of money on a jewelled Tibetan cup stand – though she didn't own a Tibetan cup; and a charming, mild friend of AW's from work spent a king's ransom on some sacrificial statues made of bronze, and clay mixed with human blood. '*They're* going to look cheerful and cosy on the mantelpiece back in England,' I couldn't help thinking to myself. But who was I to talk: I ordered a marble coffee table five foot long and my only excuse was (as I kept telling AW) that marble in India is cheaper than wood. But, as he kept telling me, we didn't need one in wood either. I suddenly realized why England is full of objects like elephant-foot umbrella stands and what my sister calls Nairobi Knick-knacks. They are the panic purchases of departing ex-pats.

The Indian grapevine was incredibly efficient. Long before even we knew the date of our departure, cards came through the letter-box asking things like 'Do you wish to sell any of your house holds?' Needless to say, the one item we couldn't sell was our curtains. The man taking over our house didn't want them – it's an infallible rule, they never do. Nor did he want to buy the TV aerial. AW and I debated whether we should take it off the roof in revenge for him not wanting to buy it, or whether life was too short to bother, but before we came to a decision, Hari had climbed on to the roof and taken it down anyway, so we gave it to him.

Nor did the new man want to take over Lucky, the cat in the garden. I decided to call an organization in Delhi named Animal Friends – hollow laughter here, for what Animal Friends did was to go round putting unwanted animals to death. When I told Hari they would be coming, he was appalled. 'Madame,' he said, 'you are not God.' I tried to explain that I was only doing this because I didn't want the cat to suffer when we'd gone, but he asked how did I know it would suffer and who was I to decide when a creature should live or die, so in the end I cancelled Animal Friends.

When the packers came, having such a lot of stuff made me feel so guilty that I kept following them round asking if it was normal for a family to own so much, but they just looked puzzled. This time we had one load going to Somerset and one to the Gambia, and a decision had to be made on every object. What did you do with the Bhutanese national costume that seemed such an exciting purchase at the time? Should it go to Africa, England or on to the garbage tip? Should you throw away the Mother's Day cards that your children made last year, or will you regret it? Some people have the philosophy of when in doubt, chuck it out, but I found myself looking ahead to the time when my daughters might have become drug-crazed topless go-go dancers who never came home any more, and hung on to the Mother's Day cards. As a matter of fact, half the time that I was agonizing over decisions the packers had already made them, and sent things – such as all my shoes – to Africa.

We said goodbye to Hari and Meena and their sons and our little house and the beggars at the traffic lights (if there had been an organization called Human Friends, I would have been tempted to call them then to put us all out of our pain), and we moved back into a hotel for our last week in India.

This was slightly complicated by the fact that the tailor hadn't finished the last-minute things I'd ordered, so he had to move in too. The hotel people soon discovered that I was harbouring a tailor in my room – it seemed to be worse than having a lover in there – and said he had to go, but the clothes still weren't quite ready, so we had to smuggle him up the back stairs every morning.

It was horrible in the hotel – everyone thought we were tourists, and each time we took a taxi the driver invented some new surcharge. It was almost a relief when the time came to leave.

Actually, the *time* came to leave, but we didn't: the computer at Delhi Airport crashed, so no one could check in for the flight. AW and Claudia draped themselves over their trolleys and went to sleep but I had a fascinating conversation about human trafficking with a handsome young man in the queue who was in the Hong Kong Vice Squad.

We'd been worried about the overweight charges on our mountain of suitcases, but the computer wasn't up to weighing luggage, so it all went on free. Then we worried even more that the pilot wouldn't know how much everything on the plane weighed, so that we'd crash on take-off. But that seemed to work out all right as well, and soon we were back in the greyness of England. (My sister Moira used to say that in her memory our childhood in India was in Technicolor and that when we came back to England it all became black and white.)

When next day I went to the local supermarket to stock up on food, I suffered severe reverse culture shock. It was so extraordinary to be buying meat and chicken without a hanky over my nose and feeling sick. No one was throttling squawking chickens or spitting; there was no blood on the floor, no buckets of yellow claws, and no legless beggar dragging around in the dirt. But nor were there any traders flicking flies off their stalls with balloons on sticks like mad morris dancers. There were no mounds of spices, no tender young vegetables picked that morning, no bargaining, no laughter. And was it right, I kept wondering, for people to be so shielded from real life – should we be allowed to forget that a family pack of eight skinless, boneless, chicken breasts once belonged to four hens?

10

Always Have Something to Do on Mondays

When I read the Post Report on the Gambia, a curious nugget of information caught my eye: apparently it was difficult for women to get their high heels re-tipped there. 'Should you wish to bring a supply of heel-tips with you,' it said, 'the office handyman will be happy to hammer them on.' I hadn't envisaged tottering round the Gambia in stilettos, but I thought it was nice that somebody cared; then when I read the section on 'Opportunities for Wives' and found the usual exhilarating list (bridge, amateur dramatics, Scottish dancing, madrigal singing, etc) I was plunged into gloom.

AW headed off to Africa to take up his proud new posting as Ambassador, but it was a while before he could report back on living conditions. In AW's business, the outgoing boss is supposed to sign off and depart before the incoming boss arrives, but when AW landed in the Gambia he found that the outgoing boss was having some kind of crisis and had shut himself in the bedroom of the Residence and was refusing to come out, let alone *leave* . . .

AW didn't know what to do, so he whiled away a few days exploring the country from his hotel – popping back to the Residence every now and again to talk to the outgoing boss through the bedroom door, trying to persuade him to hand over, but without success. In the end he gave up this approach and simply went to the office, rang the bell, introduced himself to his surprised staff, and started working.

The outgoing Ambassador eventually left, AW moved into the Residence and then reported back to us in Somerset.

'What's it like? What's it like?' I shrieked down the phone. There was a long pause.

'Put it this way,' AW replied, 'we may have to take up golf.'

But he got a lot more cheery a day or two later when he discovered that our night watchman was armed with a bow and arrow.

In September 1988 Hester and Claudia and I followed him out (the night before we caught the plane I dreamed that I was doing a headstand on top of a 300-foot ladder held only by the children). We were a complete family again, because I had had to keep my promise to take Hester out of school if she was still miserable after a year. In fact, I don't think she was miserable at all, just felt left out and wanted to come and explore Africa with us: I didn't blame her. She may have secretly regretted her decision – it was her thirteenth birthday soon after we arrived, and since we didn't yet know anyone, the most exciting thing we could think of to do was write HAPPY BIRTHDAY HESTER in giant letters on the beach. We walked her along the cliff to see them from above and she took one look and burst into tears.

AW's office was in the capital, Banjul, which is on an island connected to the mainland by a bridge. It was about half an hour's drive from our house, which was a rambling, rather battered bungalow down a dirt road in a small town called Fajara. It had acres of patched and rusting corrugated iron roof and when it rained the noise was deafening, but somehow rather reassuring and cosy. On the garden side of the house there was a big verandah enclosed by tropical plants, which was where we mostly lived.

Hester and Claudia were booked into the American school this time – the only place that catered for the small number of ex-pat children – and AW used to drop them off on his way to the office with his handsome driver Malik, who had been a champion wrestler (wrestling is the national sport of the Gambia). We had not one but two night watchmen armed with bows and arrows; they came on alternate nights. Then there was the day watchman, Saneh (known by us as Insaneh), who was a bit slow and grinned happily all day long (his job was really charity). We had a gardener, Bakari, as well, and a cleaner called Sukai. In the kitchen was our cook, Old Pa Momodou, tall and skinny and trained, he told us, by the Royal Army Catering Corps – when or where, we never knew. AW had recruited Momodou, and though he couldn't read or write, he could tackle any new recipe if you laid all the ingredients out in the right order on the work surface: a knob of butter, a spoonful of oil, onions, garlic, a pinch of salt, carrots, chicken etc. Momodou had a dreadful cough – he was a heavy smoker – and used to spit in the sink when I wasn't watching, but he was a sweet man.

The 'character' in the house, we soon discovered, was our steward, Ceesay (pronounced 'Seesay'). AW had inherited Ceesay from the outgoing boss, who had been his first proper employer – Ceesay, we discovered, had spent most of his life as a kind of slave, working for a family in exchange for his keep, and had only recently managed to extricate himself from this situation and find a paid job.

The family's first meeting with Ceesay was at lunch on our first day. He sauntered into the dining room to serve the meal wearing a tattered T-shirt that said NUDE IS NOT LEWD, a baseball cap on back to front, and a cigarette tucked behind his ear. AW looked at him coldly and said, 'Please go and change into your uniform.' Ceesay went out for a minute or two and reappeared looking immaculate in white. I never did understand why he had challenged AW in this way – it was like throwing down a gauntlet. AW never took to Ceesay the way I did. (Not that Ceesay ever seemed to appreciate that he lived on the edge of dismissal. When we left he took to writing to AW, through a scribe, signing his letters 'from your old pal Ceesay'.)

I loved Ceesay – life was always a bit unpredictable when he was around. Soon after this confrontation I noticed that all sorts of things were disappearing from the kitchen – eggs, flour, sugar . . . I told AW and he asked Valerie the receptionist in the office to come and translate while I held an investigation. It didn't take long. Valerie asked Momodou if he had taken anything from the kitchen, and he replied gravely that he hadn't. Then she asked Ceesay, and he said yes, he had taken many things. Valerie and I were completely taken aback by his honesty – 'Why did you take them?' she faltered. 'Well,' said Ceesay, 'these people have so much I did not think they would notice.' This was so true, that I didn't have the heart to be cross.

One morning a few months later, I was in the bath when Ceesay called through the door, 'Madame, your father is here.'

My heart stopped – my *father* was in our house in the Gambia? There must be a mistake.

'My father? Do you mean my father from England?' I called out anxiously to Ceesay, who replied solemnly, 'Yes Madame, your father from England.'

I panicked – if my father had come all the way from England unannounced it must be because something terrible had happened to the rest of my family: they had all been killed in a car accident . . . Our house had burned down with everyone in it . . . He had decided to come personaly to break the dreadful news. I scrambled out of the bath, flung on my dressing gown and skidded into the sitting room ready to fling my arms round my darling Dad, to find the Irish Catholic priest – a 'father', of course – sitting calmly on the sofa. He had just popped by to pay a call on the new parishioners.

That summer a friend came to stay, to recuperate from the sudden death of her husband. I told Ceesay what had happened, and asked him to be particularly nice to her. He did try in his way – on her first morning I found him standing over her on the verandah saying, 'So . . . your husband *dead, eh*? Leaving you *all alone* . . .'

Later, when my sister Tessa brought our parents out to stay, Dad, now ninety, got heatstroke and nearly died, and it was Ceesay's turn to disapprove of me: 'In our country,' he said, 'we do not let Old Pas travel, it is bad for them. We keep them at home.' He nursed my father tenderly – even bathing him when Dad wouldn't let either Tessa or me do it; it was very touching.

Valerie had told me, before our investigation, that if we couldn't find out who had taken the things from the kitchen we might have to consult a *marabout*. *Marabouts*, the West African version of witchdoctors, are among the most feared people in the local community, in spite of the fact that the Gambia is a Muslim country. A *marabout* could cure sickness, remove the evil eye, give you strength and good luck, and was often more effective than the police when it came to solving crimes. But he could also be hired to put the evil eye on someone, which at the very least could bring them misfortune, and in a bad case, might kill them or a member of their family. This was what local people believed, so it was no wonder that spells and talismans against the evil eye were part of daily life. For instance, the huge avocado tree in the garden had old flip-flops nailed to it. 'Why?' AW asked Bakari, who shuffled about and said it was 'good medicine'. In the Gambia rituals still existed that involved people dressing in masks and strange costumes to impersonate spirits. Once someone – or something – called the Kankaran came to our house: it was only a man prancing about, dressed all in dried grass from head to toe, but he exuded a kind of sinister power that gave us goose bumps and we couldn't wait for him to go. How Carmo would have loved all this, we thought.

Ceesay warned us never to throw hair combings or nail clippings into the waste-paper basket because a *marabout* could work a particularly powerful spell if they actually had a piece of you in their hands. I took his advice – why take any chances? And after we found a letter from my friend Sandy, that I'd thrown away weeks before, wrapped around a baguette we bought in our local bakery, I paid more attention to everything that went into the waste bin. Later, AW and I were horrified to find that the sheet of paper round our bread that day was the result of an AIDS test done for one of his colleagues; it was negative, thank goodness, and we kept quiet about it, but it made us wonder what other people knew about our family from their bread wrappers.

Our first social invitation in the Gambia was from a sweet family called the Homans whose son was a school friend of Hester and Claudia. It sounded lovely – a day-long picnic excursion on a boat up the Gambia River. We all assembled at the jetty with our baskets of food, but just as we were about to board we noticed a *marabout* blessing a group of fishermen, so we rushed over to watch. I was a little nervous about intruding, but the others said 'No, no, look! He doesn't seem to mind us at all.' Not half. About an hour later our boat, threading its way through the mangrove swamps to the open river, got firmly stuck on a sandbank. We were there all day – first in the blazing sun and then, as dusk fell, being eaten alive by mosquitoes.

At that point it was decided to send the boat's dinghy back with some of the women and smaller children (there wasn't room for us all) and to get help. To my astonishment I saw AW clambering into the boat with the women and children, the only man among them.

'What are you doing?' I yelled.

'Someone has to go with them for protection,' said AW importantly – turning to flash me a beaming false smile as they puttered off.

I was seething with rage – I knew he was bored out of his wits and using any excuse to escape, but I had to keep up the pretence that he was being noble or he would have looked so dishonourable. As a matter of fact I have never really forgiven him: the rest of us were on that boat for another four hours or so. I still tend to think that the *marabout* on the jetty was responsible for our plight – but if he was, he only inflicted a very tedious day on us. A couple of years later, however, we were to encounter the true terrible power of a *marabout*.

It was odd being posted to West Africa, the departure point for the slave ships, having spent four years in the Caribbean, their destination. The people who live in West Africa today are not the descendants of slaves; their ancestors were the lucky ones who escaped capture, and they are entirely free of the burden of past suffering which weighs on those with slave ancestry in the Caribbean.

The physical difference between the two opposite sides of the Atlantic was vast. In the Caribbean the sand was white and the sea turquoise, and smart hotels sat cheek by jowl along the beach; on our West African coast, the sand was grey and the sea was black because of the silt pouring into it from the Gambia River. There was a handful of resort hotels, but far, far less money and much more real life. Along the coast were small fishing villages where the men went out half-naked, in boats called *piroges*, dug out of enormous tree trunks, and brought their catch back to the local markets, or to the village smokeries. A mouthwatering smell of

smoked mackerel hung in the air in these places, but the taste of
the local smoked fish, *bonga* it was called, didn't live up to it. And
from the day I first saw the heaps of hammerhead sharks in a market
– presumably caught not so far from shore – I decided that swimming was not for me: my recreation would have to be walking.
This was not a hardship – the beaches were immense and almost
empty, lit by a beautiful silvery-grey luminous light.

Even the sex-tourism was different in the Gambia. In Barbados
the beach boys and the women visitors looking for sex were cool
and good-looking, and the visitors clearly quite well off; but in the
Gambia the visitors tended to be plump package tourists from
England, and the beach bums, rather unsophisticated village boys.

It wasn't long before we acquired a dog to walk on the beach
with us. It was the usual story: someone telephoned to say they'd
found a pathetic starving puppy in a ditch and would we like to
see it, and of course we would and did – and ended up bringing
it home. But in the case of Toy, as she had already been named by
the people who found her, it was the best thing we ever did. Toy,
a black and white mongrel, turned out to be the most humorous,
characterful dog, and we all still have a pain in our hearts because
we had to leave her behind when we were moved four years later.
Toy was terrified of AW, but at the same time she wanted him to
like her, so she would give him an obsequious smile when he came
into the room, but her teeth would be chattering at the same time.

Then one day in Banjul market, I saw a green parrot stuffed
into a cage so cruelly small it could barely stand. I knew all the
arguments for not buying it: it would be creating a market for
another one and so on, but I bought it anyway; I couldn't walk
away. As soon as I got home I released the parrot from its cage and
was just feeling rather pleased with myself, when Toy shot across
the room and snapped it up in her mouth. We had to capture the
dog and prise open her jaws to release the parrot – which was
unharmed, but I could almost hear it complaining 'Why didn't this
silly cow leave me in the market where at least my *life* wasn't in
danger.' (I seemed to be a weapon of mass destruction as far as pets
went at that time: the previous week I had advised Claudia to take
her turtle out of the water butt – I thought it must be tired of

swimming round and round all the time – and make a better home for it in a flower bed; Toy crunched it up immediately.)

We called the parrot Ziggi, and once the dog understood that she had to leave it alone, we let it free in the house and garden; it couldn't fly away because its wings had been clipped. Ceesay especially loved the parrot and would go round the house doing his chores with Ziggi perched on his head, claws anchored into his thick hair. We tried to teach Ziggi to speak, but all it learned to imitate was the sound of Momodou's terrible cough, which it did so perfectly that everyone who came to the house asked us if we realized that our parrot was sick.

It took some weeks for Ziggi's wings to grow back so that it could fly – and then one sad or happy day, it took off with a flock of wild parrots passing through our garden, and we never saw it again.

Life was pleasant and extremely peaceable – for most of the time almost nothing happened. There were days when I felt so soporific in the humid heat that I wondered if the chemist could possibly have given me Valium instead of malaria tablets. It seemed typical that when the wall of the main prison fell down in the rains, not a single convict made a dash for freedom. You could see them all calmly exercising in the yard in their batik uniforms just as if there was no huge inviting gap where the wall had been.

Our diplomatic life was not exactly a whirl: apart from AW, the entire Diplomatic Corps numbered six ambassadors – Nigeria, United States, Sierra Leone (an ex-boxer), Senegal, and the British High Commissioner, Alec Ibbott and his wife, who were exceptionally nice.

The American Ambassador was posted in the Gambia for a rather odd reason: the Gambia is on the same trajectory as Cape Kennedy, and could therefore be used as an emergency landing-place if a newly-launched Space Shuttle ran into trouble. For this reason, before any Shuttle launch in the US, the Gambia was more or less taken over by Americans, and huge nets were prepared at the airport to catch the craft should it have to abort its mission and come down. This also meant that from time to time an astronaut or a VIP would come to the Gambia on a goodwill visit. They would always be taken to the American school to talk to the children and Hester and Claudia would report back excitedly – meeting the astronauts and asking them about going to the lavatory in space was a thrill. The girls were less impressed by someone called George W. Bush, Governor of Texas. 'Bor-ing,' said Claudia. She got his autograph though – but typically, now that he is seriously famous and it might be worth something, she seems to have lost it. Oh, well. My mother never believed a word about the huge nets at Gambia airport to catch the Space Shuttle, and as I write this I can hardly believe it myself and wonder if I dreamed it.

A curious thing happened in the Gambia which I have often thought about since. Very soon after the Lockerbie plane disaster, an ex-Interpol detective came to dinner with us. He was in the Gambia investigating some kind of fisheries fraud for the EU. Over the meal we discussed Lockerbie and he said, 'Oh it will all come out soon. That plane was carrying drugs to the US as part of a deal over the American hostages in Lebanon.' He went on to tell us that in order for the drugs to get through unimpeded it was arranged that the cargo of the Pan Am plane would not be inspected. What happened then, he said, was that, via the Lebanese/Hezbollah/Iran connection, the extraordinary fact that the plane's cargo would travel unchecked, came to the ears of Iranians seeking revenge for the shooting down of an Iranian civilian airliner by the US not long before; somehow they arranged to put a bomb on board.

Though the detective said that this story would be all over the papers in the following months, it never was. I have told it to every journalist I know, but no paper has ever taken it up – though there was a book published years ago called *The Octopus Trail*, which told more or less the same tale. Last year, not long before he died, I happened to tell Paul Foot the story and he urged me not to let it lie – which is why I am putting it into this book.

Near our house were a golf course and a Club, and is there any place in the world that doesn't have Scottish dancing and the Hash Hound Harriers running/drinking group? The Gambia certainly had both; we managed to avoid the Hash Hounds altogether, but in our first year AW and I were trapped into celebrating Burns Night with the Scottish dancing enthusiasts. It was okay, but AW is half Dutch and I am Irish, and we somehow lacked the necessary zeal, so when it came around again the next year, we decided to give it a miss.

In the Gambia the group of ex-pats was so small that you dared not lie about being 'previously engaged' – everyone would know it wasn't true. So that second year we were racking our brains for a reason to refuse the Burns night invitation, when we read in the paper that the Pope was to say Mass in Guinea Bissau, a neighbouring country – and on Burns Night day itself. Here was our excuse! We *had* to hear the Pope saying Mass, so we drove all the way to Guinea Bissau (it took a day), heard the Mass, stayed with our EC colleague overnight, and drove back again. It was one way of seeing Africa, if not the Pope – a tiny figure in the distance across the stadium. (Later, though, he came to the Gambia and, in the receiving line at the airport, we kissed his ring and were both impressed by his extraordinary aura.)

Now that AW was an Ambassador, I had to pull myself together and give dinner parties without hyperventilating or getting plastered in the process. I got better at it, but there was an additional complication in the Gambia: successful men there often had several wives. If you were particularly fond of one wife and wanted *her* to come with him to your dinner, you had to find out which nights she spent with her husband, and then make sure your dinner invitation was for one of those – otherwise, we learned from experience, a wife you'd never clapped eyes on before would turn up on his arm.

Another problem was that lots of people had the same family name, so it was easy to get muddled and invite the wrong N'gums, Jallows, N'jies or whoever. We learned this from experience too, the night we had the Deputy Minister for Tourism to dinner. AW told me that the Minister loved trees, so if I got stuck for conversation, that's what I could talk about. I enthused about trees all evening, wondering why AW kept giving me funny looks – only after the guests had left could he tell me that he had no idea who had been at our dinner that evening, but it was certainly not the

Deputy Minister. (And he was certainly not interested in trees – I could tell I was boring him to death.)

An old hand in India once gave me two rules for ex-pat happiness: one was Always Have Something to Do on Mondays, and the other was Make Your House Feel Like Home Before Anything Else. Early on, following her advice, I had found a tailor to make new cushions and alter the curtains from India – which had already been altered *for* India – so that, apart from the tweed sofas and chairs supplied by the EC, our house was looking quite nice and there was nothing more I could do with it. I had no writing projects either – my book on Kashmir was done and due out any time, and *Punch* had terminated my column (which was just as well as I don't know what I would have written about every month), so I was desperately looking around for something to fill my time.

Then I was invited to join a group of ex-pat ladies learning vegetable carving. I should explain that vegetable carving is nothing *useful* like vegetable peeling – oh no, we're talking about carving a yam into a lobster or a carrot into a rose. Shirley Conran once wrote that life is too short to stuff a mushroom – I remember fuming to myself that she'd obviously never been a wife overseas, when it is sometimes long enough to think of carving a white radish into the Taj Mahal . . . I thought of my successful journalist friends like Sandy in England, and before going to the lesson, I stomped round the house kicking the furniture and yelling at AW: 'This is wonderful! VEGETABLE CARVING is what my parents saved up and gave me a private education for . . . This is the stimulating, intellectually challenging career they wanted for me . . . This is why I came to Africa . . .' and so on. But as a matter of fact it was impossible to resist being intrigued – the Thai girl who gave the classes was so skilful, it was just a crying shame she wasn't doing it in granite or marble.

One day, chatting to Joko, who sold batik clothes to tourists in our local market, it occurred to me that perhaps I could design my own batik patterns. Joko said that if I drew my patterns on paper, the woodcarver would make them into blocks, and she would print the wax on the cloth with them, and do the dyeing.

I designed the most un-African patterns I could think of (various versions of daisies and spots) to make them different from Joko's own range, and they came out surprisingly prettily. Then, copying a friend's kimono, I had a couple of sample dressing-gowns made up in my fabrics, and the next time I went on leave I showed them to Liberty in Regent Street, who actually *gave me an order*. Not far from our house was a Chinese factory which made djellabas for export to the Arab world, and they agreed to make the kimonos for me. I delivered my first order to Liberty's a couple of months later, and felt like a real businesswoman. But unfortunately the project ground to a halt when the supply of white cotton from China dried up for some reason, leaving us with no cloth to print on. And then, by the time cotton deliveries to the Gambia began again, AW had heard he was being posted to Syria.

The first copy of my *Travels in Kashmir* book arrived in the post – I thought it looked awful and cried with disappointment on AW's shoulder while we walked on the beach. The colours had come out wrong so that the cover, which was supposed to be a watercolour picture of spring in Kashmir, looked more like autumn. But the inside was excellent (though I say it myself) and we organized a small book-signing at the Club. Kind friends loyally turned up and I was so grateful – but I found in the heat of the moment that I couldn't remember anybody's name . . . One by one they asked me to write in the books they'd just bought, but my hand was paralysed because I couldn't remember what they were called.

In desperation I thought up a strategy: 'Oh, I am so stupid,' I'd say, 'I can't remember how, exactly, you spell your name?'

'J-O-H-N,' the kind supporter would say, or 'M-A-R-Y.'

'Oh, so you don't have an 'i' in it then?' I'd bluster, trying to cover up.

When I cried on the beach AW came out with his usual, 'Don't worry, it will all be all right' – and as usual he was correct. A few months later, Oxford University Press in Britain bought the book from OUP in India and published it in the UK. This would have been good in itself, but it was a glorious revenge for me, because OUP UK had rejected it in the first place. Now they'd bought it without realizing that they'd already turned it down. However, when I did a book-signing for this English edition at Liberty's in London, they put me and my books at the back of one of the huge ground-floor windows, and a group of lager louts spotted me from the pavement and jeered and laughed through the glass. It was mortifying.

Nothing ever goes quite the way you think it will, especially if you have an imagination like mine. I could see sales of *Travels in Kashmir* soaring, royalties rolling in, glittering travel-writing awards – but in fact soon after the book was published in Britain, the troubles in Kashmir came to a violent head and tourists dared not go there any more . . . I live in hope that peace will come to Kashmir again one day.

AW would occasionally disappear 'up-river' for a few days at a time, to look at projects in the bush. We always hoped to make a family trip out of one of these excursions, but the girls were never keen to leave their friends. The first time, I tried to whip up enthusiasm by describing night falling on the jungle (not that I'd ever experienced this myself). 'And then,' I said excitedly, 'men with flares will come through the forest to light our camp.'

'Oh God,' said Hester, 'they're not still wearing flares there, are they?'

A group of us ex-pat spouses used to meet at the Club some days for a swim or a coffee and a chat. Once, we boldly decided to give a coffee morning for the President's younger wife. The woman who was chosen to host the party baked a magnificent chocolate cake that sat as the centrepiece on the table, while we gathered around with our mouths watering, waiting for Lady Jawara to turn up. As soon as she did, the delectable-looking cake was cut up; we all took a piece – but the first person to bite into it discovered it was made with salt instead of sugar. An urgent whisper sped round, and someone was detailed to remove the plate with the cake on it from Lady Jawara's hand and quickly insert a substitute with shortbread or something. We laughed about it for months.

Apart from the British High Commissioner who succeeded the nice Ibbotts, we became fond of everyone we met in the Gambia:

there was Cynthia, the glamorous VSO who was with me the terrible day I parked on the beach and then lost the Land Rover key and the tide was coming in and AW was away. (The Land Rover survived the experience, and someone walking on the beach found the key next day, but not before I had ordered a new one from London, to be couriered out at vast expense.) Then there were the Whittles (he was an eminent doctor at the Medical Research Council in the Gambia) who came and fetched AW – even though he sounded drunk on the telephone – in the middle of one night, when he woke, terrified, to find his whole mouth paralysed. He was unable to speak properly for days – we never found out why.

But the person who made our West African experience into something unique was an extraordinary woman called Janis Carter. I had heard of her before we left England – I think on a radio programme about wildlife – and from Day One had wanted to meet her. When I asked about her in the Gambia, I was told that she was reclusive and unapproachable, but that if I was prepared to have my head bitten off, I could probably find her on the beach where she sometimes walked her dogs. After that, every time I saw a woman on the beach with a dog I bravely went up and asked if she was Janis Carter – and one day she was, and though wary, she did not bite my head off and became a great friend of the family.

Janis was an American, beautiful in a Sigourney Weaver way, and she had originally come to the Gambia with a chimpanzee called Lucy in order to rehabilitate her into the wild. As an experiment Lucy had been raised as a human child by a couple in the States who wanted to see what would happen to her if she grew up in their environment. What happened was that despite having her own bedroom and television set and pets and clothes, and despite being mentioned in encyclopaedias for her record-breaking ability to communicate in sign language – and even to understand the human concept of right and wrong (Lucy once admitted she'd lied about doing a mess in the hall) – as she grew up she became strong and dangerous and more chimp than human. Eventually the couple who had 'adopted' her could no longer cope, and wanted to get rid of her. But what was to happen to Lucy? She couldn't go into a zoo because she was effectively half human . , .

Janis was at university in the US studying psycho-linguistics when she heard about Lucy, and she decided to take her to the Gambia where there was already a project to return to the wild chimps who had suffered at the hands of humans. When they arrived Lucy was temporarily put in a cage with some other chimps, whereupon she signed to Janis that she didn't like the dirty monkeys, and she wanted to go home and have a Coca-Cola.

Unbelievably, Janis then spent *five years* with Lucy on an island in the Gambia river, teaching her to be a chimp. Janis lived in a cage and Lucy lived in the forest, returning to Janis for advice from time to time. It took a long time, but Lucy did become a proper chimp again, and even found a mate. And then tragedy struck: some poachers came to the island one day and Lucy, accustomed as she was to humans, rushed up to greet them. They were terrified, and shot her dead. Janis was heartbroken, but had stayed on in West Africa to continue working on other chimp projects. She is still there.

We went with her to see her camp in the forest and she showed us photographs of herself with Lucy which made us cry — no one who saw them could ever think of a chimp as being 'just' an animal ever again. Then we ourselves made friends with a lowland gorilla from the Cameroons called Julia, who had been found as a baby when her mother was killed, and was another candidate for re-habilitation into the wild. Julia was being kept in the same cage as Lucy had been a few years before, in the Abuko Nature Reserve, run by a charming elderly Englishman called Eddie Brewer. (Eddie's daughter, Stella, had started the chimp rehabilitation project that drew Janis to the Gambia.)

When Eddie took us to visit Julia, our eleven-year-old Claudia and the gorilla struck up an instant friendship through the bars of the cage, chasing each other round and round, sitting staring each other out, playing like two kids. Claudia longed to *really* play with the gorilla outside the cage, and since I was completely under the spell that being close to wild animals seems to cast over humans, I drove Claudia to Abuko one morning, timing my arrival to co-incide with the hour that Julia's keeper (I knew) walked the gorilla in the forest. It was possibly the most foolish of all the foolish ideas

I have had in my life. Julia the gorilla was off her lead; she grabbed Claudia and made her sit on her lap on the forest path, where she explored her hair and face and then took her fingers, bending them back gently one by one. It was seeing Claudia's small white fingers in the powerful hands of the gorilla that made me realize what a dangerous thing I had done. The gorilla could snap them all, one by one; she could snap Claudia's neck for that matter. I was sick with fear.

The keeper and I stood motionless, he as scared as me. Julia played with Claudia for a while, then she changed places and sat on Claudia's lap, and then – glory be – the novelty wore off. She seemed to get bored, and when the keeper calmly indicated they should continue their walk, she went along with him quite happily. Claudia and I fell into each other's arms – though Claudia was nowhere near as scared as I was – and went home. It was a long time before I dared tell anyone – least of all AW – what I'd done. Julia never made it back into the wild: it was thought that her rehabilitation would only be successful if she went with a companion gorilla, and none was found. She was sent to Jersey Zoo.

Ceesay asked if he could talk to me about a problem. Of course he could, I said, and he began telling me a complicated story, which I couldn't understand: it seemed to be about a piece of machinery that wasn't functioning properly. I thought he was telling me in a roundabout way that there was something wrong with the fridge, so I said, 'Ceesay, wouldn't it be simpler if we went into the kitchen and you just showed me?'

Ceesay let out a shriek of horror and I finally understood that the thing that wasn't functioning properly was Ceesay – he was trying to tell me that he was impotent. Once we had got that sorted out, he explained that the reason for his problem was that his wife had not made the correct sacrifice when her father died, and he wanted an advance on his salary so that he could pay for his wife to go back to Guinea Bissau (where she came from) and make the sacrifice.

'Mmmmm,' I said, 'Let's talk to Dr Peters about this.' Lenrie Peters was our doctor and good friend, and being a Gambian, I thought, he'd be able to advise on the right thing to do. Lenrie told me that since this type of problem was often in the mind, sending the wife to make the sacrifice was as good an idea as any other. So Ceesay got his advance and his wife went back to her village.

A few months later Ceesay told us his wife was pregnant – we were delighted, and I said to AW, 'You see, in Africa things are different. We would have scoffed at the idea of that sacrifice in England, but it worked.'

It turned out not to be that simple. When Ceesay brought his wife to the house so that we could congratulate her, she was young and beautiful – and not the same wife he had had before.

'Ceesay,' I said, 'this is not your wife . . . what happened?'

Ceesay beamed. 'No Madame,' he said, 'while my wife was in Guinea Bissau, I met this one. She is my *new* wife.'

So it had worked, but not at all in the way we had expected, and I don't know what happened to Ceesay's poor ex-wife.

Time for Hester was running out – the GCSEs could wait no longer. She had spent a year in the Gambia with us and would soon be fourteen. Now she really had to go back to school in England. I was desperately sorry to lose her but couldn't help feeling the time was right. Both children seemed to be running wild with the rest of the ex-pat gang – they were blissfully happy, but we practically never saw them, and had precious little idea of what they were up to. We went to look at a school in Wells, Somerset; it seemed pleasant and Hester liked it, so we booked her in for September.

In the meantime, three mysterious bumps that looked like enormous boils had appeared on my thigh. Boils would almost have been a blessing compared to what they really were: tumbo fly maggots. Let me explain: in the Gambia at a certain season these flies would lay their eggs on damp surfaces – which could include washing hanging out to dry. Unless the eggs were killed by careful ironing, they hatched into miniscule worms that burrowed their way into your skin and sat there eating your flesh and getting bigger until it was time for them to come out as huge fat grubs. These

were what I had in my thigh. The worst part about tumbo maggots was that you couldn't extract them until they were ripe and
ready – at which point a sort of crater developed in the top of the
lump and you could squeeze them out through it; until then you
had to put up with the tickling feeling of them chomping on your
body. I got them out in the end (Meriel was staying at the time
and was gratifyingly revolted), but looking back, it was as if being
eaten alive by maggots was the harbinger of bad times to come.

The first sign of these was one night when we went out to a
supper party, leaving the girls at home alone with a friend who
was sleeping over. We got back at about midnight and the first
thing we noticed was that the night watchman – whom we'd left
about four hours before looking perfectly sane and normal – was
now wearing two hats and a plastic bag on his head and had pieces
of red cloth stuffed in his nose and ears. He was waving his bow
and arrow around wildly, and telling us to hurry hurry into the
house as there were bad people around trying to gas us. Slightly
dazed, we went inside and found that Hester and her friend had
raided the drinks cupboard: Hester was staggering like a stage
drunk, and her friend had passed out in the bathroom. We were
appalled, but we put them to bed, tried not to worry, took the
nightwatchman home, and next day gave Hester the first of many
long and serious talks.

That autumn we left Hester at her new school in Wells, and
once again the phone calls started – only this time they were not
so much from a homesick Hester as from her teachers: she had
dyed her hair pink, she was insolent, she ignored the rules . . . I
began to dread answering the telephone, especially when it gave
what we called the International Click as you picked it up, indicating that the incoming call was from overseas.

Soon it was not enough to try and sort things out on the telephone – someone had to go back to England and see the school-
masters and mistresses face to face. Of course it was always me,
since AW was tied down at the office.

The Headmaster of Hester's school probably grew to think that
she came from some sort of dysfunctional family because I never
seemed to have a whole sensible outfit to wear when I went to

see him, most of my clothes being in Africa, and all my visits being last-minute emergency ones. I distinctly remember going to one meeting wearing harem trousers with Timberland walking shoes – they were the only things I could find to put on. Even worse was the time I forgot my toothpaste in the Gambia and had nothing to clean my teeth with. In desperation I looked all around the house for the stub of an old tube, but could only find some Monkey Brand black toothpowder that I'd put in Hester's Christmas stocking when we lived in India. I cleaned my teeth with this and thought no more about it until, driving home from my appointment with the Head, I looked in the rear-view mirror and smiled, to reassure myself that I looked like a credible mother. To my horror I saw that all my teeth had thick black outlines, as though someone had drawn round them with a felt-tip pen. The only consolation was that the meeting had been grim, and I didn't think I had smiled very often.

I spent less and less time in the Gambia with AW and Claudia and more and more in England . . . Then suddenly, there was a new drama – AW went for his annual medical check and was told that he had to have a bypass operation immediately. At least it meant we were all in England together for the next few months. We enrolled Claudia into the same school as Hester and then, when AW recovered from his operation and was able to go back to work in the Gambia, it seemed sensible to leave her there as a boarder.

With two of them at school in England, life over the next couple of years became more and more like walking across a minefield. You know . . . green grass, sun shining, birds singing and then the explosions. Your daughter has been suspended for smoking! Your daughter has been arrested for shoplifting! Your daughter has been caught dealing in speed! Your daughter's best friend has been expelled from her school for smoking marijuana that YOUR DAUGHTER gave her! Please remove your daughters from our school!

I thought of those Christmas letters from friends which say things like: 'Phoebe is doing Grade Eight piano this year, and we're very proud of Louise whose brilliant A-levels have secured her a place at Oxford, and Matthew who has spent his gap year working in a refugee camp in Jordan and now speaks Arabic fluently.' Our letter would read more like this: 'Our girls have given up piano, flute, violin, reading, working and all known hobbies and interests outside pop music; both girls have been asked to leave their schools, and our youngest is much enjoying her year on bail.'

It was all such a shock – we were such a close family and I'd never expected *my* children to give us problems. I remembered going to lunch with friends in India and being astonished at the way their sixteen-year-old behaved: she was sullen and rude and cast a shadow over the whole occasion. On the way home in the car I'd gazed smugly at our own two little angels on the back seat and said to AW, 'I can't imagine why they let her behave like that; I just wouldn't put up with it myself, I really wouldn't.' Now I realized that our friends were probably hanging on by the ragged ends of their fingernails and it was a miracle they'd got their daughter to lunch at all, forget about her being pleasant.

How did all this happen? I wondered. How – seemingly overnight – did our sweet little girls suddenly turn into these grumpy teenagers with ears pierced in several places and enormous boots out of all proportion to their spindly legs? And why did cruel Fate organize people's lives so that their children's and their parents' difficult years exactly coincided – leaving those of us who were both mothers and daughters squashed in the middle? My own mother had become perpetually anxious (she later developed Alzheimer's disease) and so my parents had gone into a home and were having all kinds of problems there . . . I seemed to spend most of my time on the road driving to the school in Somerset, or the home in Hampshire. It was a miserable time for everyone, and there seemed to be no way to make it better – though once, in a wild moment, it occurred to me that perhaps my mother and daughter should swap drugs – my mother's spirits would be lifted by Ecstasy and my daughter's subdued by Valium.

I could hardly remember the time when life in the Gambia had been calm and placid and almost nothing happened and we didn't dread the phone calls from England. I'd grumbled about how dull it was, but now I would have given anything to go back to those peaceful uncomplicated days.

★   ★   ★

But by that time days in the Gambia were not peaceful and uncomplicated at all. I'd just arrived back there from England and was typing up my diary one morning when AW rang to tell me that the army had mutinied and that I must be ready to flee without him to Casamance (in southern Senegal) should things turn nasty. I said 'Yes darling, of course darling,' but I certainly wouldn't have fled without him – apart from anything else, I would never have found the way.

AW had discovered about the mutiny first hand. He was running late for a meeting in the big Senegambia Hotel on the mainland; the President was to be there, and AW didn't want to arrive after him, so, finding himself at the end of a long queue of cars at Denton Bridge he told Malik, the driver, to put the flag on the car, switch on the headlights and overtake the whole line. Malik obeyed, and they shot ahead, but to their horror when they reached the bridge they found themselves staring into the gun barrels of dozens of very angry and jumpy soldiers. 'Put the car in reverse, Malik,' said AW, thinking quickly, 'and get out of here as *fast as you can*.' They whizzed backwards past all the cars, and took shelter in a peanut-processing factory, and AW rang me from there.

In the event, the Government paid the soldiers, and the mutiny fizzled out, though only for the time being. A few years later, after we'd left, there was a coup, and the army took over the country; a young officer, Lieutenant Jammeh, became President, and still is.

Then a truly terrible thing happened: an Englishwoman, Penny, who was house-sitting for Eddie Brewer of the Abuko Nature Reserve, was horribly murdered. Eddie had had to return to Britain to have a hip replacement operation, and Penny had volunteered to come out and look after his dogs. I was away again at the time, and Eddie asked AW to keep an eye on her and make sure she was happy; AW rang her every day to check that all was well. One morning the maid answered the phone and said she was worried as Miss Penny was not in the house. Since she usually walked the dogs in the morning, AW was not too bothered; he would call later, he said. Within an hour the maid rang him back in a terrible state: the dogs had returned without Miss Penny; the staff had gone to look for her and found her decapitated body in the bush; her head was lying a few yards away, as if it had been dropped by someone running away.

There was no obvious motive for the murder, but the general belief among the local people seemed to be that the killer was a wrestler, acting on the orders of a *marabout*. Their theory was that this wrestler had asked a *marabout* for a spell to ensure he won his fights, and that the *marabout* had told him that with a human head he would be able to work the most powerful and invincible of all spells. What bothered AW (and me and Eddie when we came back) was that neither the British nor the Gambian authorities seemed to be investigating the murder as doggedly as they should have been, or indeed, making much of an effort to go after the wrestler who, according to the local grapevine, had fled to Casamance. I wrote a story about it for the *Sunday Express* to try to spur some action, but nothing happened.

In the end Eddie put up a reward, and AW went to Casamance himself several times, to talk to the Chief of Police there. In due course we heard from him that the murderer had been found – dead: killed by some villagers he had menaced. But we never discovered if this was really the case, or what happened to the *marabout*, and the truth is that no one will ever really know what happened or why, to poor innocent Penny. It was a tragic, ugly story that cast a shadow over our last months in Africa.

For by now AW had been told that he was to be posted to Syria. It was very exciting, but there was one sadness: we would be living in an apartment in Damascus, and Toy was not an urban dog. AW decided that, for her own sake, she should be left behind. I tried to make him change his mind by taking Toy to his office one day to prove how well she could manage in a formal environment. As soon as the door was open Toy dashed in barking and skidding on the shiny floor; Valerie the receptionist screamed; people came running; Toy became hysterical – it was pandemonium. I had managed to prove that without any doubt we had to leave the dog behind. We found a good home for her with a young English vet – but all of us still miss her to this day.

★   ★   ★

AW was to take up his new post in Syria in the spring of 1993. The rest of the family, it was decided, would go with him for the Easter holidays, and then return to their schools (or, in my case, trouble-shooting activities) in England. Just before that happened, all the problems with the children came to a head like some huge poisonous carbuncle. Perhaps the best way to tell it is through the diary I kept over what I called at the time, 'The worst weeks of my life so far'.

Day 1

Telephone call from Westminster School to say that Hester has bunked mock A-levels, and disappeared off the face of the earth. Spent the day ringing round her friends trying to find her. Failed.

Day 2

Millfield School rang to say that since Claudia has been sitting under a tree for three days, rocking, they are putting her on a train to Waterloo.

Day 3

Collect Claudia off train.

Day 4

Telephone call from Westminster School to say that Hester has returned, but is being suspended. Can I go and fetch her? Just one thing though: she has to finish a 5,000 word A-level History of Art dissertation by Saturday (this is Thursday) or she will not be allowed to sit the A-level exam. Collect Hester from school, return to flat. Think I am behaving like a saint – smiling (falsely), no nagging and no recriminations as have been told by experts that these serve no purpose.

Day 5

Try to persuade Hester to get up and work on dissertation. Fail. Try again. Succeed in getting her up, but she says she is going out with friends. My eyes go red. 'Try thinking more than one nanosecond ahead,' I suggest, 'and do the dissertation.'

'Leave me alone,' she says, and starts putting on her coat. Something snaps in my brain. Hurl myself across the room to strangle Hester. She grabs my hands; undignified arm wrestle takes place, and something snaps again, not in my brain this time but in my hand. Go to hospital.

When you are drowning you are supposed to see your past life go by; when you break your finger, you see your future life flash before your eyes. How you won't be able to wash your hair, drive the car, do up your bra . . .

In two weeks AW is due to take up his post in Syria, we are supposed to be going with him for the holidays – how am I going to pack with one arm?

Doctor asks, as he plasters me up, 'How did you come to do this?'

'Trying to strangle my daughter,' I reply.

'Oh yes,' he says quite unmoved. 'She's a teenager is she?'

Day 6

It's Mother's Day, ha ha ha. It's also term time. Both my daughters are supposed to be at boarding schools for which we are paying thousands of pounds a year, but both are at home with me, and I have a broken finger.

Day 7

Hester spends day with friends, eating, smoking and watching telly. No work at all. Point out that A-levels only a few weeks off. Row erupts. Hester leaves.

Days 8–15

No sign of Hester. Stress. Tension. Anxiety. Sleep at night with jaw clenched. Is Hester going to return in time to go to the Middle East with the rest of the family? Cliffhanger.

Hester returns two nights before we leave. Is she coming with us? She doesn't know.

Rise at dawn the morning of departure. Appropriately enough (with hindsight) it's April Fool's Day. Hester decides she will come with us to Damascus, but only for one week. AW (just back from Brussels) says we'll discuss that later.

We go through the airport formalities at Heathrow, get on the plane and do up our seat belts. I glance up and am flabbergasted to see Hester leaving the plane. I get up to go after her but the air hostess stops me: 'I'm sorry, madam, you may not leave the aircraft now.' I explain that I've just seen Hester go out of the door. Her jaw drops. 'Your daughter has left the plane? You must get her back immediately.' If I do not, she says, it seems that all the passengers will have to disembark and identify their baggage, and it will cost us thousands of pounds.

AW goes after daughter, finds her detained by Security in Departures, persuades her to return to the plane. She agrees – but only if we will let her come home after a week. Lying through his teeth AW says yes. AW and Hester return to the plane. Glance at AW, he looks as crumpled as a walnut and so do I. Do really high-powered people have problems like this when taking up new posts? Did Chris Patten's daughters try and escape from the plane on the way to Hong Kong when he was appointed Governor?

Days 16–30

We are in Damascus. We are staying in a modern hotel built between two motorways and a flyover (because the chap AW is replacing has not yet left the Residence). There is nothing for the children to do; there is a heatwave but the hotel pool has no water because it is not officially summer yet. Masses of historic sights to see, but children not interested. Can't think how to pass their days, so make lots of appointments for them in hotel beauty salon for waxing – by the time they leave they won't have a hair left on their bodies. Send them for shampoos and blow-drys, but they come back in sulks to comb out their new Arab Big Hair. It is all extremely difficult, we don't know a living soul, we are trying unsuccessfully to find a flat, and Hester has thrown the hotel fruit from the bowl in our room at me, twice. But wait a minute: we are still all four together and we've even had some laughs. The hotel lift has a sign saying 'In case of stoppage dial the operator for a talk', and the hotel brochure says it is providing new luxurious rooms for 'effluent' visitors. Things could be looking up.

Hester did leave early, after two and a half weeks (and a hotel phone bill for £100), but she was different: being together as a family seemed to have brought her back to us. She sat her A-levels that year and got into Edinburgh university.

Claudia and I went back to England just before the end of the holidays; we had to get her packed up to go back to Millfield, where she had been given a last chance to settle down. At home in Somerset, the day she was due back at school, Claudia went up to her room to sort out her trunk. She seemed to be taking hours, so I went up to investigate – her room was locked from the inside; there was no reply when I shouted. I looked round the house, there was no one there, I checked the garden – and on the doorstep I found a note telling me she had run away and hoped to see me at some time later in life.

I leapt in the car and drove up and down all the roads leading out of the village – no sign of her. I called Millfield and explained what had happened, and said that we'd be late. Don't bother coming at all, they said.

When evening came, I rang the police and a nice officer arrived to talk to me. I was just giving him a description of Claudia, when the phone rang. It was a friend of Claudia's to tell me I mustn't

worry, she was fine – the policeman grabbed the phone and persuaded the boy to tell us where she was: camped in a field near
the school she'd been expelled from before going to Millfield. The
policeman went to fetch her home.

I wasn't cross; I just had a feeling of immense relief that a decision about Millfield had been forced on us. Now we had to look
for another school. Eventually we found Frensham Heights in Surrey,
and after a rocky start – Claudia ran away again before we even
reached the front door – she settled down there happily.

By the autumn of that year most of the problems seemed to be
over. I just had to get Hester off on her gap year to India – she
was going to stay with the Singhs – and then I could go and join
AW in Syria. I dropped Hester off at British Airways to get her
injections and popped round the corner to do some shopping.
Luckily I wasn't too long: Hester – a hypochondriac – had been
working her way through the menu of immunizations available,
each one costing upwards of £25. She was just toying with Japanese
Encephalitis for another £35 when I appeared and cancelled it.
Even so, by the time we'd bought hypodermic needles, and catheters
for blood transfusions and a water filter with a straw for sucking
clean water out of muddy rivers, the bill was almost as much as
the air ticket. (I doubted if Hester, staying with the Singhs, would
ever need to drink out of a muddy river, but she can be very convincing.)

I took her to the airport to see her off on her great adventure.
She looked so tiny in Terminal 4 with her huge backpack – a bit
like a dung beetle – it tugged at my heartstrings. I loved her so
much, but at the same time I couldn't help feeling relieved that
she was going to be six thousand miles away and I could get on
with my own life for a while.

11

My Road to Damascus

The city of Damascus grew up in layers, like an onion – or perhaps I should say in rings, like a tree, because the rings reveal its age. Right at the core is the Great Mosque, built within the walls of a Roman temple that was, itself, constructed on the already thousand-year-old site of an Aramean place of worship. Around this ancient place presses the rabbit warren of the Old City with its Roman remains – including the Street Called Straight where St Paul found refuge, and its courtyard houses, *hammams*, and caravanserais. Then there is the city wall, originally Roman, but restored and repaired and added to all through the centuries from Saladin's time to the present day. Outside the walls come the thirteenth and fourteenth century mosques and schools and bathhouses of the Mamluke period with their distinctive black and white striped walls; and then the first Western-style buildings, put up at the end of the nineteenth century when the ruling Ottoman Empire became fascinated by everything European. These are followed by a layer of pleasant villas with louvred shutters in tree-lined streets that belong to the period between the wars when the French ruled Syria, next come the first low-level modern suburbs, now considered rather posh, and after them, a terrible sprawl of cement high-rise buildings.

When we first heard we were to be posted to Syria, I asked my cousin Simon – who was the only person I knew who'd ever been there – what it was like. 'Hmmm,' he said, 'Damascus reminded me of. . . .' He paused, and I waited for him to say 'Paradise,' but 'East Berlin,' he said.

By the time I joined AW in September, he had long since unpacked our stuff from Africa and settled into the Residence – a rather gloomy apartment in the French layer, near the centre of Damascus. He'd hung up our pictures and made it all quite cosy, but when I looked into my wardrobe I was mystified by the peculiar clothes I found hanging there – there seemed to be a Red Indian squaw's fringed suede tunic among them. I was racking my brains, trying to remember how or where I could possibly ever have worn a squaw's outfit, when it dawned on me that this was the contents of the children's dressing-up box, all carefully washed and pressed by the maid. She must have wondered what on earth the new boss's wife was going to be like as she ironed a witch's outfit, a tiny nurse's uniform and various tatty old dresses that were used as Cinderella's rags. The other misplaced item was my Indian foot scraper which – oh dear – I found next to the cheese grater in the kitchen cupboard.

This apartment was the first of three places we were to live in over our five and half years in Syria. When our lease ran out only a couple of months later and the landlord decided to sell the place, we moved to a glitzy ground-floor flat in Mezze (one of the posh modern suburbs), where the taps were gold-leafed swans. Within a year, living there became a nightmare because the powerful general who owned the top floor started to expand it like a mushroom cap, building out on pillars set in our garden to gain more square metres, so we moved again, into a nice simple house a couple of streets away.

As always, I spent the first twelve months of our new posting feeling lost and lonely, this time much more so than usual, for Syria was the first place I'd gone to without the children and I missed them and all the life they brought with them – I found myself even longing for the bad bits. (Though not so much when faxes appeared in AW's office from Hester in India: 'I hate it here . . . am so homesick . . . hate the Singhs . . . feel like a prisoner, am not allowed to wander round town . . .' Later: 'The Singhs are so kind . . . I like them . . . we have interesting conversations.' Later: 'The Singhs really understand how hard it is to be a teenager in the Nineties . . .' Later still: 'If only I'd had wonderful parents like the Singhs . . .' and so on.)

The Syrian winter was much colder and damper than I had

imagined it would be, and I had no friends. Making it worse was the fact that AW's Number Two and his glamorous wife had been there for a long time and were tremendously popular – it was as if they were the real Number One – and AW and I, inadequate impostors. Life in our second flat was continuously stressful because of the mushroom work going on upstairs. I had a little office with a French window on to the garden, but you couldn't go through it for fear of being killed by the red–hot molten metal and lumps of cement that fell like rain from above. One morning out of the corner of my eye I saw a *man* falling past the window. I rushed out, dreading the crumpled broken mess I would find, but miraculously, though he'd fallen four floors he seemed to be unscathed, and gulped down the aspirins I gave him and the cup of tea I made (with shaking hands) quite calmly – I was the one who was having a nervous breakdown.

In those days I used to write my diary on an electric typewriter and to make life even more frustrating, every time I felt inspired and placed my fingers on the keys to begin, there would be a power cut. So when we moved for the third – and last – time, to the nice house round the corner, I decided to follow the local custom and make a sacrifice to ensure that our lives would be happier there. I couldn't tell AW what I was planning because he had by then become a Buddhist, so Marcelle, the cook, and I (well, more her than me, I have to admit) secretly killed two chickens and dabbed their blood on all the doors. Not long afterwards I confided this to a friendly EC colleague visiting Syria, and he told me that when he was posted to Algeria he had sacrificed a ram before moving into his house, and four days later there was an earthquake and all his kitchen cupboards fell off the walls. In our case though, I think it worked – we were suddenly issued with a generator and I could type all day long.

You do learn to behave – and believe – in slightly odd ways when you've lived a lot in the developing world. Once, a particularly attractive house plant we had in Syria started to wilt – 'Oh dear,' I said to Bing, the butler, 'I suppose we forgot to water it.'

'Oh no,' he corrected me, 'someone must have touched it when they had their period.' Bing used to put an egg in the garden every time we had a party, to make sure the weather was nice – and it always was. And when our Filipina maid slipped downstairs, she told me that she must have trodden on a little fairy and all the others were so angry they pushed her feet off the steps. 'Mmmm, that's an interesting idea,' I said.

Now it is hard for me to remember those first lonely months in Syria, for, in the end, Damascus was my road to Damascus – it changed my life. But that came later; first of all I had to learn how to be a *proper* Diplomat's Wife. The Dip Corps in Syria was big and serious, with a clever and experienced bunch of ambassadors, it was not the easy-going world of the Gambia.

At this stage I should make it clear that we EC wives don't get any instruction or help with learning how to be an ambassador's partner. In Germany the diplomats' spouses get their own allowances and a pension; in the British Foreign Office there is a particular person whose job it is to look after Heads of Missions' wives; the HSBC bank gives the wives of officials posted overseas a nice little sum of money with which to buy a computer, or pay for retraining in something that might be useful. But no one back at head office in Brussels has ever spoken to me about anything; I don't know if they are aware that I exist. We certainly don't get sent on courses about how to lay the table for a formal dinner, or what exactly to do with the huge silver under-plates we have in our official kit, or whether to sit the Papal Nuncio above the US Ambassador, or what to call the Prime Minister; we have to use our common sense and fly, pilotless, by the seats of our pants.

I had no idea, for instance, when I arrived in Syria that I was supposed to pay 'courtesy calls' on the wives of fellow diplomats – thank God for AW's secretary, Dora, who was experienced and told me these things. Courtesy visits are supposed to last for about twenty minutes, but when another ambassador's wife paid a call on me she stayed for three hours telling me about her dreams; I didn't know how to get her to leave and was beginning to get a claustrophobia attack, when AW came back from the office, saw me rolling my eyes, and pretended we had to leave immediately for an urgent appointment.

But who am I to talk. At my first official meeting – to discuss the annual European Bazaar – I noticed that in pride of place on the chairperson's desk, facing us, was an ostrich egg on an elaborate carved stand. 'That's a bit dodgy,' I thought to myself, 'someone is bound to knock it over.' Someone did – me. I went up to the desk to look at the map showing the measurements of the different countries' stalls and where they would be placed in the hotel ballroom. 'How big is a metre and a half? Is it roughly like this?' I asked, flinging my arms out wide and flicking the ostrich egg off the desk and on to the floor, where it shattered.

There was a collective gasp from all the other assembled ambassadors' wives, but our chairperson was charm itself. 'Oh, please don't worry. I have others – it is nothing, nothing at all. I am not in the least upset.' But a couple of weeks later I was in a shop in the souk and the owner said to me, 'I have been asked to repair something so difficult. It is an ostrich egg in a hundred pieces.' When I next went home on leave I found an old ostrich egg in our attic – heaven knows how it got there – gave it a good scrub, and took it back to Syria for her.

The time came when we had to give our first dinner party. Who to ask was the difficulty, since our predecessor had not left us a guest list (no one ever has, but we always do). AW and I knew we wanted to invite the American Ambassador and his wife whom we'd met and liked a lot; the problem was we didn't know who to have with them since we hadn't a clue who their friends were in the diplomatic community in Damascus. Then I had a brilliant idea – we would ask AW's driver to find out. Ambassadors' drivers, I reasoned, all know each other because they spend night after night waiting together while their bosses attend parties and receptions, and of course, every driver knows where he takes his boss most regularly, and overhears his comments from the back seat. So we asked AW's super-efficient Syrian driver to find out from the Americans' driver who we should ask to a small dinner, and sure enough, they came up with the answer: the other guests should be the Russian Ambassador and a charming Armenian couple.

The dinner party went like a dream – the most surprising part being the bonhomie between the Russian Ambassador and the rest of us. In all our previous postings the Russians had been the enemy, and we never had anything to do with them. Now all of a sudden the Soviet Empire had collapsed, the Cold War was over and we could all be best pals. Indeed, the next Russian Ambassador became a very good friend, despite putting all my diplomatic skills to a severe test one evening.

Once again we were having the American Ambassador and his wife to dinner – this time it was a small birthday party for him. Eight people (his choice) were invited – the same Armenians, the Russian Ambassador and his wife, and an American couple we didn't know. The rest of us were assembled and making polite conversation when the Russians tottered in, obviously the worse for wear, and asked for whisky. Bing the butler handed out the drinks, the Russian ambassador took a sip and then cried 'What is these sheet? Give me Black Label . . .' The evening went downhill from there. I don't know how we got through it actually, with the Russian declaring his love for the US Ambassador every three minutes in yet another toast.

'Ees not jus' that I like you, I loooove you. No, I am IN LOOOOVE with you,' he would cry, looking soulfully into the embarrassed American Ambassador's eyes. Dinner ended with a sort of grand finale in which the Russian Ambassador emotionally invited us all to a party he was giving the following week – all that is, except for the new American couple, because, as he announced loudly – unmasking them in front of us all – they were 'CIA sheet'.

I am hopeless at remembering names (definitely not good when you are an ambassador's wife), especially when they are Wojtaszek or Dimirikipoulis or Djangotchian and I don't know how to pronounce them in the first place. In Syria I used to study the seating plan at official dinners and try to memorize the names of the men sitting on either side of me. Usually this worked quite well, except for one evening when I was feeling so pleased with myself for remembering my neighbour was called Mr Shukri that I inserted his name into every phrase I uttered – Mr Shukri this, Mr Shukri that, 'What do you think, Mr Shukri?' Suddenly he said, 'Mr Shukri is the gentleman on your other side. I am Mr Hamid.'

My other problem was titles – we once went to a dinner at which a fellow guest was one of the several Syrian Patriarchs of Antioch and All the East. After a couple of glasses of wine I couldn't remember whether he should be addressed as Your Beatitude or My Beatitude – or even His Beatitude, as in 'I think Your/My/His Beatitude would like the salt, please.' And then I had to resist a frightful childish compulsion to say: 'Isn't that a platitude, Your Beatitude?'

I was brought up to believe that it was my social duty to keep dinner party conversations going and fill those awful silences that can descend on a table. AW says that this means no one else can ever get a word in edgewise, but in Syria at formal dinners where often many people spoke little or no English, it was quite useful training. Though it could go wrong: once I was at a table with a group of Eastern Europeans who spoke very, very little English and for some reason that I can't remember – I sincerely hope it made sense at the time – to fill up an embarrassing conversational gap, I told the story of the Pied Piper of Hamelin. The trouble was my fellow guests believed I was telling them about something that had just occurred – that all these children had disappeared with some frightful paedophile in the last few days – and they were horrified: 'No!' they cried, 'is terrible . . .' 'Cannot believe . . .' 'What police they do?' It took me ages to make them understand that it was just the old Pied Piper legend that everyone knows; they must have gone away totally baffled.

At a dinner given by the charming Cypriot Ambassador I was seated at a table that included the Indian Ambassador. No one spoke, it was awful, so I thought I'd start the ball rolling by introducing the subject of markets, since everyone knows something about them. I chatted about markets in the Caribbean, Africa, India etc, but no one joined in; I continued doggedly – and then I noticed that the Indian Ambassador had actually fallen asleep. In desperation, I pretended I hadn't noticed and droned on. I had just got on to the subject of potatoes – sweet potatoes, new potatoes, big potatoes, small potatoes – when he woke up suddenly, said '*Fascinating!*' in a loud voice, and then slumped back into sleep.

Having not had much social life in the Gambia, we now had too much – there was some function nearly every evening, usually attended by the same group of people – the same diplomats of course, and the same social circle of Syrians around them: the Groupies, we called them. We loved the Groupies, a mixture of both Muslims and Christians, always elegant, warm and friendly and funny – we made good friends among them – but why always them? We were mystified: were others not permitted to meet us? Did they have to report on us to the Secret Police? We'd heard that most people did . . . I don't think any of us foreigners ever really understood much about what lay beneath the surface of things in Syria – which certainly contributed to AW's and my undoing later.

We presumed our phones were tapped, and that we were monitored by one or other branch of the Mukhabarat (secret police), but it was never at all obvious. Only the military attachés and the American Ambassador seemed to be openly followed when travelling outside Damascus, and even this became a bit of a joke. The American Ambassador was once *en route* across the desert to Palmyra when he noticed the security car was not behind them. He said to his driver, 'Something must have happened, we'd better go back and see if they are okay,' so they turned back and found the security car had had a puncture. The US driver gave them a hand fixing it, and then they set off again in tandem.

The British Military Attaché led us for miles and miles into the desert once, to picnic at a remote archaeological site called Jebel Sis; there were no roads and we got hopelessly lost and would have actually welcomed a little guidance from the Secret Services but, strangely, that time no one was following him.

As far as we knew, AW and I were only tailed once, when we went off exploring in the far north-east of Syria where the Iraqi, Turkish and Syrian borders meet. We got lost in the town of Qamishle and AW drove us ten times round a roundabout looking for the correct exit with the poor security car following round and round behind us. They were laughing by the time we found the right road. We were with our friends Sandy and Adrian who had come out on holiday, and we were staying in Qamishle with the

Armenian bishop who, apart from wearing a long black robe lined in purple silk, looked exactly like Robert de Niro.

On the way there we had stopped at the famous archaeological site of Tel Brak, where Agatha Christie's husband, Max Mallowan, had spent many digging seasons discovering the roots of our civilization. The site was empty: this year's archaeologists had all gone, but Adrian spotted on their rubbish dump a whole lot of ancient, not-very-broken pots they had thrown away. It was like finding a treasure trove – we wondered if it could be a mistake, but no, the pots were lying among empty water bottles and plastic bags and potato peelings. We took as many as we could carry and packed them carefully in the back of the Land Rover – but when we arrived at the Bishop's house we were a bit nervous. Suppose he saw them and reported us to the police? They'd never believe we found them on a garbage tip, so we hid them under the picnic rug. But that night, after dinner at the Armenian Club (I am still making my version of the delicious aubergine, lamb, garlic and tomato dish we ate there), the bishop showed us his own collection of things found in the fields around that his parishioners had brought him as presents.

He also told us his story. He had been a child when the Turkish massacre of the Armenians took place; the fleeing Armenians were pursued into the Syrian desert, and his parents were killed, but he was saved by a local Syrian family who took him in and brought him up. They were devout Muslims, but when he was about thirteen they reminded him that he was Christian, and proposed that he should learn about his religion. Now here he was, a bishop, no less. (It's not usually acknowledged that Syria has offered refuge to many desperate people – Iraqis, Armenians, Palestinians, Kurds, Sudanese . . . life is not easy for these groups, who still often live in refugee camps, but at least they are not in danger.)

In England a middle-aged woman like me is usually invisible. I've endured so many conversations in which the men in the group have never looked in my direction once – only at the younger women. But in Syria I used to get admiring glances, which made me feel terrific – until I read a booklet written for American new arrivals which said something like 'No matter how old or fat you are, in Syria, men will always notice you . . .'

That should have brought me down to earth, but I still felt good in Syria – more alive somehow, and I felt at *home*. I decided that it must have something to do with being Irish. It was obvious (to me anyway) that the Arabs and the Irish share so many characteristics: bad ones like being hot-tempered, vengeful and jealous, and good ones like charm, emotion, warmth, a liking for good company, and a love of words – a famous poet died while we were in Damascus and AW and I were astonished at the numbers of ordinary people who turned out for the funeral.

I once heard the American Ambassador telling a nervous group of tourists from the Smithsonian Institute in Washington that the gravest danger in Syria lay in overeating, because of the locals' hospitality. He was right: I've never been anywhere where the people were so anxious to make you welcome or where the food was so delicious. In Syria, the longer the hostess spends preparing a meal – chopping, stuffing, shaping, mincing, grinding, rolling (Syrian food is very labour-intensive) – the more she shows love and honour to the guests. Dinner-party tables would be groaning, and so, very soon, would we, for who could resist the tiny baby vegetables stuffed with spices and meat, minute *kebbeh* oozing pine nuts and juices, lamb in a gravy of quinces, sea bass coated with almond sauce, walnuts crystallized before their shells had hardened, miniature aubergines crammed with pistachios, and the most scrumptious thing I've ever eaten – bubbly pancakes with rosewater syrup and 'cream' made from the skin of the milk? And then there would be mounds of sweetmeats – delicate mouthfuls of pastry and nuts . . . and wonderful local chocolates made by Ghraoui (a total surprise – AW and I had not expected Syria to be the home of delicious chocs.)

There is an Arab saying, 'If you love me, eat', and sometimes AW and I came home feeling that we'd been through a trial by food. Everywhere you went people would offer you coffee or tea. AW and I drank coffee in Bedouin tents; in a soldiers' bivouac (we had to ask them politely to shift the Kalashnikov so it wasn't pointing

directly at my thigh); with beaming Druze families living in original Roman and Byzantine houses in Bosra; and of course, in shops
in the Damascus and Aleppo souks, cosy and soundproofed by the
layers of rugs hanging on the walls.

As far as food in our own house went, we inherited our predecessor's Indian cook, but she had already found another job and
was anxious to leave. We were wondering what to do when a
bright, attractive Filipina requested an interview. Marcelle had experience as a maid, but she asked if we could take her on as a cook
and train her.

'Oh God,' I said to AW, 'I just *can't* go through this all over
again,' but he said helping people to acquire skills was the most
important thing we could do and that I should try.

It turned out brilliantly – Marcelle was a natural; she learned
so quickly that our awful inaugural dinner for fifty people became
a distant memory – though it certainly helped the two of us to
bond together more like comrades-in-arms than boss and cook.

Some months after Marcelle came on to the payroll, our Sri
Lankan butler disappeared and we took on Marcelle's partner,
Bing. I could write a book about Bing – hang on, I *am* writing
a book about Bing. He was an extraordinary character: small,
hardworking, obsessive; he was meticulously tidy and the first
thing he did was put up notices in the kitchen area saying CLEAN
AS YOU WORK, WORK AS YOU CLEAN. When AW was looking for
a screwdriver soon after Bing arrived, he found all the tools had
been newly arranged in height order from the smallest screw to
the hammer.

Meriel came to stay and asked Bing how he got his name. He
told her that his mother had been playing bingo when she went
into labour. Meriel turned to me and said 'Bridge,' that being my
nickname, 'knowing your mum's passion for cards, you could have
been called . . . Oh Lord, you *were*!' Our guests always adored Bing:
they were fascinated by him – and he was a never-ending source
of anecdotes. William Dalrymple even wrote about him in the
preface for *From the Holy Mountain*.

My own favourite Bing story took place after AW was invited
by a friend to visit his factory, which made all kinds of paper prod-

ucts – disposable nappies, tissues, toilet paper, etc. As he left he was presented with boxes and boxes of these, which he brought home and asked Bing to divide equally between himself and Marcelle, Nabila – our Palestinian maid, Khaled the gardener, and AW and me. Soon afterwards AW and I were having a quiet drink with a friend in the drawing room when Bing flung open the door.

'Excuse me, madam,' he said in ringing tones, 'do you still use sanitary napkins?'

Then there was the time that AW had to go to Aleppo to meet the Governor, a most important figure. Ever since I'd taken his dinner jacket instead of his dark suit to the office for the State Opening of Parliament in Barbados, AW has never trusted me to pack his bags – in Syria he always asked Bing to do it for him.

We arrived in Aleppo after a long drive and found a message at the reception desk saying *'Le Gouverneur d'Aleppe vous attend'*, so AW rushed to our room to get dressed – and found that Bing had forgotten to pack a tie. Panic! We ran into the hotel shop and bought their only one, a lurid looking thing, and AW hurried off to his meeting. Afterwards we went to dinner with friends and returned to the hotel at about 11 p.m. – to find Bing sitting patiently in the foyer with ties draped all over his lap. He had discovered his mistake and had *taken a taxi* for the five-hour drive to Aleppo, bringing a choice of ties. Of course AW had to pay the taxi fare; grumpily, he sent Bing back on the bus.

(The next time we visited Aleppo, AW had to chair a meeting at the Chamber of Commerce. They gave him a magnificent throne to sit on at the head of the table, but while he was speaking its legs collapsed, and in mid-sentence AW slowly slid under the table and disappeared from sight.)

Not long after the tie episode, AW and I came back to Damascus after a weekend away exploring archaeological sites and Bing opened the front door to us, immaculate as ever in his white uniform – but with two black eyes and a huge dressing on his nose. He had been in a fight with another Filipino, and AW had to defend him in court.

★　　★　　★

A friend in Brussels sent us a present when we were posted to Syria. It was a book called *Monuments of Syria*, and it became our most valuable possession. The author was Ross Burns who had been Australian Ambassador in Syria in the 1980s and become fascinated by the country. The Syrians should give him a medal for his work – back in Australia, between postings, Burns researched and wrote about almost every archaeological site in the country, from Neolithic through Hittite, Aramean, Greek, Nabatean, Roman, Byzantine, Umayyad, Abassid, Crusader, Mamluke, Ottoman and everything else in between.

It was Ross Burns's book that directed us to the Burqush valley, half an hour's drive from Damascus, which became AW's and my choice for walks in the evenings. It was in a military area, but since we had diplomatic number plates our car was allowed in. Burqush was perfect, and I wish I could go back there right this minute. In the valley was an ancient well to which, at the end of the day, shepherds brought their flocks of sheep and goats, making the whole scene look exactly like an illustration for the Bible. On a hill above the well stood a Roman temple and a Byzantine church, and dotted all about the hillsides were the tombs of the people who'd worshipped there two thousand years before.

At weekends, our lives became entirely dictated by *Monuments*. AW would look through it and find something that sounded interesting, and we would take off – often with the driver, who by now had become what Victorian travellers in the region called a dragoman, i.e. our guide and interpreter. Our favourite two-day trip was south to Bosra, where there is a Roman town and amphitheatre – and also a good hotel – and from there we would explore the region. In the course of our travels we became friendly with all kinds of shop-owners, local 'experts', children – and tomb robbers. Syria is so teeming with ancient remains that treasure-hunting is quite a profitable hobby – I dread to think of the priceless artefacts that have found their way out of the country.

I remember visiting the great site of Apamea – everyone there seemed to be walking bent double, staring at the ground. Was this some genetic fault in the population? No, it had rained heavily the night before and they were all searching for antique coins or curiosities that might have been exposed in the newly washed earth. Once AW, walking in the desert, kicked up a stone – except it wasn't a stone, it was part of a child's toy chariot, we were told by the museum, dating back three thousand years.

In some ruin or another in Syria we met a young man who told us that he knew someone who had found the skeleton of a giant eight metres tall, buried in the desert. I got frightfully excited about this, because in Ross Burn's book it mentions that some people believe that there *were* once giants in the area – plus, I had visited Abel's tomb and it was exactly eight metres long. It all made perfect sense. The young man said he would ask the person he knew to come next day to meet us, bringing proof of his discovery (a colossal toe?), but sadly he never showed up. AW said he knew all along that it was rubbish, but I still believe every word.

When we first went to Syria with Hester and Claudia for the Easter holidays, we were taken round Bosra by a guide who showed us what he called the Pig Breast's house and the Pig Breast's place of worship. Who or what on earth could the Pig Breast be, we wondered? We imagined some porky version of the wolf that suckled Romulus and Remus . . . but we soon realized that Arabs mix up Ps and Bs (they don't have a P in their alphabet), and that our guide was talking about a Big Priest. (On the backs of Syria buses are written the touching words GOOD PYE.) This reminded me of the guide my sister and I once hired in Bangkok who kept telling us about the famous ruler Lama Frip – we only discovered when we read the guide book later that he was actually called Rama V.

In Bosra there was a pleasant shop-owner whom AW and I saw every time we went there. I always forgot that he belonged to a Muslim sect that cannot touch women, and used to hold out my hand to shake his, and he would put his hand on his heart. After this had happened about five times, I apologized for my thoughtlessness and he said, 'Oh Mrs, I would so much like to handle you, but I cannot.'

★   ★   ★

It was a wonderful, hopeful time to be in Syria. Bill Clinton came for talks with the President, Hafez al-Assad. Peace between Syria and Israel seemed imminent; it looked as though the Golan Heights would be returned, and the people of Syria were bubbling with excitement and joy. An end to hostilities – normality – was what everyone longed for. All the Syrian businessmen began buying land along the old road between Damascus and Jerusalem – the road on which St Paul was struck from his horse by God – suddenly now known as the Road to Peace. They believed that their plots would be great investments for hotels and restaurants and petrol stations and so on, needed by the flood of tourists from Israel. And then came the catastrophe: Rabin was assassinated; peace talks collapsed. The dizzy euphoria that had gripped everyone evaporated – Syria was plunged into the deepest gloom. It was a tragedy.

For us, downcast and disappointed as we were, the country was still enthralling. Even the annual Remembrance Day service held in the British War Cemetery in our suburb of Mezze was gripping. Not only was it led by a mullah, an Anglican vicar, an Orthodox priest and the Papal Nuncio, but the place where we were standing had been the scene of one of the saddest battles of the Second World War, when the Vichy French and the Free French fought each other through the vineyards and orchards for control of Damascus. British, Indian and Australian soldiers supported the Free French; African soldiers from their colonies supported Vichy. The thought of Africans and Indians dying in Syria, in a European war, seemed almost too poignant to bear. I wrote a little piece about this for the *Daily Telegraph* and received a letter from an old Indian officer: he remembered fighting his way through the war cemetery, he wrote, and resolving that he would not join the dead already lying there.

AW and I liked to go and sit in the Great Mosque of Damascus at the end of the day, during the evening prayer; we went so often, in fact, that I had my own *chador* made so that I didn't have to go through the tourist entrance and hire one every time. We found the mosque such a calm and spiritual place, which was not surprising, I suppose, since people had been praying on that site for more than three thousand years: it had been a place of worship for the Arameans, the Greeks and the Romans; then it became a Christian church and finally, in the seventh century, a mosque. It was not quite so calming the evening AW went by himself and, when he came to leave, discovered that someone had stolen his shoes. He had to steal someone else's – old white winklepickers were the only ones that fitted – just to get home.

Damascus was the kind of place in which you felt that odd, inexplicable things could happen – and indeed, it was there that I heard of a young woman who had had visions of the Virgin Mary and owned an icon that leaked oil. I went to interview her for the *Independent* feeling quite nervous about chatting to someone who talked directly to God, but in fact Myrna Nazzour turned out to be a perfectly normal twenty-nine-year-old, with a hairdresser husband, Nicholas, and two children.

Myrna's tale hinges on a small, cheap reproduction of a Russian icon of the Virgin and Child in a tacky white plastic frame. Nicholas, then Myrna's fiancé, bought ten of these in a souvenir shop in Bulgaria on his way back from a trip to Eastern Europe in 1982, as presents for his Greek Orthodox family. He was not in the least religious, but the little pictures were a snip at 25 cents each.

Eight of them were distributed among his family but two were left over, and when he and Myrna got married, they put them on their bedside table. Six months later, Myrna noticed what seemed to be water on the table. She started to mop it up and realized that it was oil, not water, and that it was leaking out of one of the little icons. She put the icon in an ashtray but the oil spilled over and she had to put it in a mixing bowl. Next thing, the by-now-frightened Myrna found that the palms of her hands were leaking oil. (The oil has been analysed: it is olive oil.) News of all this spread around Damascus, and very quickly the Greek Orthodox church sent priests to investigate what was happening; they were swiftly followed by two men from the Secret Police who arrived with a doctor. The policemen took the icon out of its frame and tore off a small piece of one corner to take away for examination, then they made Myrna wash her hands, and the doctor examined her to see that nothing was hidden on her arms. He rubbed her palms to see if anything was secreted on them: there wasn't, but immediately more oil seeped out. The police, a bit rattled by now, put the icon back in its frame, whereupon oil began to leak out of it again. They left saying 'God is Great'.

People began to flock to the house to ask Myrna to pray with them. Nicholas told me that it was all a bit of a nightmare: they had been married for only six months and suddenly their house was full of people and they never had any privacy. Then one day Myrna was on the flat roof of her house hanging out the washing, when the Virgin Mary appeared to her. Myrna said she was frightened and wanted to run away, but she knelt down and put her hands on the Virgin's feet – 'They were warm,' she told me. I thought that was an extraordinary detail that no one would think of inventing.

The Virgin appeared four more times in the next couple of years. Her message to Myrna was always the same: she should ask people to pray for peace and for the reconciliation of all the Christian churches – indeed of *all* believers. (This is particularly apt in Syria where there are so many different versions of Christianity: Greek Orthodox, Greek Catholic, Anglican, Syriac, Nestorian, Armenian, Armenian Catholic and so on.)

I believed the story – I still do. I don't understand it but I know they are not making it up. They gained nothing material from it (no donations are allowed), and their lives were completely altered. As the Papal Nuncio said, when I asked him about it: 'Neither of them was religious at all, and now they lead a life of prayer. You could possibly fake that for a few months, but not for twelve years.'

Long after I'd done the interview, I'd pop in and see Myrna and Nicholas because as well as finding the story intriguing and liking them, being with Myrna gave me an extraordinary sense of peace. I still keep in touch and last autumn helped arrange a visit by Myrna to Britain.

Back in England, our daughters were at last doing fine. AW and I always went home for the summer holidays, and we usually spent Christmas in Somerset, but Hester and Claudia came out to Syria every Easter – once we went skiing in Lebanon, and once to visit Petra in Jordan. Hester was at Edinburgh University and Claudia half-studying for A-levels. (I say half-studying, because I am writing this years later, knowing the exam results.)

But my poor darling parents were ailing – my mother had now developed full-blown Alzheimer's and my father was trying to cope. I felt wretched that I wasn't there to help more; my sister Tessa, who lived far from them, near Carlisle, was bearing the brunt of it all. Then, in the middle of our posting to Syria, my mother's health suddenly deteriorated and she died; I didn't get back in time to be with her when it happened, which I have felt guilty and sad about ever since. She was buried on my parents' sixty-fifth wedding anniversary. My father died eight months later. Tessa and I felt utterly bereft – as everyone does when much-loved parents die. After the funeral she and Malcolm came back to Syria with us; it was February and the weather was terrible but at least, for once, we were together.

While they were with us I had to begin organizing a party for a group of VIPs from Brussels who were coming on an official visit the following month. I was on the telephone, making arrangements for the evening's entertainment with the restaurant manager, when Tessa says she was startled to hear me ask, 'Well, how many whirling dervishes *can* I have?'

Over time, AW and I explored the length and breadth of the country. We got lost in the Aleppo souk (you really need to leave a trail there, like Hansel and Gretel, in order to find your way out); we ate kebabs sitting beside the Euphrates in Deir Zor; we trudged round the big sites like Palmyra and Apamea, and found the small ones which only Ross Burns seemed to know about. Often we would find ourselves quite alone in these places. I remember visiting the crusader castle of Saône on a wild blustery day with clouds scudding across the sky; we could almost smell the fear of the European knights as they huddled in the keep and listened to Saladin's army smashing its way through to them. Sometimes we made our own discoveries: the most thrilling was when some children showed us a Roman tomb in their neighbour's garden – it had stone statues cut out of the natural rock

all around the sides. While we were in Damascus, Japanese archaeologists discovered two new underground tombs in Palmyra and
we rushed to visit them – sand had filled the vaults for centuries
and the newly uncovered carvings looked as fresh as if they had
just been finished.

Part of the excitement of sightseeing in Syria was the element
of real adventure – even danger. The sites were not sanitized for
tourists. A mud wall five thousand years old might fall on you at
Mari, or, at Resafe, you could drop through a small hole in the
ground into a vast underground cistern that you didn't know existed.
(I still shiver when I remember our narrow escape there.)

The one place we didn't explore much at that time – a bit like
never visiting the Tower when you live in London – was the Old
City of Damascus itself. For a year, I used to go there once a week
to help the Mother Teresa nuns with the elderly women in their
care, but I usually came straight back since AW would send someone
to take me home – I didn't dare drive in Damascus those days.
Middle-class Syrians didn't go to the Old City – just after we
arrived, a couple of restaurants opened in old courtyard houses
there, and the Groupies were astounded. 'Who on earth would
travel all the way to the Old City to eat at night?' they asked. But
the restaurants were hugely successful, and many more have opened
since.

In the Catholic Church in Damascus I had met and become
friendly with an eccentric English lady called Fatie Darwish.
Fatie must have been pushing eighty, but she buzzed with energy
and always had some generous project on hand, whether it was
collecting blankets for the local orphanage, making marmalade
for the European bazaar, finding accommodation for some British
student she'd been asked to look after, or guiding a group round
the Old City. She was married to a Syrian doctor and had lived
in Damascus for years – at one time she'd been a disc jockey on
the local radio. Somehow you only find Faties in places like
Damascus.

One day she asked me if I'd like to go with her to see a house
in the Old City that had come up for sale. I had never been into
one of the private courtyard houses and I thought it might be fun,

so I agreed – little knowing as I set off from my suburb that I was embarking on the road to Damascus in more ways than one.

We were let into the house by friends of the owner, and stepped through the door from a dark and dingy alleyway into a sun-filled courtyard with a fountain; there was jasmine flowering in great tumbling clumps, and all around were ornate stone doorways leading into mysterious, dark rooms. But Fatie hurried me along – she had something more exciting to show. She took my arm and led me up a flight of dirty stairs and down a dusty corridor to a window on a landing that looked into the main reception room. There she tugged open the window and pushed me forward to look through it. I gazed down into a huge, highly-decorated room that glittered and sparkled and glinted like a jewel box, and I was dazzled. I had never seen anything like it in my life before. The room was painted a pale duck-egg blue, there was a golden frieze of exquisitely carved wood all around the walls, there were cupboard doors made of more lacy gilt wood backed with mirrors, there were wall-paintings of views of the Bosphorus, marble mosaic floors and a fountain. It was stunning – but it was also full of charm and warmth. If a room could smile, it was smiling at me, and I was bewitched. From that moment on I was hopelessly, obsessively, in love with Damascus.

What made my passion all the more intense was that this house was in a terrible state; like most of the courtyard houses in the Old City, it was almost derelict. The wealthy families who once lived in these palaces abandoned them *en masse* in the early part of the last century, and moved out to the suburbs – partly because it was difficult to get a motor car through the ancient narrow streets, and partly because the huge courtyard houses needed large extended families living in them to keep them going, and these were no longer the norm. The great houses were now divided up and shared by many poor families, and they were beginning to fall down.

I couldn't bear to think that all this loveliness was on the verge of collapse. The house had to be saved. I rushed home and told AW that we had to sell everything we had, and buy the house and restore it. AW said, 'Are you mad?' so I had to think of something else. I rang a millionaire in Saudi Arabia whom I'd never met and asked him to come and see it; he came, but he didn't buy it. I showed it to a Kuwaiti princess, but she didn't want it either (she had already bought another house). My only hope was to write about the house for the *World of Interiors* magazine, and see if a buyer showed up. A photographer friend, Tim Beddow, agreed to fly out and take the pictures. Next thing, I was contacted by Nora Jumblatt, the Damascus-born wife of the Druze leader in Lebanon; she had read the article and wondered if she could see the house.

I had met the beautiful Nora briefly once before, and happened to mention that my daughter Claudia was doing her A-levels. Now, eight months or more later, she came up to Damascus to look at the house and the first thing she said to me was: 'How did Claudia get on with her A-levels?' She has been my heroine ever since. Nora bought the house and has spent the last few years restoring it – it will, one day, be the most beautiful place in the world.

This should have cured my missionary zeal, but it didn't. I lobbied academics and civil servants to do something about Old Damascus; I spent hours with the boss of Shell, trying to persuade him to put up the money to restore a small souk, and I became the biggest bore at parties, nagging at my fellow guests to buy houses and restore them. Eventually one of them said, 'If it is such a brilliant idea, why don't you do it yourself?'

That was it: I now knew I had to buy a small house and restore it – it was up to me to set the example. I began to believe that I had been specially sent to Damascus, not by the EC but by God, in order to save the Old City. The trouble was, as AW pointed out many times, we simply didn't have the money to embark on such a project. (I'd already tried to persuade him to move the EC Residence into an old house; he was getting fed up, if not slightly worried that I was becoming unhinged.) I knew we couldn't buy a house in old Damascus, but I spent every spare moment looking at what was for sale there. The cheapest house I found was a tiny place behind the Great Mosque – it had a very small courtyard and four rooms. I yearned for it, I lay awake at night designing it in my mind, but I knew it was hopeless.

And then something extraordinary happened: my sister and I each were left money by a relative we had never even met; he had been an architect, which reinforced my idea that it was all *meant*. My share of the inheritance was enough to buy the little house, and AW obligingly asked the Syrian government for permission for me to do this (non-Arabs were not allowed to buy property in Syria at that time).

The morning I received the key to my new house was the worst of my life. I let myself in and stood in the hideous little courtyard and looked at the thick grey paint all over the walls, at the stained basin and rusty taps in the corner and the filthy cement floor, and the scales fell from my eyes. I burst into tears. What on earth had I done? I *must* have been mad. No one could ever make this place attractive, no Damascene would come back to the Old City because of my house, I would never be able to sell it for what I had paid (I suspected that, since I was a foreigner, noughts had been added to the price). I wished I'd never heard of Damascus, let alone lived there, let alone wasted all my money on buying this dump.

I climbed up a rickety ladder on to the roof and was looking around bleakly at the desolate view of decayed houses, when I suddenly saw, poking up from a neighbouring courtyard, a long stick with a black flag on it waving to and fro. I was seized with fear – here, behind the Great Mosque, I must be the only Christian inhabitant. This was the Muslim area, the black flag was obviously a call for action against me – some sort of *jihad* against the intrusion of an infidel. But then a flock of pigeons landed on the roof of the black flag house and I realized that it belonged to a pigeon fancier: waving the flag was his way of calling the birds. It was such a relief; but the house was still hideous, and I couldn't confide in AW or sob on his shoulder, since he had advised against the project from the very beginning.

I asked Naim, a young Syrian architect friend, if he would take on the restoration of the little house. At that time I was writing a column for Sainsbury's *Magazine*, and I worked out that over the months my fee would cover the work. So Naim's team started cleaning off the hideous grey paint and one day he telephoned, telling me to get to the Old City as quickly as I could. He wouldn't say why, just that I would be pleased. I rushed to the house and found that another miracle had taken place: behind the grim grey paint and plaster covering the courtyard walls were all sorts of decorations: carved stone window frames, Mamluke blocks with coloured designs on them (re-used from another building), and a blocked-up doorway – indicating that my little house had once been the small courtyard of a big house next door, long since separated off.

It took a long, long time, with some serious hiccups on the way (such as when the authorities demolished my new room on the roof because they said I didn't have planning permission for it), but it was eventually finished and furnished. Three designer friends, Kaffe Fassett, Candace Bahouth and Brandon Mably, who were staying with us then, came to inspect it – their verdict was that it was perfect: 'A tiny jewel box,' Kaffe said. And so it was: Naim had done a fantastic job.

According to the local custom, I arranged for the butcher who lived two doors down the road to sacrifice a ram (I was far too squeamish to attend this ritual) and we distributed the meat to poor families in the area, and then AW and I had a party to celebrate and invited our particular Groupie and Dip. Corps friends. Afterwards we took the last of the guests to our local *sharwarma* (doner kebab) shop for a snack.

'Who are all these people?' the owner asked AW in Arabic.

'Well, they are the Dutch Ambassador, the Swiss Ambassador, the French Ambassador . . .'

'Oh yes,' said the *sharwarma* shop man, 'and I'm Mickey Mouse.'

AW and I went to live in the house – and the very next day had to move out again because the lavatory was blocked (by a floor cloth that had gone down the drain when the house was being cleaned – Bing?), but we moved back in soon afterwards. Every morning we would be woken by the haunting chorus of the dawn call to prayer from the Great Mosque, and then go back to sleep again. Later, I would walk a few yards up the road from my front door, carrying our own plates to be filled with *hummus* and *fuls* (beans) and pickles for breakfast, and on the way back I'd buy bread, still untouchably hot from the oven.

AW and I now made up for lost time and explored the nooks and crannies of the Old City – the ancient flour mills down by the river, Roman gateways in unexpected places, the wool souk, the new gold souk, the copper souk and so on – and we watched the world go by: Iranian women pilgrims enveloped in *chadors* visiting the tomb of the Prophet Mohammed's great-granddaughter, not far from my house, modest Syrian women in scarves and raincoats, other glitzy Syrian girls with big hair and short skirts. We passed tattooed old ladies wearing wimples, from Hauran in southern Syria; we met an old man who had brought a haversack of lapis lazuli all the way from Afghanistan by train and bus; we saw fuel oil delivered by horses decked out in beads and ostrich feathers. And on a stall in the Hamidiyyeh souk I found crotchless musical knickers – they worked on tiny batteries and for some unaccountable reason played Rudolph the Red-Nosed Reindeer. I bought a couple of pairs as a joke for Hester and Claudia's Christmas stockings, and as I walked away the vendor called me back: 'Extra batteries for you,' he said grinning, pressing them into my hand.

All this (well, not the knickers) was valuable stuff, for in the meantime, Tim Beddow, the photographer, had fallen as much in love with Damascus as I had, and we had decided to do a book together on the houses of the Old City. This was the plan: I would go round and find houses for him to photograph, and when I had several organized, he would come out from London to photograph them, and then I would seek out another batch.

It took months and months to do the pictures. I would knock on the doors of likely-looking houses, and when they asked who was there, I would call out in my newly learned Arabic, 'I am the wife of the European Ambassador,' knowing that the curiosity of the people inside – usually the wife – would lead them to open the door. No man could have done this, because no Syrian woman would have opened the door to him, no matter who he was, but once I'd made a proper appointment for Tim, we had no problems with him taking pictures.

One afternoon, walking wearily back down Straight Street after photographing some houses in the Christian quarter, Tim and I saw a small crowd. As we passed, we glanced across to see what they were all looking at, and to our horror we saw that it was a huge eagle – they were pulling it this way and that, holding out its enormous wings. We stopped to ask what was happening and were told that one of the men was a taxidermist, and another was his client, and they were trying out some poses to see what position the bird should be stuffed in once they had killed it.

We were appalled and decided to buy the eagle; I seem to remember Eddie (as we had already named him) cost about £12 after some negotiation. The crowd thought this was hilarious; someone fetched an enormous cardboard box to put the huge bird in, and, stopping at a butcher's to buy some lamb chops on the way, we carried it to our rendezvous with the driver who was going to take us home in our Land Rover. Tim and I were so proud of ourselves that we went to AW's office first, so that we could show the eagle to him immediately. AW came down, looked in the box and said 'That's not an eagle, it's a vulture.'

We looked Eddie up in the bird book when we got home and AW was right: he was a Common Indian Vulture – the only one in Syria, it seemed, because it was not a native bird. Don't ask me why Tim and I hadn't noticed that Eddie had a bald blue face and a red neck. I think we were tired.

First we fed Eddie the lamb chops in the garden (the tearing and gobbling was quite an unpleasant sight), and then I put on rubber gloves and wrapped my hands in towels – Eddie's beak was about four inches long and deadly sharp – and cut the string that tied his legs together. 'Okay Eddie, that's it, you are free to fly now. Go into the wild where you belong, or rather, don't belong . . .' But Eddie just sat there, shoulders hunched, baleful eyes staring at us ungratefully. We suddenly realized he didn't know how to fly.

For two days he hopped about the garden, doing massive poos on our outdoor furniture, picking up the glass ashtrays in his beak and dropping them, and terrifying Khaled, the gardener, so he refused to come to work. AW said we'd have to get rid of him, and I could see his point. A vulture is not exactly the bird of choice for ornamenting an ambassador's Residence. We decided the only place to take him – because it was the least likely one in which he would be caught and taken straight back to the souk – was our favourite walking spot, Burqush.

AW and I, plus twenty-four more lamb chops, and Eddie in his box in the back of the Land Rover, drove through the military checkpoint and stopped by a lonely cave in the valley. There was no one around. Wrapping our hands and arms in towels again, we took Eddie out of the box and put him in the cave with the chops. We went back two days later to deliver some chicken – and it had all been worth it: Eddie was standing on a rock, the sun on his blue head, the wind ruffling his feathers, looking out over his valley. Two days later when we went with more food he had gone.

'Are you looking for the big bird?' an old shepherd asked us. 'He flew away yesterday.' I often wonder if Eddie's homing instinct could have got him back to India. I hope so. Or perhaps the old shepherd had already taken him back to the souk.

The photography for our book was nearly finished, and Thames & Hudson, the glossy publishers, were interested – but only if we could get a sponsor to help with the costs. Then another of the minor miracles that had, from the very beginning, helped my Saving Damascus project along, took place. My old friend Valerie Grove (whose Dalmatian ate all the Smarties at Hester's first birthday party) suggested that we should approach Wafic Saïd, the millionaire who was then building a new business college at Oxford University, for help. She had just interviewed him for *The Times*, and they'd got on well.

'Ask him,' she suggested, 'he was born in Damascus. And mention my name.'

She was right: Wafic Saïd agreed, not just to sponsor any old book, but to pay for a lavish and beautiful production.

We should have already left Syria by then, but the year before, in 1997, AW had asked for his posting to be extended – a favour to me because the restoration of the little house and the photography for the book had to be finished. But now, even the extra twelve months we'd been given were nearly over.

That summer we went on leave from Damascus for the last time. Diplomats in Syria had a fast track through the airport, bypassing many of the formalities. As the driver shepherded us past a long queue of British tourists having their luggage searched, one of them looked at us crossly. 'It must be nice, not being Ordinary People,' she said in a loud and sarcastic voice. I thought about this on the plane going home. The ex-pat's life with all its homesickness and loneliness and privilege and perks, with its dizzy ups and miserable downs, was certainly not ordinary. And yes, at that moment, riding high, it did seem very nice.

But a few weeks later in Damascus, at 8.30 a.m. on 8 September to be precise, I would have given anything to be the most ordinary person in the world – to be anyone else in fact, except myself. After five and a half years of happiness in Syria, of so much achieved by AW professionally, and so many good relations established, something terrible happened.

This story goes back to two years earlier, when an American teacher, married to a Syrian, had begged AW to sponsor an international school through the Foreign Ministry, and he had agreed since there was no such school in Syria at that time.

There had been lots of problems with the school along the way, some of them serious, and a feud had broken out between the American Headmistress and the Syrian Deputy, which threatened to divide it into two rival camps. In the end AW, as Chairman of the Board, had asked the Deputy to resign. After a lot of argument and discussion, she had eventually agreed. By the end of the summer holidays that last year of ours, it seemed that all the problems had been resolved; the school had been re-painted, extra staff hired – including a new and well-respected Deputy – and it had expanded to 280 students, with waiting lists for every class.

AW flew off to Brussels for an EC meeting, early on that morning of 8 September; it was the day the school opened for the new academic year but he had no worries on his mind. At about the time the wheels of his plane were leaving the ground, I got a phone call from the American Headmistress – the police had come and closed the school.

I couldn't believe it – it must be some silly mistake that could be cleared up in a moment. I rang an influential minister we knew and liked, and begged him to do something. It was not so simple, he told me, gravely, AW should never have dismissed the Deputy, she had powerful friends . . .

He said that he would try to help, but that it might not be possible for him to do anything, because of the story the Deputy had told. When I heard what the story was rumoured to be (no one ever told us directly) I went into shock. The Deputy had, apparently, copied every reference to Israel in the school textbooks (many of which were the same as the ones used by the American school) and had gone to the Secret Police with a dossier, accusing us of having some sort of involvement with that country. I had never heard anything so ridiculous. AW and I? It was absurd, particularly given our strong views about the injustice inflicted on the Palestinians by the occupation of their land: we were probably the last two people on earth likely to be working for the Israelis. But in Syria – as in the old Soviet Union, where every stranger was presumed to be a spy – many people assumed that all foreigners were gathering information in one way or another, so her story fell on ground that was not infertile.

I won't go into the torture of the next six weeks – made worse by the fact that we had to try and unravel the problem before the deadline of our departure. Hundreds of children now had no school to attend; parents were telephoning all day and night wanting to know what was happening . . . as if we knew. AW appealed to people in high places (some of whom had children in the school); he used every contact he had made; our dear Groupie friends tried so hard to help; but no one was able to get the school reopened. Our ambassador colleagues were wonderful, I am eternally grateful to them: they made a *démarche* – an official complaint – to the Foreign Ministry, but even that didn't work. AW and I were sleepless and worried out of our minds; the Headmistress was on the verge of collapse.

A dark cloud hung over us. The official story about the closure of the school was that it had not conformed to all the conditions set out by the Ministry of Education – I don't know if this was true or not, but if it *had* been the case, it could have been put right in a moment, and the school reopened. As it was, the Minister of Education refused to see AW.

AW had expanded the office in Damascus, he had worked so hard and done so much to build up relations between Europe and Syria and he had a marvellous team at work whom he, and I, really liked. Now they too seemed to turn hostile – perhaps they believed the story about the school, perhaps they thought we were foolish to have got involved with it in the first place, perhaps it was because we had suddenly become so vulnerable.

Looking back, I think some of it was my fault – I act impulsively; I don't think things through. I had encouraged AW to support the school because I liked the Headmistress (and, ironically, the Deputy) and it seemed such a good idea. I learned a hard lesson from all this – never again to interfere in *anything* to do with AW's work – but I have to say, when the office is the whole reason for your being in a place, it's almost impossible not to be, at the very least, interested in it.

In the meantime my only consolation was to think of Isobel Burton who, as the wife of Richard Burton (British Consul in Damascus in 1870), had lived in and loved the city more than a century before my time. Richard Burton had upset the rich and the powerful (in particular the Jewish moneylenders) by his refusal to take bribes and his insistence on fairness – and he had been recalled from his post when his enemies complained to London. He left Damascus immediately, issuing the famous instruction to his wife Isobel to 'Pay, pack and follow.' She described the afternoon before he received the news that he would have to leave, as 'My last happy day'. I felt the same now about the day before the school was closed – though AW was not being recalled or leaving early, but on the scheduled date, for a new posting in Brussels.

We went through the formalities of departure – presentations, farewell parties – as though nothing had happened, but we all knew that AW and I were still under a cloud; and the school remained closed. I cried all the way home on the plane – it was the first time in my life that I didn't worry about it crashing, in fact I almost wanted it to – for the pain of leaving a place I loved so much, for

the unfairness of it all, and most of all for the miserable way AW
had been rewarded for all his hard work and genuine love for the
country.

AW went back to work in Brussels for the first time in sixteen
years, and I stayed in England to finish the book on Damascus.
Strangely, I felt sad, not angry, and I was homesick enough to keep
my watch on Syrian time. I remembered the story about the scorpion who asks a frog to give him a ride across a river.

'But you will sting me to death,' says the frog.

'No, no, of course I won't,' says the scorpion, 'If I did we would
both drown, so what would be the point?'

So the frog agrees, and the scorpion climbs on to his back.
Halfway across the river the scorpion stings the frog. As they both
start to drown, the frog asks 'Why, oh why did you do it?'

'I'm so sorry,' says the scorpion, 'I couldn't help it: it's my nature.'

There are lots of versions of the story, and I have been told it
to illustrate the way people behave in every country I've lived in,
from the Caribbean to India, to West Africa and to Syria. AW's
and my story, I told myself, was just another example of the unpredictable side of human nature. It was just a hell of a shame that
we'd had to be the frog.

Damascus: Hidden Treasures of the Old City was published eighteen months later, and to our delight (and amazement) the Syrian
Ambassador in London threw a party to launch it. Then yet another
of those strange miracles happened: I met Suzy Menkes, the powerful fashion editor of the *International Herald Tribune*, at a magazine
party and she reviewed the book for her paper, giving it the prized
back-page slot. It was odd that I had been invited to the party,
odder still that I was for once in London and able to go to it, and
oddest of all to bump into her there, for I had not seen or spoken
to Suzy for twenty-five years, since we were both young fashion
journalists and friends. If that wasn't Fate, I don't know what it
was – for her review led to my being asked by the World Monuments
Fund to lecture on the Old City at the Royal Geographical Society
(a prospect so terrifying that I actually threw up in the photo lab
when I went to collect my slides) and to guide a prestigious group

of their Trustees around Damascus. When I went back to Syria with the group we were made welcome everywhere. I felt that I had somehow been redeemed and restored.

Wounds seemed to have healed in Syria, and our own were scarring over, but perhaps they were still a little sore back at head office. Or was it mere coincidence that when AW was due for another posting abroad a couple of years later, he was sent to Kazakhstan – land of the Soviet gulags? Whatever. The fact is that we are there now – and he loves it.

12

The Fearful Road to Samarkand

Almaty, 20 April

I flew back to Kazakhstan yesterday. A grumpy security woman at Heathrow confiscated my nail clippers and tweezers, and took a corkscrew off the man standing next to me. He and I started to joke about hijacking a plane with a pair of nail clippers and a small corkscrew, but the stony-faced security woman overheard and ticked us off.

'You may think you are very amusing,' she said, 'but this is a serious matter.'

On the other hand, she let a man go through with a picture in a frame. Mr Corkscrew and I agreed that it would be easy to smash the glass and use the shards as a weapon, but we didn't say anything.

It was pouring with rain and pitch dark when I arrived, but this morning it is as though I am in a different world from the one I left a month ago – everything was black and white then; now it has turned into Technicolor. And, on top of everything else, Nina spoke a whole sentence in English to me at breakfast.

The rain has washed away all the snow, revealing that we live on a garbage tip . . . all the humps and bumps under the snow that I thought must be picturesque boulders and grassy hillocks turn out to be rusting containers or lumps of concrete with wires sticking out, or the carcasses of cars.

Down in the town the opposite has happened – the shabby stained concrete buildings with bits falling off are now concealed by the dense greenery of the trees that have come into leaf. The Russians planted trees on an incredible scale in this region – in Monica Whitlock's book about Central Asia, *Beyond the Oxus*, she describes how they sent no less than six million tree seedlings to Tashkent on the Transcaspian Railway in the early twentieth century, for planting in their new towns in Central Asia. And not just any old trees either: in Almaty, they planted a mixture of oriental planes, elms, limes, maples, poplars, oaks, chestnuts, and of course the tree of Russia – the silver birch. All the old streets are lined with rows of these and it is hard to believe that you are actually in a city at all. It may not always look like this though. It's said that the Kazakhs, being people of the steppe, don't care much about trees, and are cutting them down. However, right now Almaty is green and looking out of my attic window I can see, across the top of it, that the steppe is green too. I can feel my spirits lifting.

AW has a group of officials visiting from Brussels and we are giving a reception for them this evening – *eighty* people have been invited. I heard about all this in the middle of last night and almost got back on to the plane again, but it seems that Nina has the whole thing under control and all I have to do is arrange the flowers and smile.

When I was in London I heard from friends that all the time I've been here feeling lonely, so has a young woman called Lucy, who crossed Central Asia by horse and camel a couple of years ago with a group of pals from university; she has come back here to learn Russian. (Strangely enough I've met two other girls who've ridden through Central Asia, as well as a young woman and her husband who were doing the journey on a tandem tricycle – which means I now know more people who have crossed Central Asia in peculiar ways than ones who've just taken planes.) I invited Lucy to AW's reception this evening and she said she'd love to come if we didn't mind her wearing trainers, as she hadn't got any other shoes.

Later. The reception went very well; goodness knows how Nina did all the canapés and things without showing any signs of stress. I am going to shadow her every move in future, and learn how to be more organized.

Lucy (in her trainers) was lovely: quirky and funny, she could be a *friend*, even though decades younger. Also at the party were two archaeologists that AW has made friends with while I was away. Jean-Marc (Belgian) and Renato (Italian) came here a few years ago from China and India to work on the Late Bronze Age period in this region. Both are Buddhists, small, thin, wiry and poor as church mice – trainers are the least of their clothing problems; in fact when they came through the front door I was just about to say politely but firmly, 'I am sorry but I am afraid you have come to the wrong house,' when AW rushed up and they all hugged each other. They have already taken AW out exploring and, he says, they will change our lives.

22 April

Yesterday was Sunday and, led by Renato and Jean-Marc, we took the official visitors out into the steppe to look at the one sight there is to see in Kazakhstan – petroglyths. These are primitive stick-man drawings of people and animals, scratched on to rocks by tribes wandering the region in the Bronze Age. The ones we saw yesterday – at Tamgaly, about 120 kilometres from Almaty – are the best known. Renato had arranged for us to have something to eat nearby in what used to be a collective, but has now evolved into a normal village. We sat on the floor round a low, plastic-covered table in the Headman's wooden cottage, and had delicious hot fried bread dough, butter, cream, jam . . . a sort of Kazakh version of a Cornish cream tea.

The wild flowers – especially ravishing little yellow tulips – are coming out and if it would just stop raining for a bit, everything would look wonderful.

Bishkek, 23 April

Yesterday AW and Gainee, his assistant, plus the Brussels team and me, drove to Bishkek, the capital of Kyrgyzstan, which is about three hours away from Almaty. For some mysterious reason I believed Bishkek would be like a picturesque village in the Black Forest in Germany and I almost cried when we drove in and I saw it has just the same old Soviet-style crumbling apartment blocks and tacky shopping complexes as Almaty – only on a smaller scale, and more decrepit. Actually I was feeling pretty miserable anyway as this is a business trip for AW and he has no time to talk to me; I am completely redundant.

Spent today wandering round by myself and realized perhaps I'd been a bit unfair about the town. Bishkek is even greener than Almaty, full of trees and parks, but it is desperately run-down – the grass in the park is knee high. They seem to have an obsession about lilac here – the lilac trees in the parks have had all their flowers torn off and every second person is carrying a huge bunch of looted blossoms.

I went to the museum – a colossal Soviet block of a building surrounded by a vast paved piazza with fountains, but the marble facing on the façade is slipping, the paving stones are cracked with weeds growing through, and the fountains are dry and full of rubbish. Inside the huge halls the rain was dripping through the roof on to plastic sheeting draped over the display cases. I talked to a woman who worked there and she explained that, since independence, there is just no money in the coffers of the Kyrgyz government. She told me that she herself, a university graduate from Moscow, earns six dollars a month.

An enormous bronze statue of Lenin stands in front of the museum, his arm flung out dramatically towards the mountains and Afghanistan beyond. I watched people having their picture taken in front of the statue; one by one, they each copied his pose. Inside is another Lenin in the same position: it has a broken plaster hand on the outstretched arm, and the wired fingers have bent so that it looks as if he is making a very grand obscene gesture – as though he had foreknowledge of how the Soviet army was going to fare in Afghanistan years after his death . . .

AW and I are staying in the Hyatt; apparently it used to be empty, but since 11 September and the war in Afghanistan, the Americans have stationed 3,000 troops in Kyrgyzstan and the hotel is booming. It's strange to see these big, protein-fed US soldiers wandering around the lobby amongst the small Kyrgyz. It reminded me of Vietnam during the war (I went there when I was working for

the *Sunday Times* to try and make my name as a foreign correspondent – needless to say I failed, but that's another story). A plate
of biscuits was left in our room by the management and AW ate
them all, which put me in an even worse mood.

Instead of wishing I were in London with our daughters and
friends and my own life, I should accept that I am *here*, and will be
for a while, and enjoy it while I can. After all I am so spoiled, having
Nina and Ira and Yuri doing everything in the house, and I should
be appreciating that and not wishing I were somewhere else. AW
loves it here in Central Asia – he believes he was a Mongol horseman
galloping across the steppe in a previous life. I definitely know that
I was not with him in that incarnation and I really must try to stop
moaning or he'll begin to wish I wasn't in this one . . .

Almaty, 25 April

Back in Almaty and it is still raining . . . The lilac obsession seems
to have gripped people here too, everyone is carrying bunches of
it and all the little old ladies outside the market are selling stolen
branches. I bought some and, though I say it myself, did a really
beautiful flower arrangement for last night when we had Renato
and Jean-Marc and some people from the office to supper. I couldn't
help feeling rather pleased when I came into the room and found
all the guests gazing intently at my arrangement. I was going to
be very modest when they praised me, but it turned out they were
not gazing in admiration at all: they were searching for blossoms
with more than four petals because they are supposed to be lucky
here – you have to eat them and make a wish. I must say I never
thought the day would come when I'd have to contend with people
eating my flower arrangements. (Speaking of superstitions, according
to Lucy one magpie here is not unlucky – might even be lucky.
What a relief: there are a higher-than-average number of lone mag-
pies in Kaz, and now I won't have to keep saluting them all the
time and giving myself Magpie Elbow.)

I have always secretly prided myself on my talent with flowers.
The year of Princess Diana's wedding we happened to be in
Somerset for our village Horticultural Society Show. It always

has a flower arranging competition, and that year (of course) it had a Royal Wedding theme. I worked so hard on my entry – I cut every flower in our garden, combed the hedgerows, and was absolutely certain I would win. But when the judges had done and we were allowed into the hall, I saw that a hideous arrangement with tulle draped round it had First Prize, and I had just a Highly Commended card with a note written on it saying 'Very interesting but too heavy'. A farmer's wife reading this over my shoulder said 'That's always been my problem,' which cheered me up again.

It has rained so much that I am seriously worried our house will slide down the hill – or else the huge telecommunications tower on the slope behind us will topple over. I keep trying to size it up visually to see if it will fall right across our roof or just miss us and fall on the German Residence next door.

26 April

Oh God. Hester has just telephoned from Cairo, where she is working, to say that a dear friend of ours, the Egyptian writer Ahdaf Soueif, has offered to lend Hester her flat there; she is moving in day-after-tomorrow. From past experience, this could be the end of a beautiful friendship. Hester went to Australia a couple of years ago and, because we didn't know a single other soul in the whole continent, I gave her the telephone number of David Malouf, the distinguished writer, whom AW and I had met in Syria once. I told Hester that the number was for emergencies only – and I meant *life or death* emergencies. She left, and twenty-four hours later telephoned to say she had arrived safely.

'Oh darling, how wonderful,' I said, 'where are you?'

'I am in David Malouf's flat,' she said.

'*No!*' I screamed, 'what on earth are you doing there? I told you, life or death emergencies only.'

'It *was* an emergency,' said Hester, 'no one came to meet me at the airport and it was the middle of the night and I didn't know where to go so I rang Mr Malouf and he said to come here.'

Then she went on to tell me that when she drew her curtains

open that morning she had pulled them by hand instead of using the cord, and the pelmet had come off the wall, but she was sure Mr Malouf was really okay about it all, and she and her friends (whom she had finally found) were going to invite him to tea. I faxed David Malouf a grovelling apology but have never heard from him since.

Our annual Europe Day Party is on the horizon – it is planned for 24 May. AW and I wanted to have it at the newly-restored Opera House but it was too expensive. Now, by luck, we've found that someone in the office is related to one of the Opera House Director's best friends and the price is going to be adjusted so that it comes within our budget. We are so pleased.

27 April

My jaw is still giving me problems, so Elena, a doctor working in AW's office, arranged for me to see a dentist. I went along to the hospital, and the dentist had a look and then summoned an expert who suggested heat treatment. Next thing, I found myself lying on an old sofa in the expert's rather seedy office while she held a huge cigar made of 'wild grasses and herbs' (yeah right, I know marijuana when I smell it) next to my ear. I could hear it sizzling all the little hairs of my sideburns, but as the fumes wafted over my face I found I didn't care. Strangely enough it does seem to have made my jaw slightly better, but perhaps that would have happened anyway.

The cures they go in for here seem medieval. The office doctor has suggested leeches for AW's blood pressure (AW says he already has one big leech, me, and doesn't want any more). The massage lady down the road who was recommended to me for my neck/jaw (I'm trying everything) apparently goes in for 'cupping' as in *The Madness of George III*. She hasn't suggested this to me yet, but on my first visit a few days ago she advised me that I must drink tea made of *kalina* berries because, she said, she could see at a glance there was something wrong with my gallbladder. I went to find *kalina* in the Green Market (it is, apparently, what we call viburnum in England) and the juicy red berries looked positively lethal – but

Nina and Ira at home seemed to know all about it, so I'll give it a go.

I was utterly amazed at the hospital to see that Russian doctors and nurses wear tall white chef's hats – it's most unnerving having someone dressed as a cook looking at you in a medical way. Which reminds me, on the way to AW's office, we've noticed a big catering school on the right side of the road. There are pictures on a billboard outside showing a group of chefs wielding various kitchen tools, standing round a microwave oven, and a man with his mouth open looking as though he's waiting for one of them to pop a bit of pizza in it. AW and I have been impressed that Almaty runs to such a sophisticated enterprise, but yesterday, after my visit to the dentist, I was stuck in a traffic jam outside the catering school, and looking at the posters more carefully, saw that it is not a catering school at all but a *hospital*. The people in chef's hats I now realize are doctors, the microwave oven is a scanning machine, the carving knives are surgical instruments, and the poor open-mouthed man is obviously waiting for some sort of treatment.

29 April

Every time I go out for a walk near our house I come back with mud all over the backs of my trousers, and lead poisoning from the exhaust fumes of all the ancient lorries belonging to construction companies labouring up the hill with cement and bricks. There is a building frenzy in Almaty – which seems a bit odd since it is no longer the capital. Ten new houses are being built in the area where we live, and down in the town whole blocks of flats and offices in mirrored glass seem to have sprung up in a matter of weeks; the air is filled with the whine of metal saws and showers of sparks from welding.

Kazakhstan seems to be booming – it's a very different place from the one Colin Thubron travelled through soon after it became independent, when he met bewildered people who wondered who and what they were. Even Gainee (AW's assistant) has become more Kazakh: she used to dye her hair red and look as European as her high cheekbones and slanting eyes would allow – but now she has let her hair grow black, and has taken to emphasizing her Asiatic features, with red lipstick on her cupid's bow mouth (a charming feature of Kazakh faces).

The President's daughter seems to be particularly ahead of the building game. She has already opened a huge shopping mall called Silk Way and now seems to be building a version of the Great Temple at Karnak – complete with hieroglyphics – down the road from us. (Apparently it is to be a health resort – what they call a sanatorium here.) In the past couple of months two seriously flashy restaurants have opened – a Thai place with huge dragons painted on its 'oriental' wavy walls, and an Uzbek one which looks like a spectacular blue-and-white-tiled mosque. In my experience Uzbek cuisine consists of fat and gristle kebabs and greasy *plov* (rice with fat and gristle), so I am not sure why anyone would want to make a special outing to eat it; maybe that's why they had to make the building itself so fantastic.

The other day Lucy and her friends took us to eat at the place that must be the best value in Almaty – the Govinda restaurant run by the Hari Krishnas (who seem to have a big following here). For 150 tenge (under £2) you get a tray of various delicious vegetarian curries with *puris* (Indian fried bread) and wonderful creamy rice pudding. The only problem is that you can't drink or smoke in the Govinda, so once you've eaten there, the thing is to dash across the road and have a drink and a fag in the bar of the Georgian restaurant opposite.

This could also be the place to go if you are feeling depressed, because their menu translation is so hilarious. Yes, I know it's easy to laugh, and how would any of us manage even one single word in Georgian etc etc, and maybe we were just in a particularly good mood that night – but 'beef leg with giblets' somehow set us off, and then when AW noticed that lots of dishes were 'stuffed by nuts', we found ourselves weeping with laughter. (It reminded me of our first outing to a restaurant in Syria. At the top of the menu was 'Fried testicles' followed by 'Brians' – of course they meant brains, but it looked as though the testicles were Brian's. AW and I fell about.)

Speaking of food – my jaw still goes crunch when I move it,

but I think the massage may be working. I can't help feeling guilty lying there, being pounded by Milada (who is about four foot ten inches high but with the strength of ten men), except that massage is not thought of as a pampering luxury here, but as a medical treatment. And Milada tells me about what life was like in Soviet times – as with so many other people here, she is only in Kazakhstan because this is where her family were exiled in Stalin's time; two of her grandparents died in the *gulag*.

9 May

Yuri has cut me a wonderful stick for beating off attacking animals, but I must say, walks from our house are pretty dreary. You can stick to the road and set all the dogs barking behind the high corrugated iron fences round the houses, or since the snow melted, you can climb over a large garbage heap and follow a grassy path up to the top of the hill behind our house – but the trouble is there are only a couple of hundred yards of pleasant going between the heap and the deafening noise of music from the restaurants at the summit. (Normally I quite enjoy garbage tips – in fact I know someone in France who practically furnished her house from them – here though they are just full of boring lumps of concrete and rusty bits of motorcar.)

14 May

I have just been downtown and seen a huge poster announcing that Riverdance is appearing here in two days time. I'd *love* to see Riverdance in Central Asia, it would be so weird, so I asked Yuri to drive me to the ticket office – but we found all the cheap tickets had sold out and only the $50 ones are left, and I'm not going to pay $100 for a whim. But how extraordinary it is to think of the descendants of the Mongol hordes rushing to book up for Riverdance. Genghis Khan would turn in his grave.

No sooner had I written my whinge about there being nowhere to walk, than we met the German Ambassador and his wife, who live next door, coming back from a hike with their Labrador. We asked them where they'd been and now, thank goodness, we have some new places to go. One is beside a stream we didn't know existed, at the bottom of our hill. There are empty vodka and beer bottles lying around (you can't escape from litter in this country) but it's rather pretty and there are no car fumes. Another is along an old road with little wooden houses on either side. In the late afternoons there are groups of children playing tiddlywinks and hopscotch and all the games that, in the Fifties, before television, English children used to play in the street. Walking back down this road in the twilight you pass old men or women bringing their cows home from the empty lots where they've been grazing, or girls shepherding back little flocks of goats.

Best of all the new walks, if time allows (it's a short drive from the house), is a climb through abandoned apple orchards up to the top of a ridge from which you get a spectacular view of the white mountain peaks. AW and I have done it twice now and feel positively liberated.

15 May

AW gave a lunch for local journalists today. I met two Kazakh women writers who had been granted an interview by George Bush when he was Governor of Texas. They were ushered into his office and he was told they were from Kazakhstan.

'Where is that?' he asked. 'Is it near China?'

They said yes, it was actually between Russia and China.

'Is it a big country?' he enquired. Yes, they replied, it was a very big country.

'China has a great future,' he said, and they realized that was the end of the interview.

17 May

Huge scandal about Riverdance! It seems that the company that came to Almaty had only fourteen dancers and were absolutely nothing to do with the real Riverdance. Everyone is furious and wants their money back!

20 May

Off to Kyrgyzstan again, this time for AW to open the European Film Festival there. The European Film Festival is our annual nightmare – we are at the mercy of the individual European countries; we have to show whatever they choose to send out. For instance, in Syria we had the excruciating experience of having to sit next to the Governor of Aleppo in a decrepit Art Deco cinema, watching Italy's contribution: Gina Lollobrigida in a 1950s black-and-white comedy in Italian with no sub-titles. This year Spain's film launches the Festival and the Spanish Ambassador is having a freak-out because the film his country has sent is about two gays and euthanasia . . . This was the film that AW had to introduce in Bishkek, but such was the enthusiasm for a foreign film – any foreign film – that no one need have worried. It wouldn't have mattered if the subject had been watching paint dry, the tiny auditorium of Bishkek's version of Cinema Paradiso would still have been jam-packed.

AW had learned how to say 'Welcome to the audience' in Kyrgyz (a tip from the nice British Council man here), and got a standing ovation with cheering. The proprietor of the little cinema (in a pearl-studded bow tie) beamed. It was all so touching. Kyrgyz people seem to be much softer and pleasanter than Kazakhs.

23 May

Our Europe Day party is tomorrow. AW and I are in a complete panic. About 500 people have been invited but we have no confidence that any of them will turn up; our nightmare dread is that about twelve will come and our humiliation will become the gossip of *le tout Almaty*. It is at this stage, before every Europe Day party we've ever had, that AW loses his nerve and begins to invite random people he sees in the street . . .

Because the party is being held in the Opera House, some guests have rung to ask what kind of performance we are putting on. We'd like to know the answer to that question ourselves.

25 May

Hundreds of people came; we needn't have worried. In spite of the fact that the Director of the Opera House had selected *that very day* to dig up the entire parking area, it was a *success* – so much so that people were still there at 9.30 p.m., an hour after it was supposed to be over. Then, suddenly, a posse of policemen appeared from nowhere and started shooing everyone out (the police here wear extraordinary hats, like halos with peaks – they look as if they were designed by the trendy London milliner Philip Treacy). We left obediently since we'd already decided we would like to use the Opera House again next year.

27 May

Renato and Jean-Marc rang early yesterday morning, to tell us that there was to be a ceremony for Buddha's birthday in the apartment of one of the Indian Embassy people. We went along and found a motley bunch of Europeans, Indians and Mongolians, plus the only Buddhist monk in Kazakhstan (Alexei, a Ukrainian, trained in Japan), who conducted the ceremony in his saffron robes. There was a lot of monotonous chanting and one of the Indians fell asleep on the sofa and began snoring. Then the monk suddenly banged a kind of hand-held drum and the family dog started barking wildly. But in spite of all that it was rather moving, and I am glad we went.

3 June

Renato and Jean-Marc led us (AW, me, Lucy and various of their own friends) miles into the steppe to look at a site where they have excavated a Bronze Age house. It was a wonderful day; the steppe has exploded into a mass of poppies and the whole landscape, up to every horizon, is coloured red instead of green like a Fauve painting. Renato thinks Kazakhstan was the site for the Garden of Eden (it is, after all, the place where apples originated) and on a day like yesterday, even a person like me who is not stirred by vast tracts of empty countryside has to admit it is beautiful.

On the way back on a dirt track our four-wheel-drive suddenly sank door-deep into mud. We were miles from anywhere and night was falling. Renato and Jean-Marc rolled up their trousers and began to dig it out with their hands while the rest of us gathered stones to try to make a hard surface for the wheels to grip, but it was obviously not going to work. Luckily someone else in the group had a posh Toyota with an electric winch. They hooked us up, pressed a button, and with only a little bit of whining from the winch, we were pulled out.

As we continued home I began to make a list of essential items without which we must never, ever travel in the steppe again – number one now, of course, being a winch.

I have been making these lists of essential equipment ever since we got married – in Nepal, in Ethiopia, in India, in Africa, in Syria – but we've never actually got round to buying any of it. We don't even own a decent torch, for heaven's sake. This time, I lectured AW firmly, we must buy two jerry cans for diesel, another for drinking water, some planks for putting on the sand/mud when we are stuck, a tent, sleeping bags, a Butagaz burner . . . I was droning on when Lucy piped up from the back, 'Why don't you just get a Winnebago and have done with it?'

4 June

Woke up this morning to find that today Almaty is the centre of the world and has turned into a Hollywood film set. There are thirteen Heads of State in town, including Musharraf of Pakistan, Vajpayjee of India, and Jiang of China. Helicopters armed with rockets are circling above the town and black Mercs with darkened windows and flags flying are speeding around, exuding power. I got home from shopping to find messages from the Indian Control Room asking me to call urgently. I was so excited to find myself part of the action – wondering what on earth they could want from me – but it turned out to be a friend from Delhi who has come up with the Indian delegation and wants to know where to buy carpets.

★   ★   ★

Later that evening. My heart is in my mouth: Hester has just tele-phoned from Jerusalem. It had always been her plan to go and work with a Palestinian human rights lawyer in Ramullah before she leaves the Middle East and now, finally, she has got there. She sounded a bit stressed, but has found somewhere to stay and plans to commute through the check points to the office in Ramallah each day.

On the plane from Cairo to Tel Aviv she sat next to a Filipino who proudly showed her his Israeli passport. 'Why do you have an Israeli passport?' enquired Hester. He explained that his whole family wanted to leave the Philippines: his sister was trying to get to Australia, his brother to England, but he was the clever one who had thought of converting to Judaism and going to Israel. Hester was seething: Palestinians cannot go back to their country, but a random Filipino can go and settle in Israel with all kinds of grants and subsidies to help.

9 June

Hester telephoned sounding wobbly. She is staying the weekend with a friend of ours in Bethlehem. It seems that last night they were out to dinner when everyone's mobile phone began to ring at once with calls from friends warning them that the Israelis were coming into Bethlehem. Everybody fled to move their cars off the streets (Israelis run over cars with their tanks) and to get inside their homes before the curfew. This morning they woke up to find the Israelis have gone.

10 June

Frantic telephone calls all day between Bethlehem/Jerusalem and Kazakhstan. (AW will *freak* when he sees the bills.) The Israeli tanks came back into Bethlehem yesterday afternoon, and re-imposed the curfew. Hester couldn't leave the house – let alone Bethlehem – to go to work. No one knew (and they still don't) how long the Israelis will stay, so the family decided to get her out in a friendly TV cameraman's van – the Press is allowed free-er passage. The van was stopped on a back road for about fifteen minutes by a huge Merkava tank which swivelled its gun barrel right at them – Hester was terrified – but it finally let them past, and she was back in her flat in Jerusalem this evening.

12 June

Yesterday Ramallah was invaded by the Israelis . . . Poor Hester, the lawyer she has been trying to work for, told her she should leave, as no one knows what is going to happen. Since she can't do her job, she has decided to return home as soon as she can book a flight. It was a brave try, and I really admire her for making the attempt to do something.

14 June

It is getting hot now and Nina has discarded her tights and is barelegged – well, you couldn't really call them bare . . . the hairiness of certain legs here is quite startling: it's rather as if they are clad in light brown mohair stockings. Then again, one society's hairy leg is another's furry arm. The girl in the beauty salon in India used to be bewildered by us Europeans who regularly had our legs waxed, but left our arms looking, in her words, just like a monkey's. I wondered if I should say something to Nina but decided not to.

AW nominated me to tell Sukai, our maid in the Gambia, about deodorant – it was so humiliating. 'Sukai,' I said very slowly, 'in England we use this' (waving bottle of Mum) 'here' (pointing to armpit), 'so there is no bad smell' (making hideous bad smell face). She looked at me blankly and smiled, and I realized that she simply thought I was having some sort of nasty turn, waving my arms in the air and making frightful faces, and it was better to humour me. Ceesay gave her the deodorant and explained it all next day.

Nina is always jolly. She has taken to saluting AW when he comes from the office, and last week when she came to clear the table after lunch, she started making scissor movements with her fingers round his head indicating that it was time for a haircut. (AW has his hair cut by a sweet Kazakh woman in the Green Market – it costs less than a pound.) But is this too matey – do other ambassadors' cooks make snipping movements round their heads?

Wild marijuana is growing in our garden and all along the sides of the road. When I asked a friend of J-M and Renato about it she just said 'it doesn't work'. Since my terrifying marijuana experience in the jungle in Nepal, I am not interested in further research.

15 June

A Central Asian craft fair is being held this weekend. It is amazing – the Palace of Youth and Culture has become an Aladdin's cave of embroideries, carpets, jewellery, paintings . . . I was actually gibbering with excitement and came home laden with stuff – including a brass washbasin from Samarkand studded with moonstones that I now see is obviously a fake. The embroideries were miles cheaper than they would have been in London – though, as AW said rather tartly, you probably wouldn't be buying saddlecloths and wall hangings in London anyway. Most of the traders had come from Tajikistan and Uzbekistan, both famous for their embroideries and textiles; Kazakhstan only really has carpets, and one specific kind of embroidery called a Tuzkis which is made specially to decorate a yurt – I can't think of any other use for it, but I am racking my brains.

16 June

Huge excitement. AW is going to Dushambe, the capital of Tajikistan, and then on to Samarkand in Uzbekistan, and since I have been moaning for weeks that the way things are going, I'll probably live in Central Asia for four years and never see Samarkand, he thought I should come along too.

22 June

Getting back to Almaty was rather a relief. I don't want to sound ungrateful, but I have to say that our trip was more like a trial by terror than a pleasant sightseeing excursion. In fact, in Dushambe I even discovered a new form of death to worry about.

The fear began with the Tajik Air Company flight over the jagged mountain peaks (the three highest are called Lenin, Communism and Youth). AW had been assuring me that everything would be okay because we'd be travelling on 'the big plane' – but what he didn't say was that it was only big in comparison to the other, miniscule, one that plies the route, and it was packed with Tajiks and their bundles. I was terrified and had to keep taking mighty swigs of the brandy that AW had thoughtfully brought along for me (he hadn't been able to find a small bottle to put it in and had used an ex-chilli paste jar, so my lips were on fire).

One of my problems on planes is that I always imagine that I shall have to be the person organizing the orderly evacuation of the aircraft in an emergency, so when it's clear – as on this flight – that none of the passengers would understand or obey my instructions (let alone join in singing 'Nearer My God to Thee') it makes it much worse.

We flew through a thick fog with the occasional break in the cloud through which I could see Communism, Lenin or Youth about two feet below our fuselage, and ended up doing a vertical descent into Dushambe in a torrential downpour. We were met by a nice man from the office who drove us to our hotel through streets that were more like rivers – warning us (this was the new form of death) to take care if we went for a walk because many of the manhole covers had been swept away: just the week before, he said, a woman had fallen down a manhole that she hadn't noticed under the water, and had never been seen again.

We dumped our stuff in the hotel, and then he took us off to watch the Ireland versus Spain World Cup match. A group of young Europeans working in Tajikistan had organized the viewing. A sheet had been hung as a screen, beer bought, and an Irish girl among them had cut out lots of shamrocks and stuck them on pencils for us to wave as we cheered on Ireland. The members of the audience were Tajik, Uzbek, Kazakh, Swiss, Spanish, Irish, British, Italian, Danish, Pakistani, and Austrian. It was wonderful.

AW worked next day while I explored the market and wandered about Dushambe, which is a ravishing little town built in the 1920s in Russian/oriental/classical style with the buildings painted in different colours. A huge *chaikhana* or teahouse with wooden pillars and open verandahs dominates the main road and the smell of meat grilling on their outdoor barbeques hangs over everything.

Tajikistan felt much more like 'home' than Kazakhstan. The people are of Iranian descent: good-looking and charming, and it was so good to see old skills – carving and painting – used in the buildings, not just concrete.

That night the President gave a banquet to celebrate the fifth anniversary of the end of the civil war that once wracked Tajikistan. The guests of honour were the Russian, Iranian and UN officials who had helped negotiate the peace. It was all very formal until the President knocked back a couple of vodkas, and suddenly decided to turn the evening into a rave.

Male guests were ordered to take off their jackets and the President himself took to the vast dance floor, alone with one of the cabaret artistes. Everyone looked a bit embarrassed. Then something unbelievably awful happened: the President walked directly up to our table and asked me to dance. It was the sort of thing that happens in nightmares and you wake up in a sweat saying 'Goodness, I had the most terrible dream – I dreamed I had to dance with the President of Tajikistan alone on an enormous dance floor in front of two hundred people.'

My mother used to tell us the story of how once, at a Rajah's garden party in India, she was asked by the host to play tennis with two Wimbledon champions – Borotra and Cochet. She tried to explain that her tennis was really and truly not up to this, but the Rajah said 'Mrs Keenan, you are too modest,' and would not take no for an answer. She changed and walked towards the court praying that something would save her, and at the very last moment it did – she was stung by a wasp.

As I walked on to that dance floor with the President, I prayed for an earthquake, assassination attempt, heart failure – anything – to save me from this ordeal, but I did not have my mother's luck. The only good thing was that – *thank God* – I had worn my pretty shoes that evening. (I had almost come in scruffy ones knowing that no one would see them under the table.) The President, who is rather attractive in a burly Soviet kind of way, was also a good dancer. I did a sort of Arab dance with my arms in the air and prayed for it all to end. I couldn't look in AW's direction (he was at a different table) because I knew he would be falling off his chair laughing.

Half an hour after I was back in my seat, I was still shaking with fright – which is the only explanation I have for why my hand suddenly jerked and threw the contents of my vodka glass all over the distinguished UN official sitting next to me. He was wearing a pale blue shirt that went navy in large patches where the drink had saturated it. 'Was it something I said?' he joked kindly.

Next night, AW invited everyone from the Dushambe office out for dinner, and Lucy suddenly turned up at the restaurant. She had been backpacking round the area with a friend and tracked us down. We sat next to each other and I asked her what she was eating. 'Chicken cutlets,' she said, 'and I am praying there are nuts in them because otherwise, what am I crunching?'

Lucy's route to Dushambe had been along the road we were to take next day. I hate heights: mountain roads with precipices are one of my worst fears, so I questioned her closely about it. She didn't say much except that you didn't have to do three-point turns on the bends . . .

I should have taken the hint and flown back to Almaty immediately – travelling on that road was the single most terrifying experience of my life (apart from flying in an open helicopter with the American army in Vietnam). I am still having nightmares about it.

We were driven by Tahir, the Tajik driver from the office. At first it was glorious: meandering through beautiful green valleys eating peaches bought in the market the night before, with everyone (Gainee, AW, Tahir and me) in high spirits. But soon the road climbed higher and higher – way beyond the altitude where there was any vegetation – until it was just a narrow ledge carved out of the sheer face of the mountain with a 12,000 foot drop on the valley side, a crumbling verge, and not enough room to pass another vehicle. Every now and again AW would gasp '*Look – at – that – view!*' but I had my eyes closed and my body leaning away from the drop – as though I could keep the car on the rutted dirt track by will power and my weight. I was actually crying with fear at one point and when AW put his hand on my knee and said, 'It will be all right, you know,' I said, '*I hate you!*'

It took hours and hours to climb up to the top of the pass, which was covered with snow, and down the other side, and the only mercy was that there was hardly any traffic coming towards us – a lorry had got stuck, blocking the road on the Samarkand side, we discovered later.

At the beginning of the journey I had been cheerily reciting the lines of the poem by James Elroy Flecker which made Samarkand famous: 'We travel not for trafficking alone/ By hotter flames our fiery hearts are fanned/ For lust of knowing what should not be known /*We take the golden road to Samarkand.*' Later I tried to distract myself from thoughts of cars going over precipices (would the EC send an air ambulance to pick up the pieces and how would survivors contact them?) by composing more appropriate descriptions: the Scary Road to Samarkand, the Rotten Road, the Perfectly Frightful Road Which Nothing On Earth Could Ever Persuade Me To Travel On Again.

When the ordeal was over, I asked Tahir if cars ever *did* go over the edge – oh yes, he said, during the three summer months when the road is open, vehicles go over all the time . . .

In a café in Pendishkent (where we had stopped to look at the ruins of a Sogdian city) Tahir asked me very humbly if I wouldn't mind showing more respect to my bread. Bread in Tajikistan comes in a big round disc, which the host tears into pieces, one for each person. I had just taken my piece and put it beside my plate.

'Oh dear,' I said, 'what am I doing wrong?'

'I am sorry, *Khanym*' (Farsi for 'lady'), said Tahir, 'but you have put it upside down which is disrespectful.'

I quickly turned it the other way.

There is no such thing as a quick cup of tea in Tajikistan. When the teapot arrives, the host pours out a cup and then pours it back into the teapot – he does this three times. Finally he pours out a cup, puts it to one side for himself later, and only then fills up everyone else's cup.

Travellers are fond of saying that Samarkand is a disappointment because it is over-restored, and that you can see the difference between the magical luminous blue of the old tiles and the dull new ones used in the restoration. That is all true, but to me – so glad to be alive – Samarkand was the most beautiful place on earth. The city itself is not so special, but the markets are huge and the monuments spectacular. AW and I wandered round the fabled Registan – the three huge tiled buildings, housing mosques and religious schools, that once formed the centre of Samarkand – and we walked up the exquisite Shahi-Zinda, a narrow lane with the mausoleums of the dead of Tamerlane's family on either side. And we could hardly believe how lucky we were to be there, seeing these sights after the cultural blank of Kaz.

The one thing that seemed sad was that all these religious buildings are now just giant tourist shops. The only place with any feeling of spirituality was the mosque in Shahi-Zinda built over the tomb of a cousin of the Prophet Mohammed. Families and groups of pilgrims were visiting, and having prayers recited for their intentions by the resident Mullah. We asked him to pray for our family, and for the Palestinians.

Our out-of-date *Lonely Planet* guide described the remains of another great mosque, Bibi-Khanym, adding that there were plans for its complete restoration:'Are they really going to try and *rebuild* this magnificent ruin?' asked the guide book sceptically. But since that was written, not so many years ago, they have indeed done it. Gainee took a photograph of AW and me standing behind the giant stone Koran stand in its courtyard. What none of us noticed was that a large woman was crawling between the legs of the stand at the time (there is a local legend which says that crawling under the stand will bring you a baby). In the forefront of our picture is a huge female bottom.

It was extremely hot and our hotel had an empty blue pool twinkling in the sun. None of us had brought swimsuits, so Gainee and I went to the teeming clothing market and found the only stall in Samarkand that sold them. In a tiny space behind a sheet hung at the back of the booth we wrestled on various suits, sweating with the effort. The only one I could find to fit was in electric-blue shiny nylon with two huge plastic ice-cream cones to hold the bosom. We bought AW some cotton jersey Tajik boxer shorts. After all this, when we got back to the hotel we found the pool full of shrieking children splashing each other; swimming and lazing beside it suddenly lost their attraction.

Next day we flew back to Almaty from Tashkent, and I am now booking AW out for two weeks next Easter so that no visiting Brussels officials, or work in the office, can prevent us from going back and seeing more of Uzbekistan – the market in Tashkent for instance, which we didn't have time to see. *Lonely Planet* gives it a particularly good write-up, saying you can find anything there – 'from nails to nukes'. I told this to Meriel on the telephone when I got back to Almaty but she thought I'd said 'newts', and we had a most peculiar conversation in which she wondered if I should tell Ken Livingstone (a well-known newt collector), and I couldn't for the life of me think why . . .

24 June

It is becoming something of a routine to go out exploring with Jean-Marc and Renato on Sundays – often with a slightly hung-over Lucy, the extremely pleasant British Council couple, Brian (a colleague of AW's), plus whoever else turns up at the archaeologists' office at 10 a.m. Renato is in his fifties, dark and passionate and energetic; Jean-Marc must be thirty-something, pale, with a face like a streetwise angel. They met in Hanoi about seven years ago and have been in Central Asia ever since; they know every inch of the place.

AW was right, they have changed our lives; every week is a new adventure. Without them we would never have seen the ostrich or camel farms in the steppe (camel's milk yoghurt is the latest fashion here), or the rather creepy pilgrim site in the dark pine forests near Almaty where long ago three priests were shot by the Bolsheviks.

Jean-Marc and Renato have taken us up to a high pasture where they are excavating a Bronze Age burial site. It was magical: blue with forget-me-nots (Renato calls them 'do not forget me's'), ringed by white mountains, and sprinkled with wild yurts and horsemen. And we've driven to the Illi river to see engravings of Buddha cut into the rocky cliff face by itinerant monks passing through in the seventeenth century.

Yesterday we went to see a Bronze Age fortress on a hill not far from Almaty. The hill is part of a range overlooking the plain where the tomb of the Golden Man was found. It didn't look much like a fortress to me: just another boring hill, I was thinking, when I tripped over part of an ancient grinding stone. Then we were all finding Scythian pottery shards and suddenly the hill became something really interesting – reminding me of wonderful days in Syria.

10 August

The first member of the family to visit – Claudia – has come out for part of the holidays. Anything to avoid getting a job, I suspect, but I am so glad she is here. We can go exploring together.

Summer has brought out some odd sights. Panfilov Park is suddenly full of brides in white dresses and veils flitting through the trees. It's like some kind of surrealist French film. The reason is the strong tradition in this society for honouring the dead: brides are photographed in front of war memorials, and since Panfilov Park is the home of the most powerful memorial in Almaty – commemorating the Kazakhs of the Panfilov division who died defending Moscow – this is their first choice. It's one of my favourite places too: the memorial is so dramatic it gives you gooseflesh. A colossal bronze map of Russia is the background, and poking out of it, impossibly grim, are the helmeted heads of the Kazakh defenders with their high cheekbones and oriental eyes. In front of them all stands the figure of Panfilov, their Russian officer, with his arms flung wide, biceps bulging, thighs like tree trunks, protecting the homeland behind him.

Not far away, outside the Green Market, babushkas are selling flowers and fruit from their gardens, as well as bunches of wild flowers gathered in the steppe, and old gypsy fortune-tellers have set up their stalls on upturned boxes with cards, cowrie shells, and other odd bits and bobs. Their customers – usually young men or women with desperately earnest faces – crouch beside the old ladies listening intently. I long to hear their stories.

This week I saw a babushka sitting behind a table with just one enormous root on it. When I questioned her it turned out to be asafoetida; people were buying chunks of it for medicinal purposes. She gave me a little piece and told me to mash it with honey and use it as a face mask. So I did – and gave some to Nina and Ira. It certainly made my skin soft, but I couldn't get rid of its horrible pungent smell.

26 August

The Dutch Ambassador and his wife have rented a yurt and had it put up in a valley about a hour and a half's drive from Almaty. They invited us to come for a picnic and gave us directions, but we got lost, and had to stop and ask one of the most peculiar questions that has ever passed our lips: 'Excuse me please, could you tell me where is the Dutch Ambassador's yurt?' (Translated into Russian by AW.)

We got there eventually and it was lovely. I was all for us renting it next year, but got less enthusiastic when I found it was full of insects – especially spiders. A canvas tent that can be hermetically sealed to keep out all wild life would suit me better.

AW and Claudia and I went riding – if you can call sitting on a horse as it strolls along, riding (though AW did some cantering). Claudia had to share a horse with the guide, and pretty soon we heard her calling loudly: '*Mum, Dad*! I think I'd like to walk for a bit now.' It turned out the guide's hands with the reins, which were in her lap, had been straying from their job of controlling the horse . . .

The Dutch Ambassador and his wife are leaving at the end of the summer; very sad – they have been so kind to us. (A pity the same cannot be said of the British one and his wife who are also leaving – though in the end, I must admit, I have come round to liking them.)

25 October

The new young British Ambassador and his wife arrived earlier this week and we invited them to dinner last night with their baby and toddler. I really don't know what it is with us and British ambassadors but even this cosy evening went pear-shaped. Their little boy who – his mother had just been telling me – was allergic to nuts and eggs, was stung by a wasp *twice* on his ankle. We've never had a little boy in the house before, nor have we ever found a wasp, but last night, by some trick of fate, they came together in the hall. It was frightening – I thought the poor little chap was going to pass away in our arms – but in the event he recovered quite fast, perhaps because Nina was frantically dousing his ankle with iced vodka. AW started telling the story of how our brother-in-law nearly died when he was strung by a wasp, but I managed to stop him before he got too far into the graphic description of his throat closing up . . .

4 November

AW and I were woken up by an earthquake in the middle of last night. The bed was shaking and something on the roof was banging loudly and all the barking dogs were eerily quiet.

'What should we do?' I asked AW urgently.

He said he was thinking about it, so I lay there, waiting for instructions, until I realized he'd gone back to sleep. I don't think I'll go as far as the Greek Ambassador's wife who really has packed a case with essential supplies, as recommended by the American Embassy, but I will put my dressing gown and slippers by my bed every night so that, should the time come, I am not standing in the snow in my pyjamas and bare feet.

10 December

Oh dear, my diary-keeping is becoming as erratic as the deliveries of the *Guardian Weekly*. Life seems to have taken on a kind of routine – not the most exciting in the world (it's winter now), but pleasant enough. I do my emails, write the odd article for anyone who asks me to, catch up with this diary, go to the Almaty Women's Club to meet the ones who have become friends, and – this is the best bit – I scour the shops for Tuzkis and other embroideries, because I have become a Trader. I have actually found someone in England who wants to buy them from me, so I can shop, free of guilt.

I am sinking my profits into the extraordinary carpets made by the Uighurs – a Muslim Turkic tribe who live in the Xinjiang province of China (just across the mountains from Kazakhstan). Paul Bergne, the ex-British Ambassador to Uzbekistan and a great Central Asian expert, calls these 'kitchen sink carpets' because they have vases of flowers, tables, lamps – even bunches of bananas – woven into their patterns. They are intriguing; I am planning to put on an exhibition when we finally return to Britain.

In the evenings AW and I entertain officially about once every week or ten days; we are invited out to dinner from time to time and there are national days or cultural events at the various embassies. Once in a while we go to the opera or the ballet. The other day, Renato and J-M brought the Prima Ballerina of Kazakhstan, Leila, to lunch. She was exquisite – as fragile as a snowdrop; we all felt like elephants. Halfway through lunch, when I urged her to have a little more to eat, she announced that she was on a diet because she was so overweight. She is now known by AW and me as the Obese Ballerina.

When we are home alone in the evening we read, or watch videos. We tend to avoid the news on TV because we can no longer bear to hear how many Palestinians have died each day, and because George Bush and his smirk and the war in Iraq send AW's blood pressure soaring.

Last time I was in London an anthropologist friend gave me a pile of wildlife films and asked me to give them to the British Council, but they haven't got there yet because we have found *Chimps on the Move, A Tale of Three Chimps, A Chimp with a Problem* . . . excellent and calming substitutes for Bush and Blair and Saddam Hussein. We only have five left to watch, though.

2 March, 2003

For one reason or another, I have had to return to Europe a couple of times recently. The last visit was at the beginning of February; then I had to hurry back here to help with the official visit of AW's boss, Chris Patten. But at the eleventh hour, when all the arrangements were in place, his trip had to be cancelled because of events surrounding Iraq. AW was so disappointed but I was thrilled, because I was supposed to be giving a lunch for the official party from Brussels, plus the European ambassadors here – and though Nina's calm was prevailing over my total panic (just), we were suddenly off the hook.

Since there was no way AW and I could be in London for the great anti-war march (it took place on the very day Chris Patten should have been at our lunch) we suggested to J-M and Renato that perhaps an anti-war demo could be organized in Almaty. It turned out that people are not allowed to assemble in the streets here without special Government permission, so they suggested a Peace Concert instead, to be led by representatives of all the religious groups in Kazakhstan. Yesterday they asked AW and me to go with them to invite some of the more peculiar faiths. (They already have the Catholic bishop and a Russian Orthodox priest booked.)

We assembled in their office with Alexei, the Buddhist monk (in his robes), plus an Italian documentary film-maker whom Renato had met in the street the day before, and set off; AW and I followed behind their minibus with Lucy and Omar, a young Iraqi friend who has been staying. The bus screeched to a halt on the way out of Almaty to pick up another religious representative – a beaming, round, Chechen mullah – and then led us along the bleak back roads of the snowy steppe for what seemed like hours until we came to our next port of call: the Hari Krishna settlement. Polite young men, looking seriously underdressed for the cold in robes, with shaven heads, led us to the house of their leader Govinda Swami. Govinda Swami told us that he came from Nashville, Tennessee, which was almost the oddest part of the whole encounter.

His house had under-floor heating – we know, because we sat

on the floor at his feet, while his acolyte, a lovely Russian woman, handed round delicious pomegranate tea and a sort of fudge. I suddenly had the idea that, when the time comes, instead of going into an old folks' home in England (where, I've just read in the *Guardian Weekly*, 80 percent of inmates are dosed with tranquillizers no matter what illness they have) it might be better to join the Hari Krishnas. They are kind to old people, the food is delicious, the houses warm as toast, the music is nice and it would be easier to dress with arthritic hands, since there are no zips or buttons on the robes to cope with. I think I might try for a branch in the Caribbean, though, rather than on the Kazakh steppe.

Govinda Swami loved the idea of the concert, and agreed not only to participate, but to provide free food in the interval, plus the loudspeakers for the stage, and some music and singing.

Glowing with our success, we set off again behind the minibus, this time to visit a shaman that Renato and Jean-Marc have discovered living in a shack on the steppe by some caves. (Perhaps I should explain that Shamanism was the ancient religion of Central Asia; shamans, like African witchdoctors, have no 'gods' as such, but communicate with nature and spirits. All around the steppe, particularly where there is water, you come across trees covered with little pieces of fabric knotted on by passers-by as prayers or goodluck tokens – which seems to indicate that deep down, shamanism is still a lingering belief here.)

It took ages and ages to get to the shaman's place and Omar and Lucy, who had intended to go skiing that afternoon, were looking a bit bleak; AW was becoming more and more irritated, and I was bored and hungry . . .

The shaman turned out to be a fierce old woman in a turban and a long dress, carrying a big carved stick, and with a piercing look in her eye. She led us into her home (past a wet and bloody sheepskin hanging on the outside wall) and we all sat down on the rugs on the floor.

I think it was at this point that I started to feel slightly hysterical. We were such a peculiar group: the shaman, the monk, the mullah, the Iraqi, Lucy, the Italian film-maker, Renato and Jean-Marc – not to mention AW, the European Ambassador, and me, his wife. We were like the cast of that old film, *Ship of Fools* . . . Adding to the crazed atmosphere were the shaman's two male helpers who looked as though they were in fancy dress wearing long Kazakh coats and hats (which are a sort of pantomime version of Nelson's, in blue velvet with gold braid). I began to giggle, but it got worse . . .

The shaman decided we all needed 'treatment', and one by one she called us up off the rugs, whacked us on the back extremely hard with her stick, boxed our ears really violently and then spat in our faces. The sight of AW being whacked sent me into another fit of giggles, so, when it was my turn, she gave me an especially violent going over with *four* spittings in the face. As we left her house each of us had to step three times over a fire of special grasses – tears from the smoke mingled with my tears of laughter. Every time I thought of our odd group – seeing us from outside as it were – I became helpless with laughter, and so did Lucy, Omar, and AW. I hasten to say (before the evil eye strikes me down) that it was not mocking laughter – we had rather taken to the shaman, she was impressive in her way. And she had agreed to take part in the Peace Concert.

In the car on the way home I suddenly realized that it was just over a year since I first arrived in Kazakhstan. This time last March I was utterly miserable, and there seemed to be no light at the end of the tunnel. Now, here I was with beloved AW, with young friends, face aching from laughter, totally happy, as we bowled home across the steppe having spent our Sunday afternoon visiting a shaman for heaven's sake . . . I certainly wouldn't have been doing *that* in Somerset.

Twelve months ago I knew for certain I couldn't face four years here; I was planning to persuade AW to retire at the end of three at the very most – but now I am asking myself, why hurry home from a place where extraordinary days like today can happen? For most of our travelling lives I have been vaguely looking forward to AW's retirement. Yesterday, for the first time, I realized that it would be closing the door to adventure, and that, once closed, that door might not be easy to open again.

When AW asked me to marry him he said, 'I can't promise that you will be rich, but I do promise you will never be bored.' Well, he has certainly kept his promise over the years, and, though it's possibly not *exactly* the script that I would have written for myself, how can I possibly complain?

So this is what I am going to try and tell Cecilia.

Epilogue

Little did either Cecilia or I imagine at the Papal Nuncio's farewell party all those aeons ago, that answering her question would take more than two years and involve writing a whole book.

In the meantime she hasn't exactly been moping around waiting for the reply: she has learned Russian, studied acupuncture, and is working part time in a hospital in Almaty. Her husband has only about a year to go in Kazakhstan now, and they have no idea where they will be sent next. But, she says, from what she has learned in this first posting, she will be able to find her feet anywhere (which doesn't, of course, rule out crying from time to time).

As for the rest of us. . . .

Our Peace Concert went brilliantly – though it was touch and go at the beginning because when the religious leaders began to speak, the owner of the concert hall got into a complete state.

'This is not a concert,' he panicked, 'this is a political meeting. I cannot allow it. I will get into serious trouble. Everyone must leave immediately.'

He was finally persuaded that throwing 750 people out into the street would attract more attention than leaving them in their seats, so, instead, he locked the hall and the entrance gate – which meant that when the Russian Orthodox priest turned up, late, he couldn't get in. Gamely, in robe and hat, he began climbing over the wall and was then arrested by the police as a 'religious hooligan'. (He was released in the interval when it was all explained.)

AW decided not to retire after three years in Kazakhstan (as I had been trying to persuade him to do) but to see out the full four-year posting – and then go to another one. We are now in our last few months in Central Asia, anxiously waiting to hear which, if any, of the eight countries he put down as possible choices, he will be sent to.

Hester got married – to exactly the man you'd have as a son-in-law, if you could choose. She did become a barrister but then decided to do a Masters degree in human rights law; she is at university now.

Claudia eventually got her degree last year. She managed to avoid full-time work for another couple of months by helping to edit this book – but I am eternally grateful because she did it with great skill. Now she is working for a publishing company.

Bing and Marcelle (through contacts they made in Damascus) were offered work as housekeepers to a UN diplomatic family. They live in New York, where they seem to be thriving.

Ceesay lost his job last year and sent frantic emails to AW asking for help since he couldn't find work and had no income to support his family. AW decided the only thing to do was buy some land and help him build a house. (I made a poster of my photographs of old cottage windows in Almaty to help raise the money – so falling into snowdrifts and being attacked by dogs was worth it in the end.) Ceesay's house is finished now; he sent us a photo of him standing proudly beside it. One day we hope to see it in real life.

Julia the gorilla stayed at Jersey Zoo for several years, but was moved on to Melbourne Zoo in 1997 because she did not get on with Jersey's new silverback male gorilla. She has blossomed at Melbourne Zoo, and in 2000 she had a daughter, Jumatano. Julia and her child are in a gorilla group with six others and the zoo reports that she is an excellent mother. I wonder if she would recognize Claudia if we went there on a visit? You can see the gorilla group on the zoo's website (www.zoo.org.au).

We gave Tony, our beloved dog in the Gambia, to a young British vet and his wife when we left, and they loved her dearly. She earned her keep with them when, with another dog, she fought and killed a huge spitting cobra that appeared on their doorstep one day. She died of old age in 1997.

My little Damascus house seemed so far away and difficult to look after when we were posted to Kazakhstan, that I sold it. Now I wish I hadn't.

My book on Damascus, though, had just the impact I'd hoped it would — both locals and foreigners (who are now allowed to buy houses in Syria) are restoring houses in the old city. The most ambitious project is Tala Tlass's. She is restoring an enormous derelict mansion called Beit Qwatly in the heart of the Old City. When Tim and I were choosing houses for our book we thought the house was too far gone to photograph, but Tala has found all kinds of architectural treasures in it, and one day, perhaps, it will rival Nora Jumblatt's palace.

The nice British Council couple got promoted to Moscow and left Kazakhstan — as have many others I came to like, and lean on. The biggest gap was left when Lucy went home — but at least she went to Britain so I can see her when I visit.

The colossal statue of Lenin in front of the Bishkek museum — the very last one in the ex-Soviet Union left in its original place — was finally moved to a less exalted position in 2003.

Nina, Ira and Yuri are still working for us and are more loved and appreciated than ever. Nina took to shaving her legs last summer.

And me? I caught myself at a party the other day, terrifying a new diplomat's young wife with chilling tales of imminent earthquakes — and realized that I was turning into a true Almaty expat. Just as well we are moving on soon.